Sirens of the Western Shore

SIRENS
of the
WESTERN SHORE

The Westernesque Femme Fatale,

Translation, and Vernacular Style in

Modern Japanese Literature

Indra Levy

Columbia University Press

New York

Columbia University Press

Publishers Since 1893

New York, Chichester, West Sussex

Copyright © 2006 Columbia University Press

Columbia University Press wishes to express its appreciation for assistance given by
Stanford University, Division of Literatures, Cultures and Languages, in the
publication of this book.

Library of Congress Cataloging-in-Publication Data

Levy, Indra A.

Sirens of the Western shore : the westernesque femme fatale,
translation, and vernacular style in modern Japanese literature /
Indra Levy.

p. cm.

Includes bibliographical references and index.

ISBN 0-231-13786-9 (casebound : alk. paper) —

ISBN 0-231-51074-8 (pbk.)

1. Women in literature. 2. Japanese literature—1868—History and criticism.
3. Japanese literature—Western influences. I. Title.

PL726.58.W64L58   2006

895.6'093522—dc22   2006017785

Casebound editions of Columbia University Press books are printed on
permanent and durable acid-free paper.

Printed in the United States of America

c 10 9 8 7 6 5 4 3 2 1

Contents

5

Haunting the Laboratory of Vernacular Style:
The Sirens of "Shōjobyō" and *Futon* 147

Part Three

Staging the New Woman:
The Spectacular Embodiment of "Nature" in Translation 195

6

Setting the Stage for Translation 201

7

Gender Drag, Culture Drag, and Female Interiority 232

Final Reflections:
Gender, Cultural Hierarchy, and Literary Style 267

Acknowledgments

The ideas elaborated in this book were first germinated in Paul Anderer's graduate seminars and Kojin Karatani's modern Japanese literature colloquium. Paul created the optimum environment from which to confront the modern Japanese literary text in all of its linguistic complexities. Karatani, by the sheer force of his intellectual passion and critical acuity, implicitly demanded that one consider the multiple ramifications of such a confrontation. To both of these mentors I owe a profound debt of gratitude for not only providing the initial inspiration but also the many years of encouragement, guidance, and patience that enabled me to bring this book to fruition.

I extend heartfelt thanks to the many others who have read, listened, and responded to this work at various stages in its development. As readers for my dissertation, Andreas Huyssen, D. A. Miller, Haruo Shirane, and Tomi Suzuki provided invaluable critical perspectives. I owe a special thanks to Haruo for many, many years of intellectual guidance and support and to Tomi for her invigorating enthusiasm and generosity of spirit and intellect. I also benefited from the careful readings and encouraging responses of Sabu Kohso, Seiji Lippit, Mizutamari Mayumi, John Mertz, Suzanne O'Brien, and Timothy Wixted. The two anonymous readers for Columbia University Press offered extremely useful advice on the structure of the book as a whole. I am especially grateful to Jennifer Crewe of Columbia University Press for supporting this project at a time when market pressures have come to bear so hard on the genre of literary criticism.

Though they are too numerous to name here, many people provided opportunities to present my work to live audiences whose questions invariably helped to clarify my thinking. In particular, the late novelist, critic, and teacher Gotō Meisei most kindly and unexpectedly invited me to speak on Futabatei Shimei for a public lecture at Kinki University when I was still a struggling graduate student. This opportunity to test my ideas in Japanese before an extremely well-informed audience of readers and scholars proved critical to the development of the work presented here.

For intellectual camaraderie, moral and professional support, I am especially thankful to Gus Heldt, Kohno Taeko, Kumono Ryōhei, David Lurie, Makino Kyōko, Mori Kyōko, Nagasaka Kanoko, the late Naitō Yūji, Nakajima Fumi, Dan O'Neill, Giles Richter, Satoru Saito, Sekii Mitsuo, Sugiura Naoyuki, Sugiura Sahoko, my former colleagues at Rutgers, and my colleagues at Stanford.

The research for this project was generously supported by a Fulbright/IIE doctoral research fellowship administered by the Japan-U.S. Education Commission (JUSEC) and a Shinchō Fellowship for doctoral research administered by the Donald Keene Center for Japanese Studies. Publication support has been provided by the Division of Literatures, Cultures, and Languages and the Center for East Asian Studies at Stanford. Thanks to Connie Chin and the Center for East Asian Studies, I was afforded the able assistance of Julie Marie Gibson, who undertook the painstaking process of copyediting the entire manuscript before it was sent to press, and Chieze Okoye, who helped to track down Japanese citations. Miri Nakamura worked tirelessly to locate and prepare the illustrations. Joanna Sturiano provided invaluable assistance in the creation of the index. Naomi Kotake of Stanford's East Asia Library generously availed me of her expertise and support in the final stages of this project. Thanks are also due to Susan Pensak of Columbia University Press for the expertise, precision, and fine linguistic sensibility that she brought to bear on my final revisions.

The Waseda University Theatre Museum in Tokyo, the Archives of Japanese Cartoon History, the Saitama Municipal Cartoon Art Museum, Chikuma Shobō, and Kawakami Hatsu kindly granted permission to reproduce their photographs and cartoons. (Although every effort has been made to secure permission to reprint the photographs in this book, in some cases the owners could not be located. Please contact the Press for details.)

Finally, I would like to thank my family. Max Terry has been an indispensable source of strength through many years and many journeys. The title of my book, which he effortlessly produced after reading an early draft, will always remind me of my ridiculous good luck in finding such a companion. Owen Kichizo Terry has joyfully shared with me the good fortune in his name, and the incredible vitality that radiates from his entire being. Ian Hideo Levy has both shared with me the rare delights of laughing between languages and served as a moral compass in my thinking about languages. Michiko Kawatani Levy has given unstintingly of her support and encouragement. My parents, Henriette Liu Levy and Howard Seymour Levy, created the very conditions from which my love of language grew; the courage, humor, and avid interest they each brought to their relations with foreign cultures and languages have sustained me in ways that I cannot even begin to express. I dedicate this book to the memory of Howard Seymour Levy and my brother, Lincoln Isidore Levy.

Sirens of the Western Shore

Introduction

> Despite its exotic title, [this book] cannot be about such things
> as the tropics or coconut trees, the colonies or Negro souls, nor
> about camels, ships, great waves, scents, spices, or enchanted
> islands. It cannot be about misunderstandings and native upris-
> ings, nothingness and death, colored tears, oriental thought, and
> various oddities, nor about any of the preposterous things that
> the word "Exoticism" commonly calls to mind. Even less so can it
> be about those writers who gave Exoticism this meaning. For it is
> in this way that "Exoticism" became compromised and bloated.
> —Victor Segalen, *Essay on Exoticism: An Aesthetics of Diversity*

In its broadest sense, exoticism is a mode of experiencing and manifesting otherness; how we define the term beyond this point will
affect how we apprehend difference, self and other, and the kinds of
exchange that take place between the two. This is surely what motivated Victor Segalen's desire to purge the term of its provincial associations with the French colonies and extend its meaning to manifold
experiences of difference. Moving away from the typical places suggested by the "tropics or coconut trees," Segalen took his theoretical
meditations on the exotic to a host of other realms, from the opposite sex and animals to the past and future and the worlds of sound
and smell. Following his lead, this study willfully dissociates the term
exoticism from its historic roots in the Western side of modern Western expansion—the poetics and prosaics of modern travel (colonialism and tourism), the nostalgic yearning for a primitive past, and
the unflappable self-confidence of the Euro-American "Exote" (Segalen's word for the subject of exoticism), impervious to the manifold
epistemological, phenomenological, and spiritual crises that lurk in
the space between languages—in order to examine some cases, not
particularly foreshadowed by Western precedent as we know it, of

how the "shock of difference" was experienced, embraced, and made manifest by those for whom the encounter with the other was not entirely a matter of choice.

Here, the exotes are modern Japanese writers, some of whom never actually used the term *exotic* per se. However, they are not positioned as the modern Japanese equivalents of the self-proclaimed exoticists of modern Europe, for the objects of their fascination do not fall within the familiar bounds of the European model. Instead of the racially and geographically differentiated other, these writers were enthralled by the sights and sounds of women from their own country who appeared to take on the exotic airs of the West and by the exotic textuality of the modern Western literatures that inspired their own acts of writing. This study argues that the culturally hybrid archetype of the Westernesque femme fatale and the sirenlike call of modern Western vernacular writing were the privileged objects of an exoticism that underwrote the creation of Japanese literary modernity itself. Specifically, I will demonstrate that the Westernesque femme fatale comes into being in modern Japanese literature as a siren who inhabits the interlingual gap between reading Western literatures and writing in Japanese. As such, she embodies a form of exoticism that appears to stay at home, yet in fact traverses one of the most confounding of all foreign spaces: the uncharted and unruly expanse that stretches between languages.

Considered in tandem within the context of modern Japanese literature, the Westernesque sexual other and the Western textual other become mutually illuminating in significant ways. Careful attention to the rich complexity of the Westernesque femme fatale's appearance in and as language will reveal this hybrid archetype to be much more than a facile attempt to represent cultural and gender differences. Positioning her as one of the most powerful expressions of the textual exoticism that fueled the radical vernacularist movements in modern Japanese literature will also enable us to foreground the aesthetically prized opacities of the literary style known as *genbun-itchi* (literally, the "reconciliation of speech and writing")—exotic elements that have long since naturalized themselves to modern Japanese writing. We will further come to see that such stylistic opacities, as well as the enigmatic nature of the female archetype who was engendered by them, can be traced to a practice, aesthetic, and ideology of translation that played a central role in the formation of Japanese literary modernity.

In retrospect, the rhetoric of linguistic transparency that characterized the expository discourse on genbun-itchi has come to assume an appearance of naïveté that is difficult to shake off. But it would be dangerous to impute the same naïveté to the actual practices that gave birth to this new style, tempting as it may be. To do so would be to wrongly assume that the writers themselves had somehow failed to recognize the sheer complexity of the linguistic conditions out of which they wrote. Such a move would effectively cast them as unwitting victims, rather than self-conscious producers, of written language, problematically reproducing the discursive divide between the West as text and the rest as raw material. Put in another way, this would be tantamount to viewing the modern Japanese writer as a colonized primitive who can be observed as a product of a "writing lesson" received from Western masters[1] or as a mere reflection of the "West itself as portrayed in the eyes and handiwork of its others."[2] As crude as these terms may seem, they accurately capture the self-serving conceits that bolster the hierarchical set of binary oppositions pitting translation against original(ity), style against imitation, and exotic other against Western self.

The following chapters examine the intertwined strategies of gender representation, translation, and stylistic innovation by which three pivotal figures in modern Japanese fiction and theater—Futabatei Shimei, Tayama Katai, and Shimamura Hōgetsu—navigated the interlingual gap from which they worked. As concrete textual and contextual analyses will show, the particular combination of these strategies in the literature of Meiji Japan (1868–1912) poses a critical challenge to the associations implicitly attached to these terms: *representation* (vernacular realism), *translation* (imitation), and *style* (originality). While the Westernesque femme fatale certainly emerged as part of a well-documented historical movement toward "modern realism," a slippery signifier for a set of mimetic practices that was not native to Japanese literature, she also happens to inhabit texts that are especially concerned with the controversial status of modern literary language, existing within their pages as a metapoetic figure for both the promise and the dangers of the genbun-itchi project. What relationship between language and reality is suggested when the object represented is not only a positive social identity—such as the figure of the Meiji schoolgirl upon whom many Westernesque female characters were based—but also, and perhaps even more important, the embodiment of a deep-seated suspicion about the impossible promises of vernacular language itself, harbored by the very writers who served as its most impassioned advocates and practitioners? And what happens to our notions of imitation and originality when literary translation is recognized as one of the key sources of stylistic *originality* in the target language, rather than simply a pale derivative of the "original" text?

What these questions force us to confront is the primacy of written language in the formation of modern Japanese literature—not only as material medium but also as the object of a metanarrative on linguistic betrayal that lends the Westernesque femme fatale her particular resonance. Karatani Kojin's radical critique of the notion of self-expression that once dominated critical approaches to modern Japanese literature has firmly situated the genbun-itchi movement within the realm of phonocentrism—the perception of written language as a derivative of speech identified by Jacques Derrida as central to the Western tradition.[3] Much critical attention has since been invested in documenting, analyzing, and deconstructing the illusion of the human voice—i.e., interiority—as the basis for national literature. Yet, in terms of actual practice, the literary translations, compositions, and aesthetic judgments that have shaped the canon of modern Japanese literature were also driven by an implicit valorization of the exotic aura of the Western vernacular text, which thereby achieves an exalted status more akin to logos than phonos.[4] The attempt to capture this exotic aura in the modern Japanese vernacular style clearly stood in the way of the seamless functioning of phonocentrism, particularly in the formative period before genbun-itchi became firmly established as a self-evident form of self-expression. The siren call of Western vernacular writing lay not only in the seductive appeal of the voice of the modern subject it constituted but also in the strange beauty that emerged from the process of tethering vernacular Japanese writing to both the Japanese colloquial voice and the exotic Western text. The sense of betrayal figured by the Westernesque femme fatale can be read as a function of the desire to span the gaps between Japanese speech, Japanese writing, and the exotic Western text that motivated the development of genbun-itchi.

Why Westernesque?

Westernesque is a neologism I coined to name a distinct lineage of femmes fatales in modern Japanese fiction. Neither ethnically nor culturally "Western" per se, yet distinguished by physical appearances, personal mannerisms, lifestyles, behaviors, and ways of thinking that were perceived within the Japanese context as particularly evocative of the West, these women emerge in literature as the alluring embodiments of Japan's cultural assimilation of the modern West. More familiar than actually Western women, yet endowed with an exotic cachet that set them apart from images of Japanese women that resonated with preestablished gender conventions, Westernesque women would assume prominent roles as femmes fatales in landmark works of modern Japanese fiction.

No doubt the best-known of these figures is Naomi in Tanizaki Juni'chirō's *Chijin no ai* (translated into English as *Naomi*, 1925), a young woman who unwittingly attracts the protagonist narrator through the Westernesque possibilities in her name, only to conquer him completely through a consciously calculated performance of Westernness that guarantees her sexual freedom through his sexual enslavement. Seen within the context of 1920s Tokyo, Naomi presaged the emergence of the Modern Girl, that urban phenomenon widely discussed in the media of her day who continues to fascinate both cultural historians and the popular imagination. When considered within the overall trajectory of modern Japanese literary history, she also lays claim to a genealogy that traces back to the Taishō New Woman, who shared with the Modern Girl in her marked capacity to personify, most provocatively, the latest twist in Japanese modernity.

While there are significant differences between the Shōwa Modern Girl, the Taishō New Woman, and the Meiji schoolgirl, the term

Westernesque seeks to incorporate these three different species under one family name. Words like *haikara* ("high-collar") and *batakusai* ("reeking of butter") have also been summoned to describe these kinds of female characters in Japanese, but each word has its own particular connotations and historical resonances. Perhaps the closest approximation to the generic breadth of Westernesque woman is *atarashii onna* ("new woman"), a term that derived from the international phenomenon of the New Woman as it rose to prominence in the Taishō period but is often used to designate all women who were perceived as "new" in their respective eras. Rather than relying on existing terms that each have strong ties to discrete eras of Japanese cultural history, I chose to create a new category, the Westernesque, in order to emphasize the association between women, the exotic aura of Westernness, and the ever elusive vanguard of Japanese modernity that persisted throughout these three eras.

Westernesque approximates the connotations of the Japanese *haikara* and *batakusai* in the sense that these words refer specifically to the *Westernness* of the Japanese, as opposed to that which is simply *Western*. In English, of course, there is also a word to describe the Westernness of non-Westerners: *Westernized.* To some this term might even seem to offer a more transparent English approximation for the Japanese adjectives. Yet there are crucial differences in nuance between these terms. An easy way to get at these differences is to consider how the words function in Japanese. The Japanese translation for *Westernization* is the Chinese compound *seiyō-ka, seiyō* meaning "West" and *ka* being a suffix equivalent in function to the Latinate "ization." To convert this word into the adjective *Westernized* requires one to attach the passive, past-tense form of the verb for "to do," as in *seiyō-ka sareta.* This quite literal Japanese translation underscores the fact that the adjective *Westernized* automatically places the modified object in a passive relationship to an unspecified subject, provoking the question: who does the Westernizing? In other words, who or what is the subject of this already completed act? The implication seems to be that only the West itself could possibly be the *subject* of such an act. Perhaps this embedded assumption is the reason why the term *Westernized* in the Japanese idiom is so rarely used to describe people, because it so completely objectifies the person so described. Notably, when Tsubouchi Shōyō, in a rare exception to this rule, used the term *seiyōka* to describe his friend Futabatei Shimei, he attached the *active* past-tense of the verb *suru,* or *shita,* indicating that Futabatei was both the subject and the object of this transformation. The most accurate translation of his usage back into English would be "Futabatei, who had Westernized himself." In terms of common usage, one might say, for instance, that public education was Westernized by Mori Arinori, Japan's first minister of education, but one would not refer to Mori himself as a Westernized man. The operative word here would be *haikara.* While *Westernized* implies a complete process of transformation, *haikara* and *batakusai* simply describe aspect. Thus the latter reign as the adjectives of choice for the personal realm, applying to mannerisms, personal effects, apparel, ways of thinking, and lifestyles.

Another problem is that the word *Westernized* assumes an unambiguous understanding of that which is Western. Certainly, numerous attempts have been made to define the contents of this loaded term, but few could withstand the critique of cultural essentialism. By contrast, the word *Westernesque* limits itself to a perception of what seemed strikingly Western enough to merit special comment in the Japanese context at specific points in time. For instance, it may not be entirely clear to the modern-day reader why a character such as Mineko in Natsume Sōseki's *Sanshirō* (1908) should be seen by the men around her as reminiscent of an "Ibsen woman," but the fact that she was perceived that way qualifies her as Westernesque. For these reasons, I believe that the term offers a useful alternative to the ideology embedded in the word *Westernized.*

Why Westernesque Femme Fatale?

In large part the specific attributes that elicit descriptions like haikara and batakusai within the Japanese context are dictated by the vicissitudes of taste and sensibility; hence, the use of these words cannot be reduced to a simple binary distinction between the "Western" and the "Japanese." Furthermore, there is often a marked difference in the use of these words to describe men and women. For instance the word *haikara*, which first appeared in print in 1900, was initially a pejorative epithet for pretentious Westernist snobs. In 1901 an article in *Kokkei shinbun* (Comic news) listed some of the qualifications of haikara as "being full of pretension and affectation; praising the West and denigrating Japan; using imported goods for everything; quoting examples from abroad in every other breath; using foreign words gratuitously."[5] Several years later, however, the same word came to mark a desirable trait in women, particularly schoolgirls. In a 1907 *Shumi* (Taste) special feature on the varieties of female beauty, one commentator uses the word *haikara* to signify the beauty particular to schoolgirls.[6] A similar trend can be observed in early Shōwa, when the Modern Girl's rise to media stardom posed a stark contrast to the fate of the Modern Boy, a figure described in the media as lackluster, if not simply shallow and foppish.[7] (As for the Taishō New Woman, there was no clearly marked male counterpart to speak of.)

The value attached to Westernesque aspect changes according to gender not only in the mass media but in literature as well. In the realm of literature the Westernesque as an aesthetic asset pertains almost exclusively to female characters. An abridged catalogue of such characters would include Osei in Futabatei Shimei's *Ukigumo*, an erstwhile schoolgirl who reads the liberal women's education magazine *Jogaku zasshi* (Women's education journal), wears a shawl and spectacles, and keeps her hair in a Western-style bun (*sokuhatsu*); Yoshiko in Tayama Katai's *Futon* (Bedding, 1907), the graduate of a "high-collar" Christian girls' school in Kobe who reads Western novels, writes in the modern vernacular style, and associates freely with men; Mineko in Natsume Soseki's *Sanshirō*, another Christian schoolgirl whose seemingly flirtatious manner mystifies the men around her; Yōko in Arishima Takeo's *Aru onna* (A certain woman, 1919), a highly self-conscious and sexually liberated divorcée; Yumiko/Aki-kō in Kawabata Yasunari's *Asakusa kurenaidan* (The scarlet gang of Asakusa, 1929), a denizen of Asakusa whose self-conscious performances of multiple genders and cultural typologies prove to be literally fatal; and Tanizaki's Naomi, mentioned above.

Whereas the qualities that distinguish female characters as West-ernesque in modern fiction mark them as the coveted symbols of modernity for the male characters who pursue them and the male authors who create them, the attributes that merit special comment in male characters tend to function in the parodic register. If the French suffix in Westernesque captures the positively exotic appeal of high-collar women, then perhaps the sardonic tone of pseudo-West-ern would be more appropriate to describe the high-collar man.

One of the most memorable examples of the pseudo-Western man is Seki Kin'ya, the protagonist in Oguri Fūyō's novel *Seishun* (Youth, 1905). The main subtext for this work is Ivan Turgenev's *Rudin*, which enjoyed a broad and enthusiastic readership in Japan after its transla-tion by Futabatei Shimei (*Ukikusa*, 1897). As the first novel to focus on what Nakamura Mitsuo dubbed "Japanese Nietzscheans," then a grow-ing contingent within the intellectual class, *Seishun* likewise enjoyed popular and critical success in its day. While the subject matter of *Sei-shun* guaranteed its enthusiastic reception in the short term, however, its protagonist's hollow caricature of youthful Westernist pretension would cast a long, dark shadow over its literary posterity, as Nakamura pointed out.[8] Seki Kin'ya is an up-and-coming practitioner of *shintai-shi* (New Poetry) who enthralls young women with the passion of his words. Like Rudin, Kin'ya is an eloquent speaker, capable of moving others but incapable of committing his words to action. What distin-guishes Kin'ya from Rudin, however, is his self-conscious identification with Turgenev's fictional character. He is not simply a parody of the original Rudin, but a caricature of the parodic idolization of Rudin in Japan at the time. There are two kinds of parody at work here—first, the self-conscious parody of *Rudin* by the author of *Seishun;* second, the unintended parody of Rudin enacted by the novel's protagonist. This is what prompted contemporary readers to complain that Fūyō lacked proper sympathy for his protagonist and what led later critics to decide that *Seishun* was too superficial to be considered pure literature.

What aesthetic formula is suggested by the fact that Westernesque airs acquire exotic value in women while eliciting derisive laughter in men? To begin with, what is the underlying relationship between exoticism and parody?

From Parodic to Exotic: The Spectrum of Manifest Difference

Since parody is almost synonymous with imitation, it is not surprising to see a connection between parody and Western affectations within the Japanese context. One need only glance through a few early Meiji comic magazines to see that the adoption of Western customs and attitudes provided ample material for contemporary lampoonists. As we can see from these examples, women "under the influence" of Western material and intellectual culture were by no means exempt from the caricaturist's gaze.

While contemporary Japanese were able to find humor in the dis-orientations of the rapid social changes they were experiencing, one notable European found the Japanese adoption of Western manners to be parody at its most abject. In an article on Japanese women, Pierre Loti describes the first Rokumeikan ball with palpable disgust:

The first European-style ball held right in the center of Tōkyō was a true monkey house tour de force. One saw young girls dressed in white muslin with gloves reaching their elbows, holding ivory-white dancebooks in their fingers, sitting in chairs with forced smiles, and then, although our rhythms are completely unknown to them and must be terribly hard on their ears, they danced the polka and the waltz at a generally accurate pace to the songs of operettas. . . .

This servile mimicry is certainly amusing to foreign passersby, but in essence, it shows that this people have no taste, and furthermore a complete lack of national dignity.[9]

Apparently, Loti did not share the native appreciation for Westernesque airs in Japanese women. No doubt he would have preferred to see an Oriental spectacle of Japanese women in traditional Japanese dress, performing a traditional Japanese dance—in short, the kind of woman that he created in *Madame Chrysanthème*. What repulsed Loti was the lack of exotic appeal, or undiluted difference, in this scene. While mimicry borders on parody, exoticism typically seeks its opposite: the kind of singularity whose difference is not diluted by imitation.

FIGURE 1 *Marumaru chinbun*, November 14, 1885. "The Japanese Exposition of Social Customs and Manners. It is so divers [*sic*] and unsettled as to give us a complete puzzle." The paired contrasts of Japanese and Western customs range from sitting habits (*upper left corner*) and military dress (*upper right corner*) to women's clothing (*just left of middle*) and dancing (*bottom right corner*). *Courtesy of the Archives of Japanese Cartoon History, Chiba*

Of course, the above examples relate to parody as the unintended travesty of feeble imitation rather than consciously executed burlesque. In terms of the latter, one can say that parody is the art of mimicry, while exoticism is the art of representing or conveying the singular. Parody alternately entertains or disturbs by means of mimicry, a process of re-presentation that is "almost the same, but not quite," to use Homi Bhabha's words. Parody results not from the representation of difference but from the revelation of difference that inevitably occurs with any attempt to achieve sameness. Whether as unintended travesty or consciously calculated burlesque, the parodic effect results from the following general principle: the more one strives to eliminate difference, the more pronounced critical differences become.

Thus the perfect performance of a Japanese flamenco dancer, for instance, is easily recuperated as the very sign of her "Japaneseness"— which now comes to signify her superior faculty for studied mimicry. Taking transvestite performance as another case in point, the art of the Hasty Pudding Club would fall at the vulgar, comic end of the scale, in which gender differences are purposely emphasized through an exaggeration of both male and female markers, while the art of professional female impersonators aspires to parodic entertainment at its highest and potentially most disturbing.[10] What is disturbing about the most convincing transvestite performances is not simply that they make fool's play of gender differences, but that in the process of doing so they inevitably underscore the less malleable difference of sex. Someone who is female by biological and social definition might execute exactly the same performance, but its meaning and the audience's reaction would surely be different—the reason why many feminists are reluctant to embrace the transvestite's separation of gender and sex as a form of liberation.

While parody ushers difference in through the back door, as it were, exoticism enthralls or disturbs through the attempt to positively foreground irreducible difference. The paradox of the exoticist project is that such difference can only be evoked in relation to the familiar. If parody magnifies difference through the overt attempt to erase it, exoticism often erases difference in the professed attempt to manifest it, by reducing it to the purely relative status of the commensurable. This is especially a problem for the linguistic arts: how to manifest difference without assimilating it to the familiarity of our own language? This is no doubt why Roland Barthes began *Empire of Signs* by saying that the dream is "to know a foreign language and yet not to understand it: to perceive the difference in it without that difference ever being recuperated by the superficial sociality of discourse, communication or vulgarity."[11] Regardless of intent, the exotic effect results from difference–in–sameness, which is only a sliver away from the sameness–with–a–difference of parody. Although Loti's reaction to Meiji Japan would suggest that parody and exoticism are diametrically opposed, this is where the two intersect.

Why is it important to recognize the underlying proximity between parody and exoticism? Stated in the simplest possible terms, one person's enthusiastic embrace of the exotic may appear to someone else as ludicrously parodic. Indeed, love of the exotic is often displayed with such undiluted enthusiasm as to verge on comic exaggeration. Here I am not only referring to the young women at Loti's ball but also to the spectacular excesses on display at world's fairs, at the eye-popping Royal Pavilion at Brighton, in films like *Cleopatra*, *The Last Emperor*, and *Memoirs of a Geisha*, in Gauguin's Tahitian paintings, or the extravagant claims that characterize the bulk of exoticist writing from the fiction of Loti himself to the theoretical musings of Barthes's *Empire of Signs* or Julia Kristeva's *Chinese Women*. Whether such examples strike us as positively exotic or ludicrously parodic is essentially a matter of perspective. This kind of exoticism is only made possible by the denial of its own parodistic potential, the same lack of self-reflection that allows Loti to completely dissociate himself from the embrace of exotic customs exhibited at the Rokumeikan.

The particular circumstances that gave rise to modern Japanese literature, on the other hand, were not entirely conducive to such naïveté. If the enthusiastic adoption of exotic Western customs could easily give rise to the appearance of parody, the same could clearly be said of the enthusiastic embrace of the modern Western concept and practice of literature. Since the encounter with modern Western literatures provided the very basis for modern Japanese literature, the distinction between the positively exotic and the deplorably parodic would become a central concern for the critical determination of literary value. The gradually disintegrating distinction between these two poles—high exoticism and vulgar parody—also forms one of the central concerns of this study, which proceeds by juxtaposing examples of each in their historical, linguistic, and ideological contexts. Thus, the discussion of Futabatei Shimei in part 1 takes place against the background provided by the work of earlier literary translators and Yamada Bimyō, Futabatei's rival in the creation of the vernacular novel; the discussion of Tayama Katai in part 2 takes place against the background of the literary practice and ideology of Katai's first mentor, Ozaki Kōyō, as well as the ill-received attempts at literary imitation and conscious self-burlesque that defined Katai's own career prior to *Futon*; and the consideration of Shingeki (New Theater) in the final chapter compares Kabuki and Shinpa (New School) practices for performing gender and culture with the "natural" representation of the modern Western woman staged by the modern Japanese actress.

The distinction between the positively exotic and the deplorably parodic presented a critical issue that could not be arbitrarily decided by the subjective judgement of a single, authoritative aesthete, nor by convenient reference to a historical movement known as exoticism. Within this context it is significant that Westernesque women, as objects of desire, inhabit the canon of pure literature, while pseudo-Western men, as objects of derision, are generally found in works that literary history and criticism have relegated to the realm of popular literature (*Seishun* is a case in point) or assigned minor, adversarial roles to the protagonists of pure literature. Certainly, this gender division can be partially explained by the fact that most modern Japanese writers were men for whom women in themselves constituted an "exotic" other in Segalen's sense of the term. Yet the landmark Westernesque femmes fatales of modern Japanese literature are not simply representations of the female other; they are also sirens who personify the dangers of spanning the gap between reading Western literatures and writing in Japanese. In other words, they are also figures of *translation*. To understand the nature of their exotic value within the context of modern Japanese literature, we must therefore redefine the parameters of exoticism to include not only the exotic sexual other but also the exotic textual other as an object of fascination.

The Exoticism of the Prestige Language

What I mean by the "exotic textual other" is something quite distinct from the kind of exoticism typically associated with translation into modern Western languages (especially English). This other is apprehended not as the kind of textual object capable of being grasped—indeed, "mastered"—through a language student's due diligence; rather, it is recognized as the highest form of textuality itself. It is the object of the kind of exoticism perfectly expressed in Antoine Berman's statement that "the translating drive always posits an *other* language as ontologically *superior* to its own."[12] That is to say, it is the exotic textual other that is constituted by a newly encountered *prestige language*. It is at this point that my use of the term *exoticism* departs most markedly from the historical Western image associated with the all-knowing and quintessentially modern exote who looks down—hierarchically, geographically, temporally, *ontologically*—at the other. If any writing lesson is going to take place here, it is surely the exote who will play teacher. But in my deployment of exoticism it is the very desire to take this writing lesson that marks the Japanese writer as the true exote, and the prestige language is the true object of his adoring gaze.

Berman's "translating drive" is not that which motivates a translator to transport the ostensible content of a foreign text—as an eminently knowable object—to the familiar terms of her own language, but the drive to transform her native language by means of what she sees as an ontologically superior linguistic alterity. In fact, as Karatani Kojin has argued, this drive lies at the very heart of all attempts to vernacularize writing.

When Dante wrote in the vernacular, he did not directly transpose contemporary spoken language into writing. From the various idiomes (Saussure) existing all over Italy, he selected one. It is not because he selected the standard idiome, but rather because he wrote in the vernacular as a form of translating Latin, that his écriture later became the standard écriture. That act relegated the other idiomes to the status of dialect. The same can be said in the cases of French and German. The vernacular was written so as to "resemble" Latin and Greek as much as possible. In the case of France, for instance, the Académie Francaise was established in 1635 for the purpose of "giving a clear set of rules to the national language, making it pure, eloquent, and capable of handling the arts and academic disciplines." It is wrong to think of this as a reformation of the French language, however. As I said above, "French" did not exist as a spoken language; it was simply that written "French" later became the spoken language. "French" as écriture existed as a translation of Latin, which is precisely why it became a language "capable of handling the arts and academic disciplines." It is for this reason that Descartes wrote in both French and Latin, and that his French became the norm. Latin, which was no more than a single idiom of the Italian provinces, became a language "capable of handling the arts and academic disciplines" because of its development as a translation of Greek written documents, a process in which the Greeks themselves participated.[13]

While we are trained to recognize the poetic genius in a Dante or a Chaucer, to appreciate the originality of their vernacular texts, when we look to the pioneering works of modern Japanese vernacular fiction, do we not find it difficult to see beyond the acts of imitation that, according to the temporal and geographic divide of the world into the modern West and the premodern rest, are what would apparently make them "modern" in the first place? The view that modern Western vernacular literature is original, while the modern vernacular literature of Japan, for instance, is derivative—the problematic condition that spurred Rey Chow's question, "How might we read modern Chinese literature other than as a kind of bastardized appendix to classical Chinese and a mediocre apprentice to Western literature?"—can only be sustained by a persistent denial of the centrality of translation itself in the development of languages and the formation of cultural identities. In fact, it would be small exaggeration to say that the cultural devaluation of translation is one of the means by which the cult of (Western) originality has been sustained.

We need only recall the fact that Aristotle first entered the Christian European canon of classical Greek thought by means of an extremely circuitous route of translations—Greek to Syriac to Arabic to Latin—to recognize the crucial yet easily effaced role translation plays in the creation of cultural identities. In the postwar United States, where rigorous foreign language education no longer constitutes a central part of intellectual training, translations from both modern and ancient European languages play an even more powerful role in creating the "imagined community" of the West. Homer's "rosy-fingered dawn" is so completely at home in our English that we can scarcely think of this phrase as a translation; indeed, to do so would threaten to wreak havoc on many an undergraduate's notion of the integral unity of Western culture.

The self-effacing role almost universally assigned to the translator in English—what Lawrence Venuti calls the "scandal of translation"—strikes a bold contrast with the case of modern Japanese, a language so profoundly and admittedly defined by translation as to afford its best translators a fame that rivals, and sometimes even eclipses, that of the authors whose texts they recreate. Indeed, many modern Japanese novelists were equally known for their translations of Western texts, a kind of double distinction that has few real parallels in the history of English fiction (as opposed to poetry). But any temptation to generalize this cultural devaluation of translation as a defining characteristic of modern Western culture as a whole—which runs the risk of reifying both "Western" culture and the dogma of untranslatability that finds its best support in the notion of culture/language as an inviolable whole—can be easily forestalled by invoking the words of Friedrich Schleiermacher, who claimed that the translating impulse was a defining characteristic of the German people: "An inner necessity, in which a peculiar calling of our people asserts itself clearly enough, has driven us to translate *en masse.*"[14] Indeed, the prominence accorded translation in modern German literary discourse produced a theory of translation that, in its bold outlines, prefigures the relationship between translation and exoticism this study proposes as a defining characteristic of modern Japanese literature.

In *Notes on the East-West Divan* Goethe outlined a three-step progression that resonates with the discussion of parody and exoticism presented in this introduction. The first type of translation "acquaints us with the foreign country on our own terms; a plain prose translation is best for this purpose. Prose in and of itself serves as the best introduction; it completely naturalizes the formal characteristics of any sort of poetic art and reduces even the most exuberant waves of poetic enthusiasm to still water."[15] Goethe's "plain prose translation" refers to the kinds of literary representations that offer up a foreign text as an object of knowledge, an endeavor that necessarily eschews "any sort of poetic art" or linguistic materiality that might call attention to itself instead of simply "making sense." We could fruitfully expand this category to include not only translations, but also all "plain prose" works that seek to "acquaint us with the foreign country on our own terms." It is this kind of translation that critics like Edward Said and Tejaswini Niranjana have attacked as part and parcel of the Orientalist production of knowledge/power. This practice of translation as representation is what makes it possible to speak of ethnography, for instance, as "cultural translation"—a term that, ironically, cannot be meaningfully translated into a culture *of* translation, such as Japan, where the act of "translating the West," to quote Douglas Howland, precluded the possibility of remaining strictly within the confines of "our own terms." Under such circumstances the term *translation* is so powerfully associated with a transformative linguistic practice that it can scarcely be generalized to signify an integral discursive system for reproducing the anthropological other. As such, although it is this sense of translation that has arguably achieved the broadest currency within American academic discourse, it will have little bearing on the work at hand.

It is Goethe's second and third epochs of translation that are particularly relevant here; the works examined in this study oscillate between these two poles. In the second epoch "the translator endeavors to transport himself into the foreign situation but actually only appropriates the foreign idea and represents it as his own. I would like to call such an epoch *parodistic*, in the purest sense of that word."[16] If we substitute the word *exoticist* for *translator*, we get a succinct definition of the kinds of writers Victor Segalen dismissed as "pseudo-Exotes," among whom Pierre Loti held a prominent place. This type of translation/exoticism may profess an attempt to represent the foreign in a more authentic register, but ultimately it achieves little more than to loudly proclaim the author's self-conscious identification with the foreign.

It is most often men of wit who feel drawn to the parodistic. The French make use of this style in the translation of all poetic works. . . . In the same way that the French adapt words to their pronunciation, they adapt feelings, thoughts, even objects; for every foreign fruit there must be a substitute grown in their own soil.

Wieland's translations are of this kind; he, too, had his own peculiar understanding and taste, which he adapted to antiquity and foreign countries only to the extent that he found it convenient.[17]

In this case, idiosyncracies of expression that exceed the bounds of the familiar do not stand in for the foreign object itself but rather for the subject who claims it as his own.

Goethe calls the third epoch "the highest of the three." Here "the goal of the translation is to achieve perfect identity with the original, so that the one does not exist instead of the other but in the other's place." This is the kind of textual exoticism that succeeds in the often thankless task of reproducing the shock of difference for its readers.

This kind met with the most resistance in its early stages, because the translator identifies so strongly with the original that he more or less gives up the uniqueness of his own nation, creating this third kind of text for which the taste of the masses has to be developed.

At first the public was not at all satisfied with Voss (who will never be fully appreciated) until gradually the public's ear accustomed itself to this new kind of translation and became comfortable with it. Now anyone who assesses the extent of what has happened, what versatility has come to the Germans, what rhythmical and metrical advantages are available to the spirited, talented beginner, how Ariosto and Tasso, Shakespeare and Calderon have been brought to us two and three times over as Germanized foreigners, may hope that literary history will openly acknowledge who was the first to choose this path in spite of so many and varied obstacles.[18]

In Goethe's third epoch "traduttore, traditore" means that the translator betrays her own language, willfully violating its presumed boundaries. His account of the public reaction to Johann Heinrich Voss's translations could be directly applied to the work of Futabatei Shimei, the progenitor of Japan's modern literary vernacular and the first to translate a modern Western literary text into vernacular Japanese.

Goethe's emphasis on the formal, rather than the semantic, aspects of literary translation presages the kind of transformation that would take place in modern Japanese literature as well. What allows a translation to "exist not instead of the other but in the other's place" is the translator's powerful identification with the *form* of the text he chooses to translate. Privileging exotic forms and abandoning native ones to create a "third kind of text" thus constitutes the first step toward the emergence of "naturalized foreigners," writers who, while writing in their "own" language, exploit the formal possibilities imported from other languages through the medium of translation. Goethe's phrase "Germanized foreigners" neatly identifies the inversion that takes place once the third language of translation has achieved acceptance. If we think of exoticism simply as a preference for the foreign over the native, then this third type of what Lydia Liu calls "translingual practice" is thoroughly exoticist in its privileging of foreign forms. But the resulting product is a text that replaces the source of its own genesis, rendering the foreign text obsolete by offering it up for *use* (not merely "knowledge" or aesthetic appreciation) in a new linguistic environment. Once the initial resistance to this kind of translation is overcome, its use by other writers will result in the transformation of the target language and thus, paradoxically, the complete naturalization of the foreign text to the native linguistic environment. It is by means of this process that Japanese Naturalism, which found its models not only in Western writers but also in the work of Futabatei *as translator*, became "naturalized" in every sense of the word.

Once this process has been completed, we easily lose sight of the essential hybridity of the linguistic condition. The phenomenon Goethe alludes to with the term "Germanized foreigners" is superseded by an encompassing idea of "the West"; in the case of modern Japan the exotic cachet of the vernacular literary style as a form of translation is forgotten, and the vernacular is naturalized and subsumed to a universalist discourse on modern literary realism. This study of the hybrid image of the Westernesque femme fatale explores the historically productive relationship between translation and modern literature, conceptualizing translation as an exoticist practice and modern Japanese literature itself as a mode of relating to the exotic text. With its roots in the first "modern Japanese novel," the persistently recurring image of the Westernesque femme fatale provides us with an opportunity to explore this relation without losing sight of the constant workings of translation.

A final word on methodology: three decades ago Clifford Geertz boldly claimed that "ethnography is thick description." In a critical attempt to relativize the scientific authority of the ethnographer, to expose the messy and inherently unstable processes of interpretation that undergird his work, Geertz quotes a long and involved passage from his own field notes in order make the following point:

> Quoted raw, a note in a bottle, this passage conveys, as any similar one similarly presented would do, a fair sense of how much goes into ethnographic description of even the most elemental sort—how extraordinarily "thick" it is. In finished anthropological writings, including those collected here, this fact—that what we call our data are really our own constructions of other people's constructions of what they and their compatriots are up to—is obscured because most of what we need to comprehend a particular event, ritual, custom, idea, or whatever is insinuated as background information before the thing itself is directly examined.[19]

In the following pages I proceed by means of what might be called "thick translation."[20] It is "thick" in two senses: first, my translations aim to achieve a transparency not of meaning alone but also of the densely layered linguistic materiality of the Japanese texts they reproduce in English. Second, the translation-citations are thick in number and, where necessary, lengthy. This "thickness" represents my own attempt to relativize the authority of the critic who writes in academic English, taking up the position of the Western discursive subject. Rather than presuming too much upon the reader's trust and belief in the authority of this subject by frequent paraphrasing—another way of saying "take my word for it, I *know*"—I have aimed to present as many translations of relevant Japanese texts as practically possible. As for the translations themselves, I have attempted to follow Futabatei's ethic of translation as closely as possible, with one major caveat: where the absence of personal pronouns is critical to my analysis of a text, the translation-citations have gone to unusual lengths to preserve this particular quality in English; otherwise I have inserted them for the sake of clarity, even at the expense of a more formally accurate translation. The thick translations in this study are offered as one humble means of according the non-Western other with the respect due to a producer of texts by another producer of texts; it is my hope that they will be read in that spirit.

Part 1

FOREIGN LETTERS, THE VERNACULAR, AND MEIJI SCHOOLGIRLS

Roses bloom on heads, live people become pictures; in such a world, how pathetic that writings alone should have its cheeks crammed full of stiff, mold-sprouting gobbledygook, or a mouth dripping with drool from learning to speak with an immature tongue. Once I realized that this must be a matter for the union of speech and writing, I could hardly wait to seize the moment, with the winds of civilization and the fever of reform surging nigh all at once . . .

—Futabatei Shimei, preface to *Ukigumo*

With a strategically ironic use of the poetic Japanese style's economic elegance, Futabatei Shimei summed up his impetus for writing a novel in the vernacular. Here, meaning is compacted into a series of striking images: roses blooming on heads and live people becoming pictures refer to women ornamenting their hair with roses and socialites posing for tableaux vivants, while the stiff, mildewed gibberish and inarticulate wordings that plague the "mouth" of writing refer to the inherited Chinese and Japanese styles, respectively. These images serve as both a critique of the status quo and a promise for the future. First, the oblique language by which they conjure up the dramatic changes taking place in Meiji Japan eloquently evokes the disjunction between the inherited literary language and the state of contemporary society. As the influx of Western material culture rapidly changes the face of society, Futabatei suggests, it is only fit that writing too should be reformed according to the Western model. Clearly, the use of oral imagery reinforces the notion that this reform will give writing the easily consumable quality of speech. And, finally, the allusions to the Westernesque in women's fashion serve as a subtle yet tantalizing suggestion of what Futabatei's new style will be capable of bringing to Japanese fiction.

Indeed, what places Futabatei Shimei at the beginning of this study is the fact that he created the prototype for the Westernesque femme fatale in Osei, the heroine of *Ukigumo*. The presence of this particular female type in Japan's first modern novel is not an entirely fortuitous coincidence. Although there is little evidence to suggest that the persistent reappearance of the Westernesque femme fatale in landmark works of modern Japanese literature can be explained as the conscious appropriation, emulation, or parody of *Ukigumo*, when Futabatei's first novel is read in the light of these later landmarks it is possible to discern a distinct pattern of relations between new literary media and the erotic-exotic valorization of the Westernesque woman in modern Japanese literature.[1] Regardless of the degree to which *Ukigumo* may or may not have directly affected later writers, we can confidently say that Futabatei Shimei was the first to discover the Westernesque femme fatale as the figure par excellence for manifesting the complex hybridity of modern Japan. What led to this discovery, and what resulted from it?

Even in the preface quoted above we find an important clue as to what connects the Westernesque woman to modern Japanese literary media: the rise of the modern vernacular in Japanese literature is simultaneously conceived as a new turn toward the West and as a return to the native body of spoken Japanese. Thus the vernacularization of Japanese literary style known as genbun-itchi—in spite of its literal meaning as the "reconciliation of spoken and written language"—cannot be fully grasped as an ideology of returning to the native tongue. As Futabatei's preface hints and as his own literary career confirms, the successful deployment of a new vernacular literature could only be achieved by means of *translating* Western vernacular literatures. Although the vernacular style is often discussed in terms of its transparency, it is also, particularly at its inception, characterized by the opaque traces of the foreign. In other words, as a literary style, genbun-itchi began as an uneasy coalescence of the native body of speech with the exotic textuality of foreign letters.

The narrative of *Ukigumo*, constructed as Futabatei's attempt to portray the "contemporary state of the nation," can also be read as a dramatization of this linguistic dilemma. The basic story of *Ukigumo* is a fairly simply one: the protagonist, Utsumi Bunzō, falls in love with his cousin Sonoda Osei, who in turn seems to shift her affections toward Honda Noboru, Bunzō's former and infinitely more success-ful colleague in the prestigious government bureaucracy. Described as a natural-born mimic, Osei has a distinct facility for picking up on new trends and an equal tendency to discard them as soon as some-thing newer comes along. Bunzō, by contrast, is characterized by an unswerving adherence to his own ideals, making him almost com-pletely incapable of adapting to his surroundings. Within the terms of the novel, Osei is a talker, while Bunzō is a thinker—or, more pre-cisely, someone who sees everything in terms of written texts. The ever widening gap between the two, when read as the failed betrothal of speech and writing, emerges as a powerful metanarrative on lit-erary media, one that reveals a great deal more about the essential dilemmas of vernacularization than the expository discourse on gen-bun-itchi.

Moreover, as emblematic representatives of Meiji Japan, Osei and Bunzō reflect two poles in the modern Japanese relation to the West: the freely chosen adoption of Westernisms as a means of fashionable self-ornamentation (Osei), on the one hand, and the paralyzing inter-nalization of Westernisms as fixed textual realities (Bunzō), on the other. Futabatei's narrative, which spares neither of these positions from critical analysis, manifests a direct concern with the painfully parodic relationship between Japan and the West. As noted in the introduction, the problematic raised by this relationship was central to literary production itself, and Futabatei's work as both novelist and translator proposed two different approaches for negotiating it. As a prelude to our reading of *Ukigumo* in chapter 2, chapter 1 examines the relationship between literary translation, vernacularization, and composition in Futabatei's work and in his time.

Translation as Origin
and the Originality of Translation

The history of modern Japanese literature begins with translation in more than one sense. First, we have the translation of the nineteenth-century European concept of "literature" into the Chinese compound *bungaku*—not a neologism in itself, but the investment of a completely new meaning in an old and fairly recondite term. Tracing as far back as *The Analects*, the word *bungaku* 文学 originally referred to the study of written documents, and its meaning later evolved to include the study of rhetoric and the Confucian classics. It was not until the early Meiji period that it came to signify "literature" in the nineteenth-century European sense, as a category of the arts that included poetry, drama, and fiction. This reorganization of knowledge marks a watershed in the social history of fiction, raising the novel from its lowly status as frivolous entertainment to the high culture of civilized nations.[1] In tandem with the introduction of this new concept, the Meiji period ushered in an era of translations from Western languages that would have a decisive impact on all forms of Japanese literary production.

The onset of the Meiji era saw Kanagaki Robun, a professionally trained writer of the popular fiction of the Edo period known as *gesaku,* struggling to keep up with the rapid changes of "enlighten-ment and civilization." Robun's combination of formal training as a gesaku writer and lack of training in foreign languages was to become a serious handicap in the new literary (or, rather, *newly* literary) world of the Meiji period. *Seiyō dōchū hizakurige* (1870–76) and *Aguranabe* (1871–73), two of Robun's final efforts to maintain his old trade, duly reflect Meiji Japan's signature turn toward the West. The former tells a comic tale of two Yokohama merchants who travel to the West; the latter comprises a series of vignettes about the patrons of a beef restaurant in Tokyo. Although Robun studied up for the composition of these works by reading Fukuzawa Yukichi's best-selling accounts of contemporary conditions in Europe, his formal training had only prepared him to project the profound new changes taking place through the irretrievably outdated lenses of gesaku language. It was a flippant comic language that could not resist reducing the West to a series of *dajare* puns:

ゆきの普魯西もさて亜米利加も馬車で通ふて英吉利。僕はこれほど葡萄牙。きみはいつでも仏蘭西か。浮世の希臘と只印度、床を土耳其のひとつ夜着。埃及こちらへ寄らしやんせ。支那ハと取りすがり。魯西亜の見える恋のみちハアトツチリトン

fall/Prussia   rain/America
Yuki no *purosha* mo sate *amerika* mo basha de kayōte

go/England   smitten/Portugal
ingirisu. Boku wa kore hodo *horutogaru.* Kimi wa itsu de mo

reject/France?   duty/Greece   once/India   lay/Turkey
furansu ka. Ukiyo no *girisha* to tada *indo,* toko o *toruko* no

     a little/Egypt   coquettish/China
hitotsu yogi. *Ejiputo* kochira e irashanse. *Shinashina* to

     ?/Russia
torisugari. *Roshia* no mieru koi no michi . . .[2]

In this indomitable effort to assimilate Western place names to the language of gesaku, most of the double entendres (indicated in italics above) stretch homophonic associations far beyond their usual limits. Here is the closest approximation I could manage in English (it may help to imagine Groucho Marx giving a private geography lesson to an attractive young woman):

Snow may Prussiapitate and American on rain, but I shall be travelEngland by carriage. These days I am in Port-du-gal. Will you never Francy me? Hinduty to the floating world, just once she aGreece Turkish me for a night. Please come a teeniE-gyptian in my direction. Sino-ously cuddling up, Russian down the path of amour . . .

While this almost intoxicated, nonsensical flippancy might have provided a welcome palliative for the merchant classes within the staid Tokugawa hierarchical system, the sobering effects of the social upheaval occasioned by the threat of Western hegemony proved less conducive to the enjoyment of pure verbal play.

The end of the self-proclaimed gesaku was undoubtedly hastened by the work of literary translation. In 1877 (Meiji 10) Niwa Jun'ichirō published his epoch-making translation of Bulwer-Lytton's *Ernest Maltravers*—a novel that, though certainly not in itself of great literary merit, offered the reader a compelling story and a more intimate sense, however fictional, of the daily lives and sensibilities of Westerners. A sensation in its time, Niwa's *Karyū shunwa* (A spring tale of flowers and willows) set an important standard for novel writing in Japanese for the remainder of the Meiji teens. According to Itō Sei, one of the most important contributing factors to the popularity of *Karyū shunwa* was that Niwa wrote it in *kanbun-kuzushi*, a Japanese permutation of literary Chinese.[3] While Robun was working in the gesaku language of commoners, Niwa wrote in the language of the educated elite. His translation of a modern English novel into literary Chinese helped to establish a new audience for the genre.

The flood of political novels and translations written in kanbun-kuzushi that followed in the wake of Niwa's *Karyū shunwa* provide ample evidence of its wide-ranging impact. (Even Tsubouchi Shōyō's translation of Sir Walter Scott's *Bride of Lammermoor* into the rhythmic Japanese style of *gabuntai*, published three years later, follows the precedent set by Niwa in its Chinese title of *Shumpū jōwa*.) This is the second sense in which the history of modern Japanese literature began with translation. As one commentator remarks, "For the Japanese novel, the period from the publication of *Karyū shunwa* in Meiji 10 to that of Futabatei Shimei's *Ukigumo* in Meiji 20 brought forth so many translations as to suggest a dearth of compositional power in Japanese literary circles at the time."[4] Clearly, the popularity of Chinese diction and written style in the Meiji teens was not the manifestation of some Japanese preoccupation with China, but rather with a particular style of translating the civilization and enlightenment of the "West" that marked its exotic prestige by means of the semiforeign lingua franca of Chinese.[5] Indeed, the entire vocabulary of "Western civilization" was translated into Chinese compounds (*kango*), from *bunmei* (civilization) and bungaku to *sokuhatsu* (the simplified coiffure of the Western-style bun) and *butōkai* (dance ball). As the preferred language of translation, Chinese surely facilitated the acquisition of new social customs, technologies of learning, and the profound reorganization of knowledge by which Japan sought entrance into the exclusive and powerful club of modern nations. Yet, within the context of the novel itself, the transformative potential of kanbun translation was substantially limited to the sphere of narrative content.

First let us examine the language of fiction established in Niwa's *Karyū shunwa*. In his commentary on this work, Kimura Ki selects the following passages for comparison:

[*Ernest Maltravers*]

"You work at the factories, I suppose?" he said.
    "I do, sir. Bad times."

[*Karyū shunwa*]

客問フテ曰ク子、日ニ近傍ノ製造所ニ行キ以テ生活ノ途ヲ立ツルヤ。
曰ク誠ニ然リ。然レドモ方今製造所盛ナラズ。僕大ニ之ヲ憂フ。

Kyaku tōte iwaku shi, hi ni kinbō no seizōjo ni yuki motte seikatsu no michi o tatsuru ya. Iwaku makoto ni shikari. Saredomo hōkon seizōjo sakan narazu. Boku ooi ni kore o ureu.

[translation of *Karyū shunwa*]

Quoth the guest, querying, Dost thou go to the proximate factory every-day to earn a subsistence? Quoth, Verily I do. However, recently production is not prolific. I am greatly distressed by this.[6]

There is no parallel to kanbun in the history of English letters, and this gap has made a parody of my attempt to convey the highfalutin language of Niwa's text. However, it is not my intention here to suggest that Niwa's translation would seem as ridiculous to his contemporary Japanese audience as the above English rendition will surely seem to mine. Niwa was writing in a well-established idiom that was quite familiar to the educated classes of 1870s Japan, to whom a more literal, "vernacular" translation may have seemed ridiculous indeed. We might even suggest that by packaging Bulwer-Lytton's work in the prestigious learned language of kanbun-kuzushi, Niwa secured a lasting place in literary history for a writer whose original work would not merit such an honor. Nevertheless, what the above retranslation should make immediately clear is the inability of the kanbun style to approximate the pedestrian tone of Bulwer-Lytton's vernacular English. While kanbun provided a suitable medium for the translation of European concepts into "Japanese" in ways that we have already noted above, this is its most obvious drawback.

In the translation of novels, what kanbun did facilitate was the transference of exotic narrative content (i.e., stories about the West) unencumbered by the aesthetic demands and stylistic conventions of classical Japanese prose. In her study of Futabatei, Marleigh Grayer Ryan sums up the conditions of literary translation in the early Meiji period as follows:

[The translator] was forced to choose between two equally unsatisfactory styles: the cold, terse, extremely difficult intellectual language of kanbun-chō [kanbun-kuzushi] and the poetic, allusive, flowing gabuntai [classical Japanese prose]. The vogue which kanbun-chō enjoyed in the mid-1880s stemmed from the fact that readers considered this style to be more suited to Western writing than the flowery gabuntai. The images and metaphors of gabuntai were so intimately linked with past Japanese literature that they seemed singularly inappropriate to foreign fiction. The wealth of associations conjured up by the mention of a familiar image or even word drawn from traditional Japanese literary writing was likely to destroy the atmosphere of a foreign work. Such images and vocabulary had to be abandoned to forestall the possibility of irrelevant associations with past literature, but substitutions were hard to discover.[7]

The preference for kanbun-kuzushi in the translation of Western literatures is also surely related to the fact that kanbun originated as a language of translation. Neither "Chinese" nor "Japanese" in the strict sense, the Japanese practices of reading and writing known as kanbun grew out of the tradition of rendering written Chinese into Japanized pronunciations, grammatical and syntactical patterns. As a language of interlineal translation between Chinese and Japanese, kanbun was an interlingual écriture par excellence. Its greater malleability as a language of translation can be seen, for instance, in its capacity for maintaining gender (and class) neutrality in the translation of English dialogue—aside from the use of the gender-specific first-person pronouns *boku* (male) and *warawa* (female), in Niwa's translation Maltravers and his amour Alice "speak" the same stilted language. Had Niwa rendered his translation in spoken Japanese, such gender parity would have been read as a clear mark of the lower classes.[8]

While Niwa's kanbun style was able to provide the reader with fairly straightforward access to the essential elements of the foreign story, gabuntai, a language of poetic allusion rather than expository prose, had powerful demands of its own. Ryan provides an illuminating glimpse of the results:

Tsubouchi translated Scott's "had, by her frequent rambles, learned to know each lane, alley, dingle, or bushy dell" as

. . . koko kashiko to shōyō shi,
Sansui no ki o saguritareba
Keikyoku no ato o uzumetaru nobe no komichi,
Matsukaze no hibiki ni wasuru tagitsuse wa iu mo sara nari,
Kaigan arasoitachi,
Rōboku outsu taru yūkoku no sumizumi made,
Nabete eshirazaru wa nakarikeri. . . .

[Wandering here and there
exploring the wonders of mountain and river,
of paths through fields filled with brambles,
or the waterfall echoing in the wind through the pines,
every corner of the warring cliffs and ravines thick with ancient trees—
there was none unknown to her. . . .][9]

The broad divergence between the texts will surely strike the reader as gross embellishment on Shōyō's part. Yet it is not necessarily arbitrary. Rather, the poetic elaboration of Scott's descriptive prose reveals the kind of judgment call that inevitably occurs when the translator places primary authority in the conventions of the target language instead of the original text. In the case of gabuntai, the nature of that judgment call is simply more obvious than in kanbun (or modern English, for that matter).

Futabatei Shimei's dual career as translator and novelist presents us with the third sense in which modern Japanese literature began with translation. Futabatei's long-standing status as a progenitor of Japanese literary modernity derives primarily from his creation and successful deployment of the genbun-itchi style that was to become the very foundation of the modern Japanese novel. Significantly, his earliest efforts at literary translation predate his work as a novelist, though they were never published and the manuscripts have been lost. By 1886 he had translated a work by Nikolai Gogol (title unknown), and by March of the same year he had translated part of Ivan Turgenev's *Fathers and Children*. From Tsubouchi Shōyō's recollections of these translations, we know that both of them were written in a vernacular style. *Ukigumo* was published in installments over a two-year period from July 1887 through August 1889. In the meantime, Futabatei also debuted as a literary translator with the serialized publication of *Aibiki* (Turgenev's "The Rendezvous" from *A Sportsman's Notebook*).[10] As this chronology itself suggests, Futabatei's creation of a vernacular Japanese literary language was inextricably tied to the process of translation.

Although in the English context, we customarily consider translation to be a process of transference between two discrete and already established languages, Futabatei in fact used this process to create a new language in Japanese. It is in this sense that his translations from modern Russian literature constitute truly original innovations. If the age of literary translation and political novels precipitated by the success of *Karyū shunwa* effectively outmoded the comic gesaku reaction to the West, the form of literature presented by Futabatei's *Aibiki* and *Ukigumo* was so new as to ultimately create a radical divide between modern Japanese fiction and all that preceded it. For Futabatei's approach to and practice of translation manifested a new conception of literature itself. Though the effect of his work may not have been immediate, in the long run it proved to be the most incontrovertible: when Japanese Naturalists refer to the kanbun fiction they read as youths in the Meiji teens, it is almost always as a trope for their as yet immature conception of literature; by contrast, their glowing recollections of *Aibiki* almost always narrate their awakening to literature proper (*bungaku* in the modern sense of the term).

As Ryan rightly points out, to undertake literary translation in early Meiji was to first confront a choice between the lesser of two evils. What was the basis upon which Futabatei refused this choice? In an interview he made the following renowned statement of his personal standard for literary translation:

Well, in the translation of foreign literature, if you think only of the meaning and place all the weight on it, there is a danger of destroying the original. I believed that you must imbibe the rhythm of the original and then convey it, so I never disposed of a single comma or period arbitrarily—if there were three commas and one period in the original, then I would also use three commas and one period in the translation in my effort to convey the rhythm of the original. Particularly when I first started to translate, the earnest intent of conveying the rhythm of the original led to a real struggle over the form in which I tried to use the same number of words as the original and not destroy the form, but in reality it did not really turn out as I hoped.[11]

Futabatei's credo for translation serves as an implicit critique of works like *Karyū shunwa* and *Shumpū jōwa*. While Niwa's method of translation placed weight primarily in the "meaning," Shōyō's placed greater importance on the "rhythm" of the target language than the original text. At this point it must be noted that Futabatei's critique of the emphasis on meaning was by no means a defense of "liberal" translations—he himself strove for the same kind of literalness as did Nabokov in his English translation of Pushkin's *Evgeny Onegin*. This stringent standard, purely self-imposed, created perhaps the single greatest challenge to Futabatei's translations of modern Russian literature. At a time when other literary translators had few inhibitions about altering the content of the translated text and none whatsoever about altering its formal characteristics, Futabatei's pious attitude toward the original text could only be described as original in itself. And indeed, it was what enabled, even compelled, him to create a new literary language for Japanese.

Futabatei's standard for translation could not have been based on anything but his understanding of literature itself. Aside from the undeniable differences of style between himself and earlier literary translators, which will become apparent shortly, this is where he first departs from all of his predecessors and most of his contemporaries in the production—translation or composition—of Meiji literature. For Futabatei's attitude toward the text to be translated was indeed one of *piety*. With the possible exception of Tsubouchi Shōyō, he was the first of the Meiji literati to treat the novel with the respect customarily reserved for the Chinese classics—ethical philosophy, history, Chinese poetry—that constituted the essential syllabus for elite education in pre-Meiji Japan. Put in terms that would apply to any culture at some point in its development of a modern literature, Futabatei was one of the first in Japan to accord the novel with the respect normally reserved for the language of *truth*.

In "Shōsetsu sōron" (Theory of the novel, 1886), published as the prolegomenon to an aborted critique of Shōyō's *Tōsei shosei katagi* (1885–86), Futabatei defined the novel as follows:

Art is that which penetrates Ideas by means of emotion.

The two kinds of novels are didactic and mimetic, but for the reasons stated above mimesis is the true essence of the novel. . . . Since, from the outset, the novel is that which directly apprehends the necessary affective state (Idea) of the varied multiplicity of phenomena (Form) manifest in this world, in order to convey this apprehension to people it must be direct. In order to be direct, it must be mimetic. Thus it is evident that mimesis is the true essence of the novel. . . . Yet just to proclaim mimesis without defining it leaves room for confusion. To state the very broad outlines, that which is called mimesis borrows real appearances in order to depict empty appearances. As articulated above, none of the phenomena of the real world of appearance are without a necessary Idea, yet the Idea is obscured by contingent form so that it cannot be understood clearly. Certainly, the phenomena described in the novel are also contingent, but to clearly draw out the essential Idea within these contingent forms by means of verbal locution and plot pattern is the purpose of the mimetic novel. This requires that the writing be alive. If the writing is not alive, then even if there is an Idea it will not be evident. It requires that the plot be suitable to the Idea. If it is not suitable, then the Idea will not be able to develop sufficiently.[12]

While the famously cryptic language of this brief essay precluded all but bewilderment in the reactions of Futabatei's contemporaries, it nevertheless provides us with an important summation of his concept of literature. First, Futabatei defines the novel as a genre that borrows the appearance of reality for the sole purpose of revealing the Idea (truth or meaning) hidden within it. This is a significant departure from the notion of realism developed in Shōyō's *Shōsetsu shinzui*, which can still be read as an advocacy of mimesis for its own sake, and it forms the basis for Futabatei's ambitious attempt to capture the "contemporary state of the nation" in *Ukigumo*. Furthermore, he cites both verbal locution and plot construction as the key means for achieving this end. His formulation of the relationship between the calculated use of language and plot to the revelation of Idea within the novel thus lays the basis for his approach to translation: if there is something to be "translated" from a novel, it is the Idea revealed therein, which is necessarily the product of both language (rhetorical and rhythmic form) and story (narrative content).

Futabatei's attempt to translate the original text as an indivisible unit of linguistic form and narrative content necessitated the creation of a new target language. The language that he created in Japanese is known as genbun-itchi, a term that in itself provides an illuminating example of the complexities of the translation process even at the morphemic level. While genbun-itchi is the Japanese signifier for the phenomenon of vernacularization seen in European languages, its literal translation back into English is "the reconciliation of spoken and written languages." Thus genbun-itchi provides a specific gloss for the concept of the vernacular that emphasizes the relationship between speech and writing. (Another possible gloss was provided by the term *zokubun*[*tai*]—literally, "vulgar written style.") One of the most intransigent problems with translation is its ability to efface itself by naturalizing to the target language, which is precisely what has happened to the language Futabatei created as well as the very word genbun-itchi by which it has been named.

Despite its origins as a neologism that unhesitatingly and constantly announced its foreign derivation, the term *genbun-itchi* has long since naturalized itself to Japanese, with the consequence that it has been written and thought about *specifically as* "the reconciliation of speech and writing" for long enough to overshadow its original connection to any broader notion of the vernacular. As a result, the understanding of Meiji genbun-itchi literature often tends toward an anachronistically one-sided focus on the realistic representation of spoken language in writing as particular to modern Japan. An especially revealing example of this anachronism is provided by one scholar's critique of Yamada Bimyō. In *Meiji bungaku to eibungaku* (Meiji literature and English literature), Ebiike Toshiharu cites the following explanation of Bimyō's impetus for writing in the genbun-itchi style:

To begin with what motivated my conversion, first I realized that Western writing was *genbun-itchi,* and then I saw that the poet Chaucer's portrait was prominently placed in a history of English literature. This distinguished servant of his country completely changed the writing style of England—this person emerged, propounded *zokubun,* and ultimately created the English writing of today. Thinking of this extremely accomplished man, one realizes that such a person had already appeared in England hundreds of years ago. Nevertheless in Japan, no one had yet attempted to make their name from writing in *zokubun,* and I really felt from the depths of my heart that this was most unfortunate.[13]

Ebiike then takes Bimyō to task for stating that "Western writing was *genbun-itchi*" and describing Chaucer as an exemplary genbun-itchi writer. From his point of view, Western writing is not apparently genbun-itchi, and Chaucer's use of the vernacular (which he translates as *zokugo*—reconstituted into English as "vulgar/common words") is distinct from genbun-itchi by virtue of the fact that he wrote in verse.[14] What Ebiike fails to realize, however, is that for Bimyō genbun-itchi and *zokubun* simply refer to what we call the vernacular in English, not to the narrow concept of realistic prose that emerged later.

In the particular case of genbun-itchi, translation has been doubly effaced: the sharp focus on spoken Japanese has obscured the importance of translation as both the impetus for the movement and as the process by which vernacularization was ultimately realized. It is altogether too easy to lose sight of the simple fact that the call for genbun-itchi sprang from an awareness of the vernacular nature of modern Western writing (which is patently obvious even from Futabatei's brief preface to *Ukigumo*). The seeds of the genbun-itchi movement were first planted by Dutch scholars of the Edo period, who commented that the use of colloquial language in Dutch writing greatly contributed to the spread of education in the Netherlands.[15] If, on the surface, the genbun-itchi movement was a call to close the gap between colloquial speech and written language, at base it was driven by a desire to achieve parity between Japanese and modern European languages. Thus it was intralingual by definition, but interlingual in motivation. As noted in the introduction, Karatani Kojin points out

that this interlingual motivation forms the basis for vernacularization within the European context as well.[16] A critique of genbun-itchi
in modern Japanese literature and history can easily expose the lie
of "the reconciliation of spoken and written language"—for instance,
critics have pointed to gender, class, and regional biases in the selec-
tive "reconciliation" of spoken and written idioms. Yet such critiques
of representation fail to account for a crucial determining factor in
the competition between different types of vernacular writing in
Japanese: the capacity to approximate not Japanese speech itself, but
rather the vernacular languages of modern Europe.

It is no accident that one of the key issues in the development of
the genbun-itchi style, that of the copular sentence ending, was finally
decided in favor of *de aru,* a usage that derived from the established
translation for the verb "to be." Whereas early novelist practitioners of
the new vernacular style in the Meiji period were divided between the
use of *da, desu,* and *de arimasu,* often vacillating between the three,
Ozaki Kōyō's use of *de aru* beginning with *Ninin nyobo* (1892) gained
wide currency by the Meiji thirties.[17] The most casual form of the
verb, *da,* borders on rudeness, being used only in conversations that
call for the lowest level of politeness; *desu* and *de arimasu* are more
formal. All of them, to differing degrees, therefore bear the mark of
the speaker/narrator's relationship to the addressee/reader within
the social hierarchy. By contrast, because *de aru* was a form from
translation, it was able to create a neutrality for the narrative voice
in vernacular writing that was not common to the enunciations of
spoken Japanese.[18] (We are reminded of the relative gender neutrality
made available by kanbun as a language of translation.) The point is
that it took the intervention of translation, as a primarily intertextual
deployment of language, to free Japanese literary language from its
bonds to the social, wherein each utterance served to mark the class
and gender relations between speaker and auditor.

What set Futabatei's vernacular apart from contemporary rivals in
the field was not his superior ability to record spoken Japanese in his
writing, but rather his ability to translate the language of modern Russian literature into the diction of spoken Japanese. This decisive difference has been obscured by the anachronistic focus on genbun-itchi as

the realistic representation of common parlance in prose or, rather, the representation of reality in prose via the language of spoken Japanese. Even Yamada Bimyō, Futabatei's ultimately unsuccessful rival in the pioneering of a lasting standard for the vernacular novel, was aware of the need for genbun-itchi to function as an interlingual rather than simply intralingual medium. Leaving our consideration of Bimyō's basic assumptions and their practical results for later, let us now take a look at the language of *Aibiki*, which numerous critics have cited as ultimately more important than *Ukigumo* for the later history of the modern Japanese novel. Compare the opening lines of Futabatei's translation with the English translation by Charles and Natasha Hepburn:

[Hepburns' "Rendezvous"]

I was sitting in a birch-wood one autumn, about the middle of September. Ever since morning a fine drizzle had been falling, giving way now and again to warm sunshine: it was fluky weather. One moment the sky would be all overcast with puffy white clouds, at another it would suddenly clear in places for a moment, and, through the rift, the azure sky would appear, clear and smiling, like the glance of a brilliant eye.[19]

[Futabatei's *Aibiki*]

Aki kugatsu chūjun to iu koro, ichinichi jibun ga saru kaba no hayashi no naka ni zashite ita koto ga atta. Kesa kara kosame ga furisosogi, sono harema ni wa oriori nama-atataka na hikage mo sashite, makoto ni kimagure na soraai. Awaawashii shirakumo ga sora ichimen ni tanabiku ka to omou to, futo mata achikochi matataku ma kumogire ga shite, muri ni oshiwaketa you na kumoma kara sumite sakashige ni mieru hito no me no gotoku ni hogoraka ni hareta aozora ga nozokareta.

[translation of *Aibiki*]

Autumn, around mid-September, I spent all day sitting in the middle of a certain birch forest. A light rain had been falling since the morning, and in the breaks between the clouds a warm sun would shine now and then, truly fickle skies. One moment bubbly white clouds would stretch over the entire sky, only to give way in the blink of an eye to a break in the clouds, and between the clouds that seemed to have forced themselves apart could be glimpsed a bright, clear blue sky, looking like a lucid and sagacious human eye.[20]

My translation of Futabatei's *Aibiki* attempts to follow his own standard for translation, retaining the syntactical form and verbatim meaning of the source text as much as possible. Clearly, there are minor discrepancies between the Japanese and English translations of Turgenev's text, and my translation of *Aibiki* does not approach the felicity of the Hepburns' English. Nonetheless, the above translations are infinitely closer to each other in tone and meaning than the passages cited above from Niwa and Bulwer-Lytton or Shōyō and Scott.

The vernacular style of *Aibiki* is so much closer to contemporary Japanese than Niwa's kanbun-kuzushi and Shōyō's gabuntai that it almost seems "natural." For instance, Ryan understandably comments that *Aibiki* "is presented in such natural Japanese that it is difficult to believe that this is a translation and not an original story."[21] Yet this is both an unwitting tribute to the fact that Futabatei's innovation set a lasting standard for modern literary style, and a failure to recognize the radical departure from "natural" Japanese that it originally constituted. What was "unnatural" about Futabatei's translation is not apparent in my English translation either. In fact, what was "unnatural" in *Aibiki* can only be indicated in English by the degree to which Futabatei's text facilitates translation into English in expressions such as "fickle skies" and similes like "a lucid and sagacious human eye."

These are no doubt the kinds of expressions that led Ishibashi Shian, a contemporary reviewer of *Aibiki*, to suggest that Futabatei had purposely embellished the story's descriptive language to compensate for an uneventful plot. Shian found the descriptive language of *Aibiki* cloying. As a case in point, he quotes the following line: "kosame ga shinobiyaka ni ayashige ni shigo suru yō ni parapara to futte tōtta."[22] The Hepburns render this line as: "furtively, slyly, the finest of drizzles began to spray and whisper through the wood."[23] Although unavoidable differences of syntactical arrangement between the Japanese and

English translations create subtle shifts of emphasis, the two versions are close enough that we may consider them essentially equivalent for our purposes here. Again, a reading of the Hepburn text does not give us a concrete sense of what it was that jarred Shian's linguistic sensibilities. However, anyone educated in the idioms of classical Japanese and Chinese will immediately recognize why this kind of description struck Shian as excessively overwrought. While the use of this particular kind of personification to describe nature in Western literatures is as old as Homer's "rosy-fingered dawn," it had little place in the literary lexicons of classical Japanese or Chinese, much less in the figures of everyday speech. Within such a linguistic environment even a phrase like *kimagure na soraai* ("fickle skies") could not avoid having a novel and bizarre ring.

This is the aspect of *Aibiki* that tends to be obscured by Naturalist homages to Futabatei's translation. For instance, Kanbara Ariake describes his first reaction to *Aibiki* in a way that foregrounds the spokenness of the narration: "I was taken by the feeling that its rare style of genbun-itchi, with its skillful use of the colloquial idiom, was ceaselessly whispering intimately into my ear, which gave rise to both an indescribably pleasant sensation and a desire, somewhere at the bottom of my heart, to rebel against it. I just could not stand being spoken to so familiarly."[24] To be sure, the lack of distance between narrator and reader is an important aspect of the first-person narration of *Aibiki*, which employs the verbal sentence endings *da* and *ta* of casual speech and the first-person pronoun *jibun*, as opposed to something more writerly like *yo*.[25] Yet Kanbara's account elides Futabatei's inherently nonidiomatic use of colloquial diction. Ultimately, I believe that it is this subtly *exotic* stylistic feature, rather than simply the "naturalistic" descriptions of nature hailed by Kunikida Doppo, Tayama Katai, and others, that inspired emulation and adulation by Japanese Naturalist writers.

The kind of personification used throughout Turgenev's story seems so natural in English that few native readers would pause to reflect on the central role played by rhetorical convention in Turgenev's "naturalistic" description. The literal translation of alien rhetorical conventions is destined to produce the shock of the exotic in the target reader, and it is also a method of translation that demonstrates the true difficulty of separating form and content. If Futabatei had wished to produce a more "natural" Japanese version of Turgenev's story, he could have reduced the personifying descriptions of nature to a level of semantic content that could then be repackaged in the forms already available to Japanese writing, much as Niwa and Shōyō did. In theory this approach was certainly one option for Futabatei. Yet, as Ishibashi Shian's comments suggest, if Futabatei had reduced "The Rendezvous" to the core narrative content of a plot, he would have been left with very little to translate. Not only was his method of translation revolutionary, but his choice of text was equally radical. Whereas preceding translations of Western fiction reflected an over-whelming interest in exotic stories about the West, Futabatei chose to translate a work of fiction that conveyed almost no story at all. His interest in this particular work was no doubt related to Turgenev's underlying critique of serfdom, yet his radically formalist translation ultimately foregrounded the very language of the text rather than any message that might be extracted from the body of the narrative. By manifesting a modern Western literary text in and as language, Fut-abatei's *Aibiki* definitively exposed the adaptational nature of other literary translations—in other words, their apprehension of modern Western literature as mere content.

In emphasizing the importance of *Aibiki* as a radical departure from earlier translation practices, however, it is not my intention to suggest that Futabatei's importance as a writer can be reduced to a simple matter of stylistic innovation. The lasting impact of his translations—the very fact that today they can be read as "natural Japanese"—could not possibly have been achieved by the force of linguistic novelty alone. Yamada Bimyō, Futabatei's sole rival as the progenitor of the first genbun-itchi novel, provides an illuminating contrast in this respect. As noted above, Bimyō's motivation for writ-ing in the vernacular was, like Futabatei's, prompted by his encounter with a vernacular Western literary language. Indeed, the two novelists shared much in common: both engaged in forms of literary transla-tion; both possessed a certain sensitivity to the rhetorical conventions of their second literary languages; both referred to a number of the same precedents for the written Japanese vernacular in their own stylistic experiments. Yet Bimyō's approach to vernacular writing can be summed up in a single word: *ornamentation*.

With respect to the representation of dialogue in written Japanese, popular Edo fiction had already achieved vernacular realism. For instance, the work of Shikitei Sanba—one of the writers Futabatei cites as a stylistic model for part 1 of *Ukigumo*—constitutes a rare study in the written representation of spoken language for fiction, virtually approaching phonetic transcription through the use of special orthographic signs to indicate dialectical idiosyncrasies in pronunciation. Yet the use of the vernacular was still limited to dialogue, while the narrative passages were written exclusively in gabuntai. Bimyō clearly believed that vernacularization could be achieved by simply extending the spoken idiom to narration, with the addition of a few literary flourishes. Thus he introduces *Fūkin shirabe no hitofushi* (An air for the organ, 1887), one of his first vernacular novels, as follows:

When it comes particularly to novels about today's world, the dialogue has finally taken the vernacular form, but the narration still uses the classical style, with sentences ending in *nari, keri* and *beshi*; this conflict between speech and narration is indeed an eyesore. By all means, it must be fixed. But that is not easy. Because it is not easy, some people have even thrown away their writing brushes, thinking the vernacularization of written language to be altogether too much to hope for in Japan today. That is also too short-tempered. To be sure, the classical style has some things that cannot be matched by the vernacular style, but when skillfully prepared, even the vernacular style will be in no way worse than the classical style, and moreover it has regulations unto itself and an exquisiteness that cannot be put into words. I wrote the narrative portion of this novel with attention to these matters; briefly said, it is like a transcription of Enchō's tales of the human heart with decorations added on.[26]

San'yūtei Enchō was a popular *kōdan* raconteur whose performance art was immortalized by conversion into print form as *Kaidan Botan dōrō* (A ghost story peony lantern, 1884). Sakai Shōzō and Wakabayashi Kanzō, trained practitioners of the revolutionary shorthand technique developed by Tagusari Tsunaki and directly inspired by the use of shorthand in the West, attended a performance by Enchō, recorded it verbatim, and published the transcription in book form.

Futabatei also cites Enchō as one of the models for the style of *Ukigumo*, suggested to him by Shōyō,[27] and *Botan dōrō* is considered to be an important contribution to the development of genbunitchi. Yet if the vernacularization of written language were simply a matter of replicating speech in writing, as so many of its proponents claimed, then the publication of *Botan dōrō* would have represented the completion, rather than a suggestive prelude, to the development of this style. Bimyō was clearly aware that some other element was necessary to complete the process, but the kinds of "decorations" he added to the Enchō narrative style were not sufficiently literary to withstand the wear of time—which is to say that they did not endow speech with the status of writing, but reduced writing to the level of mere talk. The opening passage of *Fūkin* offers some typical examples of Bimyō's vernacular style:

This is the Nakamura Hall in Kōtō. *Standing like a sea-serpent* at the entrance is a sign with the words "Charity Concert" written in large letters, and the hanging row of electric light bulbs, calling to mind great balls of coral taken from the sea-serpent's capital, are such a sight that a country bumpkin would die of fright from one look at them—to describe the scene in a Chinese style. . . . Enter two young women, both with Western-style buns in the common fashion. They head straight up the stairs to the second floor without a hint of demure hesitation, to find the hall already full of people who all, as though by previous agreement, *set their eyes on the two like shellfish to be shucked and thrown into the soup of censure.*[28]

The italicized phrases above mark the use of complex puns that condense numerous meanings into a few syllables. For instance, in the original Japanese, what I have translated as "set their eyes on the two like shellfish to be shucked and thrown into the soup of censure" is simply "futari e me o *mukiminomisoshiru*" (pun in italics). This phrase has four distinct meanings: 1. *futari e me o muki* (to turn eyes towards the two), 2 *mukimi* (literally, shucked shellfish, but in relation to 1, also to strip the two with their eyes), 3. *mukimi no misoshiru* (a miso soup of shucked shellfish), and 4. *mi soshiru* (to censure a person). Bimyō was such a jubilant and devoted punner that it would be no great exaggeration to define this rhetorical device as one of the main "decorations" by which he attempted to complete the process of vernacularization. *Kakekotoba* puns (technically known as "pivot words" in English) have always played an important role in Japanese poetry, and hence of gabuntai, but Bimyō's puns are what is known as *dajare* in Japanese, a term that emphasizes the frivolity of the wordplay in question. The dajare is both a habit of spoken language and a characteristic feature of popular Edo fiction (cf. Kanagaki Robun, quoted above). At best, one could view Bimyō's frequent use of dajare as an attempt to replace the literary device of kakekotoba with a common spoken equivalent, but the result was undoubtedly an appearance of frivolity reminiscent of the popular Edo fiction he sought to supersede.

Among the other types of "decoration" Bimyō added to the model of Enchō's printed performance, we should include frequent personification, forced metaphors, and English punctuation (as in *!* and *?*), all employed as marks of his fashionable familiarity with English literature. A particularly egregious example of this stylistic trait can be found in *Hana no ibara, ibara no hana* (Thorn of the flower, flower of the thorn, 1887), an adaptation from an unspecified German source: "On the coast stands a stately castle, and the light of the sun glares at the very profile of the castle so that the Caucasian color of its white wall this morning is a pale American Indian color, and also the dazzled eyeballs of the windows are sparkling."[29] This peculiar descriptive language suggests that the brief but widespread popularity he enjoyed in the early Meiji twenties had more to do with the novelty value of such obviously exotic expressions as "Caucasian color" and "eyeballs of the windows" than his proclaimed use of spoken Japanese as the basis for a new vernacular style. That these rhetorical devices lose none of their novelty when translated into English provides clear evidence that they are far removed from the process of translation established by Futabatei; it is with good reason that Bimyō called the above work an adaptation.

If the popularity of kanbun translations of Bulwer-Lytton and Jules Verne had much to do with their exotic content, Bimyō's writing was sensationally exotic at the level of style. Like his penchant for dajare, Bimyō's enthusiastic use of exotic linguistic novelties reveals an essentially unproblematic relationship to language, despite his own call for linguistic reform. That this was a major contributing factor to the popularity of early genbun-itchi fiction is suggested by Ishibashi Shian's comment that the cloying descriptive language of *Aibiki* was endemic to genbun-itchi in general.[30] Yet it was also one of the main reasons for the rapid decline of the vernacular style in the Meiji thirties.

Karatani has suggested that the trend toward vernacular literature started by Futabatei and Bimyō was not abandoned in the Meiji thirties, but rather reformulated by Mori Ogai's *Maihime* (1890), which overhauled the classical style of gabuntai according to the model of European vernacular prose.[31] Technically speaking, *Maihime* is not written in genbun-itchi. However, if we consider the genbun-itchi project in terms of its relationship to modern Western writing, rather than simply its use of colloquial Japanese diction and sentence-endings, then the acuity of Karatani's insight becomes clear. In a deft fusion of writing conventions that Tayama Katai later named *wa-kan-yō setchū* (Japanese-Chinese-Western mix), *Maihime* was able to neutralize the most immediately jarring aspects of Western writing by carefully exploiting the stylistic elements of native prestige languages (*kanbun* and *gabun*). The result was an unprecedented form of first-person narrative that suggested a new realm of possibilities for the writing of Japanese fiction. It is particularly interesting that Ōgai managed this feat by deploying the figure of a Western, rather than Westernesque, siren. Paradoxically, it is the Western siren who, quite literally, speaks the language of gabuntai, while, as we shall see, the Westernesque siren speaks the new language of modern Western discourse. As this linguistic domestication suggests, the Western siren turns out to be infinitely more malleable, more knowable, indeed more *transparent*, than her hybrid cousin.

Futabatei's constant struggle with language, as both translator and novelist, could hardly provide a starker contrast to Bimyō's undiluted enjoyment of stylistic experimentation. This critical difference between the two novelists—essentially that of a literal translator and a liberal adaptationist—also clearly manifests itself in the contrast between *Ukigumo* and *Fūkin shirabe no hitofushi*, two of the earliest works of Meiji fiction to focus the spotlight on the schoolgirl, one of the most frequently discussed figures in the new Japanese social landscape.

[2]

Meiji Schoolgirls in and as Language

The first part of *Ukigumo* was published in July 1887, virtually simultaneous to the first installment of Bimyō's *Fūkin* in *Iratsume* that same month. Since there is no evidence to suggest that Futabatei and Bimyō had mutually influenced each other's choice of subject matter, we can only conclude that they conceived and executed these novels independently. The uncanny synchronicity of the Meiji schoolgirl's double debut in Japanese vernacular fiction powerfully suggests that the connection between the Westernesque woman and new literary media was not a matter of sheer coincidence. In light of notable similarities in their delineation of the schoolgirl figure, the critical differences between these two novels compel us to question the status of Meiji schoolgirls in and as language.

It is clear from Tsubouchi Shōyō's memoirs that Futabatei's work with literary translation led to an acute awareness of language as a gender marker. In *Kaki no heta* Shōyō recalls that his first concrete discussion of the vernacular style with Futabatei was sparked by this very problem:

It was a passage in a certain work by Gogol, in which a middle-class husband and wife were engaged in a rather heated discussion about something. This was the first subject matter that brought us to a concrete discussion of the pros and cons of the vernacular style.

His style for translating that piece by Gogol was a crude manner of speaking that might be likened to the parlance of the back alleys (proletarian style). When I said "I cannot see this as middle-class," he said, "But husbands and wives abroad are equals, so if I don't translate it this way, I think it will diverge from the actuality," so he had written the dialogue between husband and wife without honorifics on either side, using words like *omai, ore, sō kai,* and *sō shina.* It was the same opinion as that of Taguchi Teiken's *Nihon kaika no seishitsu* [The character of Japanese civilization], and as a theory it admitted no room to differ, "but when it comes to art, this gets in the way of associations. You know, no one will be able to see this as anything but a back-alley couple. It would be one thing if you put it into kanbun-kuzushi and replaced *omai* with *kei* and *sō kai* [*sic*] with *kou nani nani se yo*," I argued. Being the meticulous, self-reflective and skeptical person he was, he spent sleepless nights working on many different forms of vernacular style.

In those days, the language of the middle and upper classes, particularly that of women, was chock-full of honorifics, and did not at all lend itself to use in translation. There were obstacles and difficulties totally unimaginable to those writers who are accustomed to hearing and using the schoolgirl parlance that developed in late Meiji, or even more, the language of contemporary women.[1]

The contemporary feminist would have good reason to pause over Futabatei's claim that "husbands and wives abroad are equals." Nevertheless, we should not underestimate the significance of his attempt to preserve a certain kind of gender equality in language. As Shōyō points out, the crux of the problem confronting Futabatei's translation was the absence of an even remotely gender-neutral conversational language in middle- and upper-class Tokyo Japanese, a situation that continues in a less extreme form to the present day. In translation the semblance of linguistic gender neutrality could only be achieved by resorting to the abstract language of kanbun or by jarring the reader's class sensibilities. That Futabatei considered the gender equality of Russian dialogue significant enough to preserve in Japanese even at the price of sacrificing class markers reflects an acute sensitivity to gender differences *between* cultures.

While Futabatei was unique in his attempt to render these differences in a vernacular translation, he was certainly not alone in his interest in them. A major component of the discourse on civilization and enlightenment was the concept that women's status offered a key index to any society's level of civilization. Interestingly, the roots of this concept can be traced back to James Mill's *A History of British India* (1817), a work that laid the moral foundations for English expansion into India.

The condition of women is one of the most remarkable circumstances in the manners of nations. Among rude people, the women are generally degraded; among civilized people they are exalted. In the barbarian, the passion of sex is a brutal impulse, which infuses no tenderness; and his undisciplined nature leads him to abuse his power over every creature that is weaker than himself. The history of uncultivated nations uniformly represents the women as in a state of abject slavery, from which they slowly emerge, as civilization advances. . . . Not only among the Africans and other savage tribes, and the Tartars of the present day, but among the ancient inhabitants of Chaldea and Arabia, and all the nations of Europe in their ancient uncivilized state, the women were excluded from the inheritance of the family. Being condemned to severe and perpetual labour, they are themselves regarded as useful property. . . . It is only in that improved state of property and security, when the necessities of life have ceased to create perpetual solicitude, and when a large share of attention may be given to its pleasures; that the women, from their influence on those pleasures, begin to be an object of regard. As society refines upon its enjoyments, and advances into that state of civilization, in which various incorporeal qualities become equal or superior in value to corporeal strength, and in which the qualities of the mind are ranked above the qualities of the body, the condition of the weaker sex is gradually improved, till they associate on equal terms with men, and occupy the place of voluntary and useful coadjutors.[2]

Notwithstanding an undeniable difference of perspective from their Western contemporaries, many Meiji reformers were quick to grasp the central importance and broad implications of this cornerstone idea, which by the latter half of the nineteenth century had grown into a fully developed discourse.

Japanese sensitivity to the powerful discursive connection between the status of women and nations manifested itself in a variety of forms. For instance, the era of the political novel during the Meiji teens is characterized by a fairly large percentage of publications (translations and adaptations) about the lives of prominent political heroines from the West. Within a year of the publication of *Karyū shunwa*, Miyazaki Kuniyoshi came out with *Seiyō retsujo den* (Biographies of heroic women of the West), a translation of Elizabeth Starling's *Noble Deeds of Women*. Over the following decade the genre of female political biography expanded to encompass a sizable list of publications, comprising roughly 10 percent of all prose narratives about the West from the period (both translated and adapted).[3] Another obvious marker of the new representational status of women can be found in the use of Empress Jingu as a symbol for Japan on paper currency, school textbooks, and women's education magazines.[4] Where this discourse probably had the most direct affect on social reality, however, was in its interpretation by advocates of educational reform.

The case of Nakamura Masanao (1832–91, pen name Keiu) is particularly suggestive. During his studies in England Nakamura became keenly aware of the importance of women's education. A scholar of Chinese who had been employed by the Bakufu as a teacher, Nakamura went to England in his mid-thirties. In order to practice pronunciation and conversation, he first went to an elementary school and studied with young children. To his great surprise, these children were able to answer scientific questions like "Why does the rain fall?" or "What causes thunder?" for which his erudition in Chinese had given no preparation whatsoever. The children told him that they had been taught these things by their mothers. According to Yamakawa Kikue, this was how Nakamura became convinced that a failure to improve the state of women's education in Japan would render his native country incapable of competing with the West.[5]

After returning to Japan, Nakamura made the following case for women's education:

The quality of a child's mind and disposition generally resembles that of the mother. Down to the child's future preferences and habits, much resembles the mother. Such being the case, in order to improve the character and customs of the people and to advance into the realm of civilization, it is necessary to attain good mothers. . . . There is no better means for creating good mothers than teaching girls.[6]

Clearly part of the lengthy Japanese discourse on "good wives, wise mothers" (*ryōsai kenbo*), Nakamura's educational philosophy was also an important addition to the discourse of correspondence between the status of women and their nations. By the time *Ukigumo* and *Fūkin* appeared in print, the correlation between women's education and the nation had become a matter of common sense among intellectuals, even by the outspokenly conservative standards of the women's education magazine *Iratsume*:

It is indisputable that the level and character of women's education is closely related to a nation's culture. Ultimately, women's education and a nation's enlightenment mutually influence each other, so that one cannot hope to find the perfect education of women in a society whose culture has not advanced, and if women are not properly educated one cannot hope for true enlightenment. Because women are people's mothers, people's teachers, because they pass on their own character to their children and take charge of their children's education at home, there can be no argument against the fact that women's education influences the nation's culture.[7]

Having an immediate impact on the development of modern women's education, this discourse facilitated the emergence of the schoolgirl as the representative par excellence of modern Japan.

The new phenomenon of formal education for women in Japan gave birth to the unprecedented social entity of the Meiji schoolgirl.[8] In response to the strong identification of women's education with Christianity, the new custom of girls leaving home to board at or nearby their schools, schoolgirls' gender-bending preference for *hakama* (the long culottes customarily worn by men), and their facility with Chinese and English, the prestige languages of civilization, the public greeted schoolgirls with mixed reactions of respect, sympathy, curiosity, suspicion, and hostility. Of course, schoolgirls were not the only new additions to the Meiji social landscape—for instance, soldiers, as commoners participating in military functions, were equally unprecedented. However, the discourse of correspondence between women and nations endowed schoolgirls with a particularly representative status vis-à-vis modern Japan, one that often placed schoolgirls and women's education at the center of debates on national identity.

A major impetus behind modern women's education was to establish a certain kind of equivalency between Japanese women and their female counterparts in the advanced nations of Europe. An even bolder logic of correspondence guided Inoue Kaoru's strategy for securing the revision of the unequal treaties by demonstrating how European—and thus civilized and deserving of equal status—the Japanese could be. Under his leadership, in 1886, the government built the Rokumeikan, a sumptuous Western-style ballroom, to serve as center stage for Inoue's diplomatic strategy. Throughout the late 1880s the government officially encouraged schoolgirls to learn Western social dancing and etiquette for display before Western dignitaries at the Rokumeikan balls. Although this demonstration apparently did not impress the likes of Pierre Loti (see the introduction), the deployment of schoolgirls as cultural currency certainly contributed to their incipient Westernesque status as an imagined bridge between Japan and the West. In this sense the schoolgirl figure seems a fitting muse for the first vernacular novels, in themselves attempts to span the gap between Japanese and European fiction.

Moreover, two of the major forums for the discussion of women's education were also the sites of important developments in modern Japanese literature and both played significant roles in *Fūkin* and *Ukigumo*. Founded in 1885 by Iwamoto Yoshiharu (1863–1942), head of the Christian girls' school Meiji Jogakkō, *Jogaku zasshi* became the leader of Meiji women's education magazines and the breeding ground of Meiji romanticism, giving birth to the spin-off magazine *Bungaku-kai* in 1893. Not only was *Jogaku zasshi* one of the handful of publications to review *Ukigumo*, it also appears in *Ukigumo* itself as part of Osei's initiation into the vocabulary of modern Japanese womanhood. *Iratsume*, the magazine in which Bimyō published *Fūkin* as a serial novel, is the second case in point. Four of its six founding editors had studied with Nakagawa Kenjūrō, one of the leading figures in the history of Meiji women's education, and two of them, Masaki Naohiko and Nakagawa Kojūrō, had collaborated on a prize-winning essay, "How to Unify the Writing of Men and Women."[9] What is the nature of the relationship between these magazines and our two novels? Let us begin with a consideration of *Fūkin*.

Presumably, Bimyō's participation in *Iratsume* was solicited because of his advocacy of the vernacular novel, rather than any particular commitment to educational reform. As the basis for an alliance between a novelist and a group of educational reform advocates, a shared interest in vernacularization may have been a tenuous connection at best, but it did contribute to the early emergence of the schoolgirl figure in Meiji vernacular fiction. As it happened, by the time Bimyō began to write novels for *Iratsume* he had also developed a particular fondness for Thackeray's *Vanity Fair*. The forum of a women's education magazine may have struck him as the perfect opportunity to adapt Thackeray's novel to the contemporary Japanese context.

Bimyō published *Fūkin* in a section of *Iratsume* called *Himekagami* (literally, "The Mirror of Princesses"), the implications of which might be roughly rendered as "dos and don'ts for good girls." And indeed, several passages in *Fūkin* strongly suggest that Bimyō intended it to function as the fictional counterpart to his cohorts' critique of women's education articulated in the first issue of *Iratsume*. Nakagawa Kojūrō later described the original impetus for *Iratsume* as a desire "to encourage the nation's people to reflect upon and amend their ways, in opposition to the Westernization ideology then at its peak, by first taking up the woman problem and rousing public attention."[10] Because of Bimyō's aesthetic Westernisms and his reputation as a "premature baby of Westernization fever" (Uchida Roan), scholars have surmised that he did not share the conservative, anti-Westernist convictions of his coeditors at *Iratsume*. Nevertheless, the caricature of contemporary schoolgirl mores developed in *Fūkin* reflects a distinct effort to advance their critical agenda.

Following the example of *Vanity Fair*, Bimyō's novel tells the story of two friends soon to graduate from a certain Tokyo girls' school (italics indicate puns in the text).

The one called Okaku [Miss Square] is about sixteen or seventeen years old, with very good facial equipment, except that the space between her eyes is rather broad, so that one might unkindly say that it looks like a face reflected in a convex mirror. At a glance she gives a good, if not entirely flawless, impression because of her extremely white face. As for the whiteness of her face, it has been said that she whitened it by drinking arsenic, but we are still unable to ascertain the truth of this theory. Yet what makes it seem not entirely unlikely is the fact that the girl herself is much concerned with appearances and recently has been caught up in imitating European women, which may have caused her to forcibly change her yellow color to this brilliant white.

The other one, about eighteen or nineteen, has a face so round that if one covered it with a compass only the ears would remain, which is all right, but when she laughs she bares her upper gums, making her mouth look far from attractive whether seen from either side, and simply seems like a chatterbox; and indeed, such an estimation would be not be mistaken, as she was wanton by birth. On top of that, her name being Omaru [Miss Round], unfriendly acquaintances *turned the heat of Ibuki moxa* on her parents with the nasty comment that they indeed showed foresight in giving her such a name, prompting them to try to correct Omaru's babbling, but that having little effect, they thought that at least if they gave her a good education the problem would correct itself and—now this is parental benevolence—until this year they had been sending her to school, but that had rather an evil effect on the girl. Having haphazardly glanced at one or two Western books, with the conjecture of an ugly girl she began to spout sophistries with every other word—"In the countries of the West, there is even an argument to give women political rights" or

"How vexing that sexual equality is not practiced in our country"—and became a most unfilial child who looked down even on her own parents, a fine specimen of the woman stalwart, *as immovable as Narita Fudō himself*, who blinded the originally gentle Okaku, *making her over in impudent Western-style hairesies,* who would show the naturally red hairs of her *man-eating praying mantis coiffure* to people and call them "Golden hair" to be witty.[11]

Here Bimyō presents us with two basic stereotypes of Japanese women under Western influence. Okaku, the first and more attractive of the two, is mainly interested in appearances, specifically of looking more European herself. Omaru is the "woman stalwart" (*jojōfu*—a word whose literal meaning is positive but one that was frequently used in a pejorative sense): a repulsive and dangerous creature who cites Western examples to justify what the narrator suggests is a plain lack of feminine virtues. She is clearly a send-up of the women's rights movement initiated by outspoken political activists like Nakajima Shōen and Fukuda Hideko in the early 1880s. Aborted after three short chapters, the ensuing installments of *Fūkin* delineate Okaku's gradual disenchantment with Omaru's radical Westernisms and her growing idolization of Takagi Kagetō, the handsome and well-spoken young composer of the "air for the organ" that gives the story its name.

The narrator's relentless stream of commentary develops a two-pronged critique of Meiji schoolgirls: while Omaru represents the self-interested appropriation of Westernisms to legitimate a reprehensibly "loose character," the good-natured Okaku is hopelessly lacking in self-consciousness, leaving her constantly at the mercy of external influences. Within the three short episodes of this unfinished novel, the spineless Okaku emerges as the main focus of interest. The shift in her attention from Omaru toward Takagi is not a felicitous escape from bad influence, but rather a perilous regression to the lax sexual mores of an earlier age:

By this time, Okaku's heart had become an utter slave to a certain something; her outlook was rather too base. Had her outlook been debased as thanks for her fervent belief in women's rights? Had she been thrown from one extreme to the other, going back to the ways of the Tempō era? No matter how gorgeous Takagi might appear to be, to yearn for a man whose character she knew so little—my, my. Passion of the senses easily fades; true feeling doesn't change. Led astray by the easily fading, without a care for true feeling, how can you take the pledge of a hundred years? If you could, it would surely be a risk. To forget the pledge of a hundred years and get strung along by the tether of a momentary passion, and then work yourself into a fret over it—this is the behavior of beasts. Hey, does that make you a lady?[12]

Ever since she came back to her uncle's house, Okaku's mind grew even more agitated. But since she of course wanted to conceal it, her heart was all the more tormented. At times, she would paint a picture of Takagi in her imagination and gaze upon it, or if she saw a face in her picture books that looked like Takagi's face, she would go to the trouble of copying it out on a piece of rice paper, or in idle moments she would pass the time by writing out the first character of Takagi's name, but always fearful of being discovered, she would attach random characters to it. I'm just impressed that she hasn't yet looked up their compatibility in a fortune-telling book. Pitiful in the poignancy of her feelings, she was still an idiot in the narrowness of her mind. Were she already a man's wife, and these the feelings she had for her husband, there would be nothing wrong in them—rather, she would make a sweet wife. But there is nothing desirable about such thoughts in a maiden, and to the contrary one might call this inconstancy. I may be harping, but Okaku was completely taken in and blinded by Takagi's charms. There is no way Okaku could know what kind of disposition Takagi might have. Supposing that her wish were granted and she became Takagi's wife, only to discover that he had an evil disposition—what would this lady do then? This would surely damage her. Doesn't she realize? Or rather, is it just that she doesn't think of her own future? And before she used to say quite haughty things. But this is about all that she has at the bottom of her heart. Can this lead to the raising of women's status? While she had the status of being called a schoolgirl, it seems that she was a slave to men. And she will graduate next year . . . and there is one who can play the piano well . . . and is rather good with words . . . and here we have the new lady of Meiji. How fortunate [ellipses in original].[13]

To state the all too obvious, the narrator reveals that beneath the trappings of her modern education, Okaku is just a simple-minded, boy-crazy Tempō girl at heart. If there is any noteworthy resemblance between *Fūkin* and *Vanity Fair* aside from incipient similarities of character distribution, it is the narrator's staunch refusal to exempt any of his characters from his sardonic jibes.

In fact, the narrator of *Fūkin* takes such obvious pleasure in exposing his characters' flaws that some readers found the novel objectionably inappropriate for a women's education magazine.[14] One critic warned Bimyō that such a novel would only be read in the tradition of Tamenaga Shunsui, an Edo *gesakusha* known for his tales of passion (*ninjōbon*).[15] This may seem surprising to today's reader, who is more likely to place weight on the moralistic diatribe that interrupts the descriptive passages. Yet the depiction of a young woman in the throes of a secret obsession with a prepossessing young man would no doubt have struck contemporary readers as titillating, regardless of the narrator's critical comments. The fine line between social commentary and cheap titillation is even more obscure in the conversation that leads to Okaku's disillusionment with Omaru:

KAKU: "But you know that in a place like Japan, where moral thinking has yet to take control of people's minds, free marriage can only do a great deal of damage, and not a whit of good can possibly come of it . . . "

MARU: "That's what a few people argue. But when it comes to that argument, I . . . You know, even in the Western countries, which are much more restricted by religion than Japan, the actuality of things generally comes down to dancing. . . . So there's plenty of scandal, you should know. . . . That's human nature, and nothing can be done about it. . . . Ha ha ha. . . . Because it's you I can say this, but . . . "

She approached Okaku's ear and for a while was whispering something

MARU: "Well, it's just a matter of calling it free marriage to keep up appearances."

KAKU: "Oh dear, is that so? So you . . . "

MARU: "Sure, I'll go with being a *Miss* . . ."

KAKU: "Well!"

MARU: "Ha ha ha ha ha" [ellipses in original].[16]

In our day we can only begin to conjecture as to how Bimyō expected the reader to fill in the blank horror that Omaru whispers into Okaku's ear. Ultimately, the rhetoric of moral censure in *Fūkin* only thinly veils a prurient interest in the budding sexuality of young women.

Nakagawa's recollections suggest that the founding editors of *Iratsume* were not so much interested in the subject of women's education per se, but rather in its potential to draw public attention to their critique of excessive Westernization. For them the phrase *women's education* may have been little more than a marketing tool, as is so often the case when "women's issues" get taken up in mass media. The deployment of the schoolgirl type in Bimyō's *Fūkin* seems equally opportunistic, merely pasting together some common prejudices about the new Meiji woman from contemporary print media in a rather strained attempt to be timely. When read as a companion to the critique of women's education set forth by the editors in the first issue of *Iratsume*, Bimyō's fictional treatment of the moral, emotional, and intellectual development of young women does suggest a metonymic association with the development of modern Japan in its problematic relationship to the West. Yet the correlation between the schoolgirl and the nation in *Fūkin* only emerges from the text's relationship to the discourse surrounding it on the pages of *Iratsume*. In isolation from the circumstances of its publication, *Fūkin* simply reads as a pretentiously Westernesque caricature of contemporary schoolgirl mores that makes only the most perfunctory show of interest in how they reflect the current state of the nation.

Rather than the parodic relationship between Japan and the West she potentially evokes, the main focus of the narrator's critique is the sexually suspect schoolgirl herself. The strident caricature of educated women in *Fūkin* speaks not only to Bimyō's unapologetic misogyny but also to his own essentially unproblematic literary relationship to the

West. Thackeray's *Vanity Fair* suggested to Bimyō a new subject for fiction as well as a more vituperative style of narration. Yet these are nothing more than slight refinements of the gesaku deployment of fiction as a moralizing caricature of contemporary manners. Of course, it must be said that *Vanity Fair* does lend itself to being read within this paradigm, and one can see why the work appealed so strongly to Bimyō. In both translation and composition Bimyō's relation to Western literary models remained securely within the realm of adaptation.

By contrast, *Ukigumo* directly and self-consciously exploits the discursive connection between the nation and the schoolgirl: Futabatei derived the name Osei from the word *kokusei*, "the state of the nation."[17] Osei's characteristic penchant for imitation is not intended as testimony to the inadequacies of female subjectivity, but rather as a metaphor for one facet of Japan's relationship to the West. Moreover, the complex problematic of parody or imitation informs every level of the text, from its overt themes to its very composition. What is the status of imitation in the composition of *Ukigumo*? First, in terms of literary style, Futabatei described his first novel as follows:

On the whole, the style of *Ukigumo* is almost all imitation of others; for part 1 I wrote in imitation of [Shikitei] Sanba, Aeba [Kōson], and the Hachimonji-ya books. In part 2 I tried my hand at imitating the stylistic essence of Dostoevsky and Goncharov, and for all of part 3 I imitated Dostoevsky. With the intent of practicing, I tried a variety of things.[18]

We have already surveyed the enormous gap between the inherited styles of Japanese fiction and European vernaculars, the difficulty this posed for literary translation, and the innovative solutions presented by Futabatei's *Aibiki*. Yet in the case of *Aibiki* Futabatei still had an already written text from which to work. His attempt to imitate or "import" the styles of Dostoevsky and Goncharov in an original Japanese composition posed an immeasurably greater challenge. At times Futabatei even found it easier to write in Russian, then translate into Japanese.[19] His stylistic imitation of these two Russian novelists in *Ukigumo* marks the bold step from translation as a mode of reproduction to translation as a method for original composition.

This method might also be described as a feat of doubled imitation, first in Russian, then in Japanese. It is not the only doubled imitation in *Ukigumo*. The influence of modern Russian fiction in *Ukigumo* has traditionally been described in terms of the "superfluous hero," a character type named after Turgenev's *Diary of a Superfluous Man* that seems almost ubiquitous to nineteenth-century Russian fiction. Recently, however, the contemporary novelist Gotō Meisei has redefined the relationship between *Ukigumo* and Russian fiction according to much more specific terms. Gotō identifies a clear distinction between two streams of Russian fiction. First, there is the naturalist, humanist tradition represented by Turgenev and Tolstoy, which became the mainstream of Russian fiction in Japan. Then there is what he calls the "St. Petersburg school of comic delusion," encompassing Pushkin, Gogol, and Dostoevsky. In contrast to other critics, he places *Ukigumo* squarely within the latter tradition, which he characterizes as follows:

Russian modernity commenced with the construction of St. Petersburg. St. Petersburg was built in 1701 according to the "more European than the Europeans" ideology of Peter I. And what kind of city is "more European than Europe"? It is the literally hybrid/schismatic city that simultaneously gave rise to every architectural style, from ancient Greco-Roman, Gothic and Baroque to the modern styles of London and Paris. With France as the model for modernization, Peter I made French the official language of the aristocracy, intelligentsia, and bureaucracy, created the bureaucratic system we all know from Gogol's "The Overcoat," and forced people to shave the beards that were the pride and symbol of the Slavophiles, leading to an escalating antagonism between the Slavophiles and Westernists and a great debate that would divide the Russian intelligentsia of the nineteenth century.

And at the same time, the hybridity/schism of "Slavic and Western," in other words, "Slavic spirit, Western knowledge," also became a theme of modern Russian fiction. Modern Russian fiction begins with Pushkin's *Evgeny Onegin*. In a word, this novel is known as a parody of Byron, the Russian version of *Childe Harold* or *Don Juan*, but Pushkin describes the protagonist Onegin as the typical St. Petersburg "elliptical man," a hybrid/

schismatic figure. Namely, he is a "European made in Russia," a high society dilettante who is fluent in French and wears an overcoat tailored in London. This line of fiction was continued by Gogol, who created the genre of the Petersburg novel with works like *Diary of a Mad Man*, "The Nose," and "The Overcoat."

Gogol's line was continued by Dostoevsky, and I call the genealogy of Pushkin, Gogol, and Dostoevsky the Petersburg School, which is also a school of "delusional comedy." Above, I mentioned "the comedy of relational discord" [with respect to *Ukigumo*]. The discord of relations in the hybrid/schismatic city of Petersburg is the Gogolian comedy. The comedy of relational discord is humor, delusion, nightmare, the irrational, and a fear whose origins remain unknown.

Dostoevsky created *Poor People* from Gogol's "The Overcoat." Thus he said "We all came from Gogol's 'Overcoat,'" and after that he created his next work, *The Double*, from Gogol's *Diary of a Mad Man*.[20]

Gotō defines this genealogy as a series of successive parodies, beginning with Pushkin and Byron, leading to Gogol and Dostoevsky, and finally to Futabatei.[21] This redefinition of Futabatei's literary roots deftly evokes the almost gangliform convergence of imitative acts that spawned modern Russian and Japanese literatures. In a world heavily engaged in parodic imitations of the vaunted West, writers like Pushkin and Futabatei discovered the potency of literary parody as a form of "critical repetition."

While Bimyō's *Fūkin* can be described as a parodic adaptation of *Vanity Fair* to the gesaku form, it would be pure sophistry to call it a "critical repetition." What is critical about an act of literary imitation is not only the manner in which it is carried out but also the quality of the discovery that inspires the imitation in the first place. As we have already noted, what Bimyō discovered in Thackeray was the use of schoolgirls as central characters, a vituperative narrative style, and a novel without heroes—a paltry discovery that could only have been redeemed by Thackeray's exotic prestige as a major English novelist. What Futabatei discovered in Russian fiction was not an underlying similarity to Japanese fiction, nor a world-famous literary tradition, but a set of social and cultural dilemmas that suggested innumerable parallels to Meiji Japan. As Gotō points out, "Futabatei superimposed the hybridity/schism of modern Japan upon the hybridity/schism of modern Russia. This is not only because he happened to study the Russian language, but because he discovered a commonality in the modernity of both parties, namely, the hybridity/schism of imitating Europe."[22] If England and France offered models to strive for, what Russia offered was an example to identify with, for the ambiguous position of Russia vis-à-vis the modern "West" offered a particularly compelling analogy to the situation of Meiji Japan: the debate between nativists and Westernization advocates, the authoritarian bureaucratic system harshly lampooned by so many nineteenth-century Russian novelists, the clout of a foreign lingua franca (French), and so on. The historical relationship and cultural analogies between Japanese and Russian literature in the modern period should remind us that while certain aspects of modernization may be universal, there are nevertheless important shades of difference within the categories of "Western" and "modern," both temporal and geographic in nature, that make a simple, dichotomous "West versus non-West" depiction of the modern world untenable.

While scholars and critics have discovered an abundance of Russian precedents for the character of Bunzō in *Ukigumo*, Osei seems to stand in a class by herself. The only hint that Futabatei may have gotten the idea for Osei's character from his readings of Russian literature is in a talk on Russian women, in which he mentions Aleksandr Griboedov's *Woe from Wit* as a prime example of the discord between young men and women occasioned by the influx of Western liberalism.[23] As we have already observed, *Jogaku zasshi* makes a cameo appearance in *Ukigumo*, and Futabatei specialists have traced several passages within the novel directly back to the pages of this magazine.[24] Since Futabatei was no stranger to the schoolgirl as a discursive figure, it is not surprising to find that Osei in fact shares key character traits with Okaku and Omaru. Like Okaku, Osei is a highly impressionable girl whose penchant for imitating others leaves her constantly at the mercy of external influences; like Omaru, Osei also delights in brandishing her knowledge of Western thinking and social customs. As the story begins, Osei has returned home after two years at a boarding school. The narrator sums up her intellectual development as follows:

After her coming-of-age ceremony she attended grammar school at her father's wishes and learned *Kiyomoto* music after her mother's tastes, and, one of the virtues of her inborn cleverness being a quick though incomplete grasp of things, it seemed that she was good at both learning and the leisurely arts, so her mother showed great joy in both her eyes and her words, a proud, braggart parent who would blow her horn even to those who didn't ask, in a constant drool. Around that time a government bureaucrat moved into the house next door with a family of four, including a wife and daughter. Getting started with neighborly seasonal greetings, the parents grew friendly, followed by the daughters, who traded visits almost daily. The girl next door was two or three years older than Osei, gentle and ladylike, and with the ruins of a once aspiring Confucian scholar for a father she was fond of learning and so naturally excelled in it though still a child. Even when people mature they can't help imitating others, and all the more so for children, among whom Osei was particularly flighty by nature, so as soon as she came under the influence of this girl she mimicked everything from her demeanor and manners to her way of talking, suddenly abandoning the samisen and placing a quill on her Chinese-style desk. Omasa found serious things like studying distasteful, but it was something her dear daughter did of her own liking and so she let it go, during which time Osei graduated from grammar school, when it turned out that the girl next door was to enter a private *juku* in Shiba. Well now, once that happened Osei suddenly developed an unbearable desire to enter the *juku*, begging her parents at every chance, even talking about it in her sleep. In an attempt to flex their parental muscles, they once rebuked her—the *juku* was out of the question because she was too young and, moreover, there was no point in women studying—but Osei engaged in one of her hunger strikes and appealed to their emotions with sighs of "If I can't go to *juku*, there's no point in going on living," making such a display of dejection that both parents gave in, seeing that her mind was so set on it, whereupon they entrusted the girl next door with everything and, not without a measure of unease, sent her to *juku*. That was two years ago. The head of the *juku* Osei entered was a woman stalwart whose capacity for repeating opinions from the newspapers as though they were her very own had given her a very high opinion of herself, on top of which she had the spiteful spirit of a millipede, rarely making the effort to show appreciation for a meal given, but never failing to repay even the most inconsequential slight, the kind of person who would sting those whom she didn't like with fine barbs swathed in cotton wadding whenever an opportunity arose. Osei may have paraded around like a big clam in front of her parents, but being the type to shrink to the size of a tiny corbicula before strangers she couldn't bear censure and so ingratiated herself with our woman stalwart using all kinds of obsequious behavior. Rambunctious by nature, she seemed easily influenced; soon enough her demeanor had changed beyond recognition and she grew distant from the girl next door. After that she began to study English and got even more carried away: her Japanese *juban* became a Western shirt, her Chinese-style hairdo turned into a Western-style bun, a handkerchief strangled her neck, and she even put up with the discomfort of wearing spectacles, becoming a laughable specimen of conceit, a first-rate copycat.[25]

The series of conversions—from the samisen to Chinese studies and finally to English—that constitute Osei's educational résumé trace a progression from the native popular culture of the Edo period to the early Meiji boom in Chinese and finally the turn toward the West by which English would supersede Chinese as the learned language of choice. While each successive conversion leads to a new persona, none leaves a permanent impression on the nonstick surface of Osei's mind. As with Bimyō's schoolgirls, Osei's facility for adopting new personae manifests itself in the inconstancy of her affections, which provides the main drama of the novel—her gravitation away from the incompetent yet sincere Bunzō toward the slick playboy Noboru. In keeping with the new sexual morality of Meiji enlightenment, Osei's drift toward Noboru is also cast in the dire colors of potential ruin. These similarities to *Fūkin*, combined with Futabatei's allegorical intentions, would seem to suggest that *Ukigumo* is simply another exploitation of the image of schoolgirls already established in print media.

While the characterization of Osei in *Ukigumo* can be read as a more thorough development of themes roughly sketched in *Fūkin*, however, there are crucial differences between Osei and Bimyō's schoolgirls. First and foremost, Osei is not only the potential victim of her own caprice but also the femme fatale who brings about Bunzō's destruction. In Osei's hands the accoutrements of modern women's education often become a novel means of coquetry. Thus *Jogaku zasshi* makes an appearance in *Ukigumo* as a prop for Osei's self-conscious performance of the educated young woman of Meiji.

Osei came into the room with a copy of *Jogaku zasshi* in her hand, reading as she walked, briefly greeting Noboru without so much as a smile, without a word of deference taking the teacup her mother poured for her while chatting, putting it back down after one sip, and, with an air of utter self-composure, picking up the magazine again and staring hard at it—such being her usual way in the presence of Noboru. (94)

Jogaku zasshi is also an important source of the vocabulary by which Osei identifies herself as a new woman in references to the superiority of educated women, sexual equality, the theory of social intercourse between men and women, and the like. In this sense Osei represents not only the fictional manifestation of the discursive correspondence between schoolgirl and nation but also a meditation on the schoolgirl persona as a function *of language.*

Indeed, the study of languages—Chinese and English—constitutes the core of Osei's secondary education. The innate talent for verbal mimicry that makes Osei a fast learner is the very trait that arouses Bunzō's desire.

Since the beginning of the summer, when he was asked to teach Osei English, Bunzō began to open up a little, occasionally holding forth on the state of Japanese women, the pros and cons of the Western-style bun, and even the relative merits of social intercourse between men and women, whereupon, lo and behold, Osei—who until now had not given any thought to Bunzō as a man and had bragged in front of him to her heart's content—at some point became reticent in front of Bunzō, took on an air of composure, and seemed to become gentle and feminine. One day, Bunzō was surprised to see that Osei was not wearing her spectacles or scarf as usual, and, when he asked about it, she said, "But aren't you the one who said that they are actually harmful to people in good health?" Bunzō smiled in spite of himself, said, "That's an excellent thing," and smiled again. (52–53)

Clearly, Bunzō takes great pleasure in hearing Osei repeat his own words. This is the event that solidifies in Bunzō what had been a merely latent attraction for Osei, for it is the first time that Osei seems to acknowledge him as a man and herself as a woman (in his own image). It is particularly interesting that the first signs of sexual tension between them emerge from within their English lessons.

Throughout *Ukigumo* Bunzō is characterized by his inability to manipulate spoken language: the refusal (and actual inability) to curry favor with his boss that contributes to Bunzō's loss of employment at the beginning of the story, his inability to defend himself from or mollify his aunt Omasa, a veritable genius of verbal warfare, his frequent reduction to stuttering and speechlessness in moments of highly charged emotion, and, most important, his inability to secure Osei's affections in the face of competition from the silver-tongued Noboru. That Bunzō begins to open up to Osei in the process of teaching her English suggests that the mediation of a foreign language momentarily liberates him from the acute self-consciousness that usually ties his tongue. Instructing Osei in this prestige language of civilization and enlightenment bolsters Bunzō's confidence and serves as a natural catalyst for discussing "the state of Japanese women, the pros and cons of the Western-style bun, and even the relative merits of social intercourse between men and women" with an educated young woman of the new generation. For Bunzō the theoretical language of modern sexual relations seems to provide a comfortably abstract language of seduction. Yet, in the end, he is the one who is seduced. As a result of Osei's rapid assimilation of his lessons, Bunzō begins to nurture an illusion of Osei as an ideal partner, capable of the total and complete union prescribed by theories of modern marriage.

Unlike Bunzō, the other main characters in *Ukigumo* all share an easy facility with spoken language. While Omasa cannot rival her daughter in the strategic use of learned words, the colloquial is like so much clay in her hands:

"Honda-san, let me tell you, it was like this."

Once she began to jabber the story, fully embellished, of how she had been abused by Bunzō yesterday, there was no end in sight, like the turbulent gushing of a hundred rivers flooding over all at once, missing not a single word or beat, a brilliant instantaneous disquisition of ruminations that had accumulated over many years, endowed with a natural mastery of intonation and cadence, her mouth opening and closing, spinning out the words with a will that could turn even a heron into a crow. (94)

Noboru's successful career as a bureaucrat is likewise enabled by his aptitude with the spoken word:

Noboru, being a so-called man of talent, has a terrific amount of knowledge and wit, and often wears this knowledge and wit on his sleeve. With an inexhaustible wealth of eloquence, it is said that he could even take to the streets and give the best street entertainers a run for their money, but, unable to dam the water that streams down a vertical plank, he occasionally ends up blowing his horn. He is also rather clever, and though there is not a single thing he doesn't know, he does not excel in any particular art—I guess it would be fair to say that, being lazy by nature, his problem is that he easily tires of things.

Noboru is also terrifically rich in amiability and extremely good with flattery. With people he is meeting for the first time he makes an even greater effort at buttering them up; whether a lady or an elderly person, he figures out the right tune, and thus far he has never been off-key. The only strange thing is that as he gets to know a person better he gradually loses his amiability, turning his nose up and occasionally making offensive remarks or sarcastic banter. When someone gets angry and lights into him, he, if he can manage it, twists their words on the spot, and, when he can't, he just laughs it off for the moment, after which he makes sure to pay back the grudge—pardon the expression, but he slaps dog shit in a person's face.

Be that as it may, Noboru is a man of talent, and he serves the honorable bureau chief well. This honorable bureau chief is a personage who, having partaken of the waters of the West, seems to have an awful distaste for what is called the "lordly manner," constantly raising his voice to calumniate against the supercilious airs of his colleagues, but his honor, being well-known for his own difficult temperament, will flare his eyes in a fit of indignation when something doesn't suit his exalted will, no matter how minute it might be; being what we might call a despot of liberalism, this personage's poor subordinates find themselves flustered and confused over how to accommodate his delicate temper, all except Noboru. Not to mention the honorable bureau chief's gestures and tone of voice, Noboru has even imitated his way of clearing his throat, and even sneezing. Ah, the skill of his imitation—it is the spitting image, as though the very person were right there, the only difference being that when the honorable bureau chief deigns to laugh, he says "a ha ha ha" no matter who the audience, while Noboru occasionally laughs "e he he he" in front of certain people. (90–91)

Bunzō's staunch refusal to bend language to his own purposes provides the main source of conflict between himself and Omasa, and leaves the door wide open for Noboru's rivalry. The sharp division between Bunzō and these strategic talkers neatly coincides with class distinctions. Both Omasa and Noboru claim samurai roots, but the narrator quickly casts suspicion on their lineage:

The wife Omasa, who managed the home in [Uncle Magobei's] absence, was a second wife who slid her way up from a maid cum mistress, herself claims to be the daughter of a respectable samurai family, but . . . we have our doubts. (47)

Before [Noboru] comes back, this would be the right time to give a pithy little biography of this man, whose child he is, what kind of education he has had, what kind of circumstances he grew up in, but his past is veiled like the mountain goddess in the mist, just a heap of unknowns. . . . Now then, to record a sampling of what is absolutely certain, he was born in Tōkei [Tokyo], and someone who saw his resumé says he belongs to a samurai family that has a suspiciously underground stench—this at least is not a lie. (90)

The combination of water imagery and dubious class identity associated with Omasa and Noboru subtly suggests that for them language is as fluid as currency itself. Both characters deftly exploit the slippery surface of words—innuendo, insinuation, double entendres, deflection, purposeful misinterpretation—to further their own interests while evading the risks of personal accountability. From their perspective Bunzō's refusal to acknowledge or exploit language as a means of self-promotion is a foolhardiness that verges on incompetence.

Bunzō himself is not only of samurai lineage, but his father was a former retainer for the Bakufu—an extremely disadvantageous résumé in the wake of the Meiji Restoration that overturned it. Stripped of his social standing and formal occupation, Bunzō's father finds himself at a complete loss for navigating the new world of Meiji:

now a monkey fallen from the tree being a pathetic creature, his arms may have been thoroughly trained in the Shinkage style of swordsmanship, but they could not use spade and hoe, his mouth weighted down by *sayō shikaraba* could not suddenly make the sound *hei*, and to carry a balance on his shoulders would defile the family name and look shameful, so, after running his legs into the ground, he finally settled into a secretarial post for Shizuoka Prefecture, a happiness that went no further than entrance to the rank and file of walking lunchboxes [petty bureaucrats], never managing to rise very far in the world, but we are nonetheless impressed that he spared nothing of his scant financial means to give his only son Bunzō a thorough education. (45–46)

Bunzō's father is unable to "rise" after the Meiji Restoration because of his inability to shed an outmoded class identity, a dilemma constituted in part by the distinction between spoken and written language. His mouth is weighted down by *sayō shikaraba,* shorthand for the punctilious language of the samurai class. In tone, the Sinified phrase *sayō shikaraba* falls somewhere between "such being the case, therefore" and *ergo sum.* As such, it is emblematic of a spoken language that imitated learned writing, the basic foundation for a class that claimed moral and intellectual authority. Firmly anchored in the bedrock of written language, Bunzō's father cannot manipulate the spoken language of commercial negotiations alluded to by *hei* (yessir/yes'm). From the perspective of his class, *hei* is an obsequious merchant expression, a vulgar and deceptive performance of servility undertaken in the interest of personal profit. Yet, in a world no longer defined by a stable hierarchy, this inability to treat spoken language as the malleable stuff of *verbal performance,* rather than the strictly defined terms of *self-representation,* renders what was once a solid bedrock for social identity into a deadly economic albatross. Pinning all of his hopes on his son, Bunzō's father places such a complete emphasis on education that Bunzō's subjection to the written word becomes his most significant patrimony.

Bunzō's very name, which can be read as shorthand for *bungaku zanmai* (immersion in literature), suggests as much.[26] For Bunzō, reality is so thoroughly mediated by written language that even his loss of employment assumes the quality of an imaginary scarlet letter:

Startled from the middle of a dream by the wake-up call of the maid at his pillow, Bunzō lifted his flustered head and looked about to see that the morning sun was already shining diagonally across the *shōji*. "What, have I overslept?" The thought was instantly succeeded by the thickly looming two characters for dismissal that quickly choked his breast. (75)

So traumatizing is this two-character inscription that Bunzō can barely manage to force it out of his mouth in front of Omasa: 「ム、めん職 になりました」 "Mu, menshoku ni narimashita." While this statement could be translated into English as "I was de, dismissed," the Roman alphabet cannot approximate its particular orthographic configuration. The first sound, "mu," is written in katakana to emphasize its character as a stuttering sound rather than a morpheme. Of infinitely greater significance, however, is that when Bunzō does manage to blurt out the two-character compound *menshoku*, it is rendered half in hiragana, as though to reflect the speaker's desperate desire to strip the word of the meaning visually fixed in its ideographic form 免職. The subtle use of katakana, hiragana, and kanji in this brief pronounce-ment encapsulates one of the main sources of conflict in *Ukigumo*: the uneasy relationship between the indeterminate body of sounds that constitutes spoken language and the corpus of meaning fixed by the written word.

As the fountainhead of modern vernacular Japanese fiction, *Ukigumo* actually dramatizes the deep disjunction between spo-ken and written language that the genbun-itchi style was meant to resolve. While Omasa and Noboru personify the colloquial as the dominant language of social commerce, Bunzō represents a sub-jectivity formed by the lingua franca of Chinese, the written lan-guage of conceptual commerce. Ironically, this vernacular narrative portrays the colloquial as the language of dissembling, as can be seen from the characterizations of Omasa and Noboru. The funda-mental incompatibility between the malleable spoken parlance of social commerce and the inflexible, letter-bound language of ideas serves as the impetus for the entire narrative of *Ukigumo*, a novel distinguished by the fact that almost all its key events are verbal exchanges. Time and time again we see Bunzō inundated by the artful words of others; his alienation from their language initiates the internal soliloquy by which he attempts to comprehend the world around him. The movement of this almost plotless novel can be described as an escalating power struggle between two differ-ent linguistic practices—the seamless speech of Omasa and Noboru against the mental text Bunzō patches together from pieces of their words and the ethical code inscribed in his consciousness. Through-out his losing battle Bunzō becomes more attached to his own idées fixes and more insistent upon imposing them on others, engaging in a series of verbal altercations that decisively sever all connections to the world around him.

Osei is the enigmatic hybrid at the center of this bipolar struggle. Not only is she of mixed class, as the daughter of the presumably mer-chant-class Omasa and Bunzō's patrilineal uncle, but her characteris-tic use of Chinese diction situates her language ambiguously between the poles of speech and writing. The degree to which Bunzō's idealiza-tion of Osei hinges upon her use of language becomes comically clear in the following passage. One night Bunzō finds himself alone in the house with Osei, who casually invites him into her room.

Bunzō held back a little, then went all the way down the stairs and made his way as far as the entrance to Osei's room, but he did not venture inside, just stopped in his steps.

"Please come in."

"Eh, er . . . " Bunzō continued to fidget there, with an air of ambivalence.

"What makes you so hesitant on this of all nights?"

"Well, what with you being all by yourself . . . I uh . . . "

"Oh my, how unlike you . . . Who was it that once said the faint-hearted could hardly hope to put their ideals into practice?" She tilted her broad, white forehead to the side with a charming little smile in one cheek, by which Bunzō was drawn into the room. Taking a seat, he said, "Well, if you put it that way, there's nothing I can say, but . . . "

"Here, please use this," said Osei, handing Bunzō a fan, "But what's the matter?"

"Oh nothing, it's just that gossip is such a nuisance."

"Oh, that. Well you know, people are bound to talk a little. But what does it matter if they talk, so long as we are both innocent? I mean, here we are breaking the conventions of two thousand years, so you can't expect to escape some degree of tribulation."

"I think so too, but still, when one does hear the undeserved gossip it's a nasty thing."

"Well, yes, so it is. Just the other day, I tell you, Nabe had the nerve to say odd things and tease me. It finally became so annoying that even though I figured she would never understand, I tried explaining to her the theory of social intercourse between men and women. And do you know what she said? That she couldn't understand me at all because there was some Chinese thrown into my words. . . . Uneducated people are really so hopeless, don't you think?"

"A ha ha ha that's a great laugh. . . . But surely Nabe isn't the only one who thinks it's strange, doubtless your mother also . . . "

"Mother? Of course Mother is a lowly being, so she is constantly saying odd things and teasing me. Even so, I always make a point of really shaming her when she does that, which seems to have had an effect even on her, and these days she doesn't say so much."

"So she teases you? And what does she say?"

"Oh, what was it, that if we are going to be so close, I may as well take you . . . (she fidgets a little, and with difficulty says) for my husband . . . " Upon hearing this, Bunzō was immediately flustered and he stared into Osei's face. But she seemed unperturbed. "Nevertheless, we can't lay all the blame on the uneducated, you know. My fellow alumna may not be particularly educated, but they have received a, well, regular education, and do you know that there are only four in the lot of twenty-five who can understand Western ideology? And those four, well, that was only while they were still in school, and as soon as they went outside, they gave in without so much as a word to their parents' oppression, and all of them have either married into other families or taken in a husband by now. So when I think that I am the only one left saying these kinds of things, I just feel so terribly forlorn. Or I did, but now that I have you for a fidus Achates, well, it's been greatly reassuring."

Bunzō gave a little nod of deference. "Even if it's just flattery, I am happy to hear it."

"Oh, but it's not flattery! It's true!"

"If it's true, that makes me even happier, but I am utterly incapable of associating with you as a fidus Achates."

"Now what is that supposed to mean? Just why can't you associate with me as a fidus Achates?"

"Why? Because I don't understand you, and you also don't understand me, so associating as a fidus Achates is, well . . . "

"Is that it? But I believe that I understand you very well. You are learned, your conduct is exemplary, you treat your parents with filial piety . . . "

"That's why I say that you don't understand me. You say that I treat my parents with filial piety, but I am not a good son. For me . . . there is something more . . . important than parents . . . " stammered Bunzō, hanging his head.

Osei stared at Bunzō with a look of puzzlement. "Something more important than parents . . . something . . . more important . . . than parents. . . . Oh, there is also something more important to me than parents."

Bunzō raised his hung head, "What? You too have that?"

"Yes, I do."

"Wh-who is it?"

"It's not a person, it is Truth."

"Truth," repeated Bunzō with a tremble, biting his lips in a moment of silence, soon after which he suddenly let out with a stunned sigh, "Ah, you are a chaste one, a pure one. . . . What is more important than parents is Truth. . . . Ah, you are a pure one." (55–58)

Here again, we find Osei's genius for citation at work. She draws Bunzō into her room by directly quoting his own words, fends off the insinuations of her maid Nabe by spouting the "theory of social intercourse between men and women," replete with its Chinese diction (the phrase itself is a five-character Chinese compound), and further aggrandizes herself by recounting this incident to her mentor. Her final demonstration of fluency in Bunzō's learned language generates the comedy of their exchange. As can be seen from the tenor of the rest of their conversation, her grasp of Bunzō's idiom has been based on their English lessons and discussions of abstract social and ethical questions. When Bunzō suddenly bursts out that he is not a "good son" because he values something more than his parents, Osei either fails or refuses to recognize that he is speaking in the confessional mode of a tormented lover. Instead, she quickly recasts his words into the form of a test question, as though assimilating it to the language of their English lessons, and then searches for a clever answer. In the process she converts Bunzō's attempt to confess a passion that transcends filial bonds into a suggestion that new (Western) ideals supersede the old (Confucian) ones.

The word *shinri*, originally part of the Buddhist lexicon, came into use during the Meiji period as a translation for "truth," a key component of many of the new systems of thought coming in from the West, particularly Christianity, philosophy, and science.[27] As a set translation for a philosophical term, *shinri* carries the weight of written language in a way that would be better approximated in the English lexical environment by the Latin *veritas*. We might surmise that Osei has picked up the term from her reading of *Jogaku zasshi*

or something she has heard from Bunzō during their English lessons.[28] Yet she never elaborates on what she means by "Truth," nor
is her meaning apparent anywhere in the narrative of *Ukigumo*. In
fact, the question of *meaning* has nothing to do with her use of the
word in the above context: Osei simply hits upon the word *Truth*
as a clever way to keep up her end of what strikes her as a highly
intellectual conversation. Her enunciation of an absolute value in
modern Western thought reduces the term to the status of an exotic
verbal prop.

This is the constitutive difference between Osei and Bunzō. Bunzō's
speech does not simply imitate written diction; it is, in fact constituted as a form of writing. With few exceptions, all of Bunzō's spoken
lines follow the rules of expository prose—even his attempt to confess his love can only be articulated in the rigid terms of Confucian
morality. Unlike Bunzō, Osei is not subject to the written word, but
rather applies that language toward the production of her own identity. Osei deploys written signs to elevate the register of her speech,
with the virtually alchemical effect of converting the heavy materiality of letters into the weightless ephemerality of sound. While her
enunciation is quintessentially performative, however, Bunzō reads
it in the referential mode. To our thoroughly literal-minded protagonist, the word *shinri* is strictly bound to the textual sources that give
it meaning. This "Utterly Bizarre First Foray Into the Peaks of Love"
(as designated by the chapter title) is the site of a double projection.
First Osei projects the language of Bunzō's intellectualism onto his
attempted confession, then Bunzō projects the textual weight of this
language back onto Osei's hollow mimicry. Thus, when she spouts
out the word *Truth* in place of the beloved's name he was expecting
to hear (and desperately hoping it would be his own), he sees a direct
reflection of the speaker's pristine self instead of his own image inad-
vertently parodied in her performance.

Given Bunzō's inability to navigate the strange and often hostile
world created by the language of others, his mistaken identification
with Osei is as much the inevitable result of desperation as it is an
attempt at egocentric self-affirmation. Fatally smitten by her combination of physical beauty and her siren song of "truth," Bunzō repeatedly

associates Osei with the Westernesque definitions of love and female virtue that he has surely internalized from the likes of *Jogaku zasshi*.

As a rule, two mutually loving hearts, each being part of one whole, do not act separately from each other, nor could they even if they tried; thus, when one heart is happy, the other heart shares in the happiness; when one heart is sad, the other heart shares in the sadness; when one heart is having fun, the other heart shares in the fun; when one heart is pained, the other heart shares in the pain; they both feel the same pleasure and laughter, they both feel the same anger and censure, they both feel the same joy and ecstasy, frustration and anguish, their feelings in touch with each other, one heart evoking the other, never to act at cross-purposes nor to repel each other—until today this is what Bunzō thought, but why was Osei now unable to feel his suffering?

What is going on with her? Bunzō just could not swallow Osei's manner, her complete lack of concern. If the love were not mutual, there would be no reason for her to amend her way of talking, change her manners, give up her flippant ways, and become most gentle and ladylike after she grew closer to Bunzō, and with that passionate talk this summer's night there would be no reason for her to clear a path for him of her own will, to make weird eyes at him, to use rough language, or to occasionally fall into reverie.

If the love were not mutual, when he was approached by a marriage proposal, there would be no reason for Osei to tease Bunzō as an indirect means of searching his feelings, and when he quarreled with Omasa there would be no reason for her to defend Bunzō, a virtual stranger, and argue with her very own mother.

"No, it's not a delusion, she surely has feelings for me. . . . but. . . . "

This Osei, the one with feelings for him, the image of a heart that has sworn to be buried in the same grave, that part of himself who shares his feelings, shares his thoughts, shares his breath and his life, looks away from the gloomy disconsolation of Bunzō, her cousin, fidus Achates, and future. . . . husband, doesn't even press him when he says he won't go, and not only has a composed look of complete unconcern, but goes out for a day on the town with someone like Noboru, whom she always says she hates precisely because he is not a man after Bunzō's own heart. . . .

"I don't understand. I just don't get it." (117–18)

It is this very ideology of love as total communion that engenders the fear of deception and betrayal, for the expectation of absolute sameness from the loved one is tantamount to the demand for a perfect *imitation* of the self. Thus Osei's innate talent for mimicry has unwittingly made her both the perfect candidate for Bunzō's future wife and the most likely to betray him.

Bunzō's subjection to writing is not a simple matter of certain texts having been indelibly inscribed upon his consciousness, however. His entire thought process, so vividly described by the narrator, is nothing other than a form of textual analysis. The "indifference" he senses in Osei takes on the imaginary proportions of a physical object, upon which he proceeds to perform a painstaking dissection.

Still unable to understand, Bunzō grasped the double blades of imagination and discernment to dissect, from various angles, this worrisome indifference of Osei's, upon which it seemed that there was a thing that was hidden within it, yes, it was definitely hidden there. But, he could not make out its form. Hence he once again summoned his courage and concentrated his attention on this point alone, throwing all his might into dissecting this first, but, like the Broom Tree of song, just as it seemed to appear he could not grasp it, and Bunzō eventually lost patience. Then that mischievous creature delusion would come out heckling—it might be this, then again it might be that—making him grab at utter shams and groundless suspicions. Not entirely seeing through these shams and groundless suspicions, but not entirely unaware of their character either, Bunzō carelessly grabbed at whatever was thrust upon him, blowing on it, crumpling it, making it into a ball, and then stretching it out again, straining himself to turn it into a fact, and as if the thing had just occurred before his very eyes, he writhed and flailed, suffering every kind of torment, and in a burst of anger he would take the sham and smash it into a million pieces and, before he could breathe a sigh of relief, set back down to the investigation, once again being handed a sham, once again turning it into fact, once again smashing it, smashing and grabbing, grabbing and smashing, with no end in sight, constantly stuck in the same place, without progressing forward or retreating backward. When he did take a step back to have a good look, it still seemed that something was there inside the indifference, just dimly perceptible. (118)

The delusions spawned by Bunzō's mental process function as a parody of the idealist metaphysics outlined in Futabatei's *Shōsetsu sōron*, which presupposes the existence of an idea in every form, thus fostering an obsession with the meanings hidden deep inside the forms of sensory phenomena. This apprehension of the world as a meaning-laden text is also the source of Bunzō's chronic indecision, for it bespeaks an essential inability to sense reality in the contingencies of form. Thus, even when Bunzō arrives at the sudden insight that Osei might be attracted to Noboru, he is led to the disturbing conclusion that his suspicion has come from out of nowhere.

Bunzō at last exhausted himself. By now the energy to keep investigating was gone, and his courage failed him too. Then he closed his eyes, held his head, and collapsed to the floor right there, numbing his five senses and letting go the hold on his seven passions, wanting nothing more than to forget right and wrong, honor and shame, success and failure, Omasa, Osei, the fact of being himself, everything at all, striving to escape from this torment and anguish even for a single instant, and for a while he neither moved nor breathed, still as a dead man; then all of a sudden he sprang to his feet,

"What if it's Honda. . . . " he started, but didn't dare to finish, making a startled look all around just as though he were in search of something.

Even so, where could this suspicion have come from? Whether it fell from the sky or sprang up from the ground or was simply a mirage of Bunzō's sense of persecution, it emerged suddenly and came without thought in an indiscernible haze, so there was no way to know its origin, but, in any case, what he could not figure out after all that flailing, writhing, and investigating, that single thing inside the said indifference, Bunzō now had the feeling he had effortlessly and for no apparent reason just happened to pinpoint, and the hair on his body stood on end.

Nevertheless, a feeling is still not a fact. Unless the feeling came from facts, one could not easily believe in it. Hence, upon recalling Osei's behavior until now and thoroughly considering and examining it, there seemed to be no such signs. Granted, Osei is still young and her spirits have yet to settle down, her principles have surely not taken deep root. But, the sandalwood tree is fragrant from the seedling; a newly hatched snake already seems capable of swallowing a human. In Bunzō's eyes Osei is the bud of what one would call a woman lionheart, with an elevated understanding, great elegance, a straightforward manner, she is a young woman to be loved and respected, so even if she might be deceived or led astray by a false gentleman who ornamented himself with morality, or a pseudolionheart adorned in magnanimity, when it comes to the likes of Noboru, an obsequious, shallow jerk even worse than dogs and beasts, there is no way that she could be led astray even by mistake. Which is precisely why she is always kind to Bunzō but indifferent to Noboru, that she idolizes Bunzō but has contempt for Noboru. Mutual love resides next to mutual respect; to be led astray by the object of one's contempt is not the kind of behavior that we human beings can comprehend.

"In which case, maybe it's all right.... but ... " something still catches, it is still not clearly settled. Flustered, Bunzō tried vigorously shaking his head, but even with that it did not seem about to dispel. This damned *but,* able to crawl into the tiny pores of a lotus fiber or even the space between a mosquito's eyelashes, just this one, minuscule, damned little *but* is more hindering than a mote in the eye, more frightening than the appearance of a thunderhead on the horizon.

That's right, frightening. Not knowing what horror might be lurking on the other side of this *but,* Bunzō is frightened. Before it turns into something, he wants to dispel it as quickly as possible. As much as he wants to dispel it, it will not dispel. Moreover, with the passing of time branch clouds appear, the thunderhead spreads, and it seems like a great storm is about to break out any minute now, the senses reel. (118–20)

The vicious cycle of doubt that paralyzes Bunzō traces an interminable shuttling back and forth between the conceptual primacy of ideas and the palpable yet unreliable sensations caused by manifest form. Unable to place his complete faith in one or the other, we find Bunzō once again trembling before the sign of writing—the tiny yet ominous contradiction *but* beyond which his imagination dares not venture.

In fact, the overblown sense of doom that prevents Bunzō from even contemplating this realm of undesired possibility can only be understood as a function of his approach to life as a stable text susceptible to hermeneutic analysis. Writing fixes language in a permanent form;

speech is a transitory act. In lieu of his inability to negotiate speech as performative action, Bunzō fixes the linguistic performances of others as mental text, which may then assume incontrovertible and permanent meaning if properly analyzed. We might say that Bunzō is constantly plowing the vicissitudes of his daily life for a fixed meaning. So preoccupied is he with this pursuit that, when confronted by Omasa's change of attitude and Noboru's competition, it never occurs to him that there is anything he can or even should do to secure Osei's affections. For him she too is ultimately conceived as an immutable text; the only issue being whether or not he has interpreted her properly. With this perspective it is little wonder that Bunzō harbors such fear at the prospect that he has misread his beloved.

It is also little wonder that Bunzō can find no other way to negotiate his dilemma than to force from Osei an unequivocal statement of her position vis-à-vis the battlelines he has drawn with Omasa and Noboru. This is the climactic event that completes Bunzō's isolation—he has already severed relations with Noboru, and Omasa is nothing short of hostile. As the narrator sardonically points out, Bunzō first approaches Osei in the hopes of confirming his own wishful thinking. Faced with the two equally distasteful options of mollifying Omasa by enlisting Noboru's help to get reinstated, or adhering to his moral standards at the risk of losing Osei, Bunzō hits upon the third and most unlikely possibility that Osei might actively support his position, making any compromise with Noboru and Omasa unnecessary. He broaches the topic by voicing this internal soliloquy almost verbatim, hoping to hear Osei affirm him once again by speaking his language. When her response diverges from his mental script, Bunzō immediately tries to extract a decisive meaning from her words.

"On top of that, if I want to go to the boss's place, first I would definitely have to make a request of Honda, of course it's not that I don't know the boss too, but … "

"And what's wrong with that, making a request of Honda?"

"What, are you telling me to make a request of Honda?" When Bunzō said this, he was no longer the same Bunzō as before, the color in his face having changed.

"I am not giving orders, you know, just saying what's wrong with making a request?"

"Of Honda," asked Bunzō again, as though he couldn't believe his ears. "Yes."

"Of that obsequious jerk . . . boss's tag-along . . . slave . . . "

"Of all the . . . "

"Not even ashamed to be called a slave, just a dog . . . dog . . . dog or cat, nothing better, that's what he is, and you are telling me to humbly request his favor?" said Bunzō, staring hard into Osei's face.

"You probably talk like that because of what happened last night, but I must say, Honda-san is not such an obsequious person."

"Hmph, not obsequious, you say he's not obsequious," he said with a most bitter sarcasm, turning his face away, but he quickly turned back with a sharp look in Osei's direction: "What was it that you said that time when Honda made rude jokes to you?"

"So I was upset at the time, but now that I've socialized with him, I see he's not the kind of shameless person that you say he is."

Bunzō stared into Osei's face in silence, but in a manner that did not bode well.

"Last night, when we went downstairs after that, Honda-san silenced me, saying that 'if your mother hears of this she'll be sure to make a fuss, which wouldn't matter to me, but it would be trouble for Utsumi, so please don't mention it.' So I didn't say a word, but Nabe couldn't keep from talking . . . "

"The snake, so he had the nerve to say that, did he?"

"There you go again. . . . Bun-san, you are in the wrong here. After being abused by you like that, he didn't even get angry, and said it out of consideration for your benefit, and you turn around and call him a snake. . . . Well, you are mild-mannered and Honda-san is lively, so perhaps you don't take well to him, but just because you don't take to certain people doesn't necessarily make them all shameless . . . but you just pile on the abuse . . . talk about rude . . . " she clipped, with a slight flush in her face.

With an even more angry look on his face, Bunzō said, "Well in that case, are you saying that you have taken a liking to Honda?"

"It's not whether or not I have taken a liking to him, just that he's not the shameless person you say he is . . . calling him a snake and piling on the abuse . . . "

"You will first please reply to my question. Are you saying that you have finally taken a liking to Honda?"

His manner of speaking was rather vehement. Piqued, Osei for a while just watched Bunzō intently, then said, "What's the point in asking me that? Surely, whether or not I have taken a liking to Honda-san has no relationship to you."

"It does, so I am asking."

"And what relationship is that."

"It doesn't matter what the relationship is, there is no necessity for me to explain that now."

"In that case there is no necessity for me to answer your question."

"Fine then. I don't need to hear it," said Bunzō, turning his face away again, bitterly mumbling as though to himself, "Running away when put on the spot by a person's questioning, the utter height of cowardice."

"What's that? 'The height of cowardice.' . . . Very well, then, if you are going to say such things then there's no point in hiding it, I will say it. . . . Indeed, I will say it . . . " said Osei, sticking out her chest a bit, in a sharp posture, "Yes, Honda-san has taken to my liking. . . . What of it?"

Hearing this, Bunzō trembled and turned blue in the face. . . . For a while he was speechless, just staring hard at Osei's coolly composed face with a look of resentment, the corners of his eyes quickly growing moist . . . but then he suddenly recovered himself, put on a stern air of composure, and, in a trembling voice, "Well, then . . . then let's do this, everything until now . . . cleanly . . . " unable to finish, his breast having filled up. For a while, his words hung in the air, but then with determination, "let's cleanly forget it all."

"What is that supposed to mean, 'everything until now.'"

"Having come to this, why should you feign ignorance so? As long as there's going to be a breakup . . . can't we make . . . a clean . . . break?"

"Who is feigning ignorance. Who are you talking about? Who is breaking up with whom?"

Bunzō lost his patience. Raising his voice a bit, he said, "You've taken this pretense far enough now. How can you say 'who is breaking up with whom?' Cruelly playing with a person's emotions until now, and at this point . . . even having turned over to that Honda . . . and when a person reacts calmly, you go and take the offensive, what's this 'who is breaking up with whom.'"

"What did you say? Playing with a person's emotions until now. . . . Who played with a person's emotions? . . . Tell me, who played with a person's emotions!" When she said this, Osei's eyes were also getting moist. Bunzō just glared right into Osei's face without saying a word.

"That's just too much. . . . Playing with a person's emotions, turning over to Honda—you say nothing but libel. . . . Whatever dreams you may have had in your own conceit, it's no one's problem but your own. . . . Bunzō had abruptly risen to his feet before she could finish talking. Glaring at Osei, "There is nothing more to be said, nothing more to be heard. This is the last time I will talk to you, be sure of that."

"I certainly will be."

"Go ahead and have lots of . . . affairs."

"What's that you said?" By the time she said this, Bunzō was no longer in the room. (169–73)

Insistently monologic throughout, Bunzō finally forces Osei to speak with his own words by throwing down the gauntlet of an insult, muttered *as though to himself*—with clearly disastrous results. Enraged by the vision of an unrecognizable other where he had hoped to see a reflection of himself, Bunzō lashes out with a final act of verbal aggression, calling his "pure one" a promiscuous tramp.

In the wake of this traumatic event, Bunzō's internal language starts to take on a life of its own as he begins the sharp descent into nervous prostration. Curiously, his mind suddenly becomes a playground for foreign words that seem to emerge from out of nowhere. The first sign of mental disturbance occurs the night after his fateful altercation with Osei.

Since Noboru came, Bunzō lost his composure, standing up, sitting down. He could faintly make out a rattling sound, which made it all the more unendurable, so he concocted an excuse to go downstairs from the second floor and passed by Osei's room, when he perked up his ears, tread on tiptoe, and peaked inside through a gap in the *shōji*, at first relieved to see Osei lying on the floor, but she was c . . . r . . . y . . .

Instantaneously, the word *explanation* exploded in his breast. . . .

Once he set his mind on an *explanation*, he was much relieved. Because he sizes it up with his own open heart, it hardly seems such a difficult task. Just a bit more perseverance—how pitiful, Bunzō was having a waking dream. (184)

Overwhelmed by remorse, Bunzō immediately reverts to English, the language in which he first fell in love with Osei. It was the mediation of this language that gave him a feeling of intimacy with Osei; now it is the only language in which he can entertain the fantasy of regaining her affection. Needless to say, his attempt at an "explanation" ends in a miserable failure. After this last attempt at communication, Bunzō retreats to his second-floor quarters for virtually the rest of the novel.

The last four chapters of *Ukigumo* detail the developing relationship between Osei and Noboru, nestled among Bunzō's internal reflections on the entire situation, past and present. Having finally recognized his own folly and Osei's inherently capricious nature, Bunzō now becomes increasingly obsessed with the potential threat of Noboru's seduction. Once more trapped in the mental prison of an unresolvable dilemma, his psyche begins to break down into autonomous, clashing elements.

He can only lament, for though he has the will to save Osei, he cannot find the means. "What to do?" The question rises in his mind several times a day, but it always merely rises and, without getting an answer, disappears, leaving nothing behind but the three characters for dissatisfaction. In the rush to escape from the torment of that dissatisfaction, healthy knowledge shrivels, an overly forward fantasy begins to rage, becoming impossible to suppress, and, in the end, before being able to come up with a plan of action, a happy scene of having already saved Osei is flickering before his very eyes, often remaining despite his attempts to brush it away.

. . . He made various attempts to think it through, but could not hit upon a single plan that seemed possible to carry out; going round and round, returning once more to the first plan and thus agonizing and suffering, that familiar fantasy would go to work again to make him think of useless things. At times, he would get the strange feeling that all the events of recent days were just a temporary joke, that Osei did not really mean it when she turned her back on Bunzō, that she was just pretending to turn her back in order to test Bunzō, as proof of which she was sure to come up the stairs any minute now and laugh away the previous friction with that splendid, high laughter of hers, or so it would seem sometimes, but it never lasted for long; incompassionate memory would go to work, forcing him to remember Osei's face when she had that fit of bad temper, breaking up that pleasant dream in the space of a blink and a breath. (213–14)

Healthy knowledge, overly forward fantasy, incompassionate memory: Bunzō's victimization by the personified parts of his psyche here—even more alien to the Japanese idiom than the "fickle skies" of *Aibiki*—vividly illustrates that his internal monologue has never been purely a product of his own individual will.

As we have already seen, it was the shared second language of English that formed the bond, however tenuous, between Bunzō and Osei. From the start, we are made aware of Osei's susceptibility to the influence of English-language education. In her case this influence is manifest in a purely external form. Yet in Bunzō's case it is not until he begins to fall apart that the profound impact of Western language education rises to the surface of the narrative.

Incessant thinking about the same thing eventually exhausts the human mind, weakening its powers of discernment. Thus while Bunzō was constantly worrying about Osei, at some point his concentration scattered and was unable to focus on a single thing, and at times he would have haphazard thoughts about fragments that were totally unrelated to each other. Once he was lying down with his head cupped in his hands staring at the ceiling, at first thinking this and that about Osei as usual, when he happened to notice the grain of the wood ceiling, and he suddenly had a strange thought. "Looking at it this way, it looks like marks left by flowing water." Once this thought occurred to him, he completely forgot about Osei and, continuing to stare even harder at the ceiling, thought, "Depending on one's state of mind, it can even appear to have peaks and valleys. Hm, so that's an *optical illusion*." Suddenly recalling the magnificently bearded face of the foreign lecturer who taught Bunzō and the others physics, he simultaneously forgot about the grain of the ceiling. Next, he saw seven or eight students appear before his very eyes, all of whom were his class-mates, some with pencils stuck behind their ears, some carrying books, and still others opening the books to read. Upon looking closer, it seemed that Bunzō himself was among them. Now the lecture on *electriciteit* had ended and an exam was to take place, and everyone was gathered around an *electrical machine*, and, just as it seemed that they were all arguing about something he could not make out, suddenly the *machine* and the students vanished without a trace like so much smoke, and the wood grain came back into sight. Saying 'Hm, so that's an *optical illusion*,' Bunzō smiled for no reason. "Speaking of *illusion*, the most interesting book I've ever read is Sully's *Illusions*. I must have finished reading it in two days and a night. How does a person get so smart? He must have an intricately organized brain. . . . ' Though there would seem to be no relation between Sully's brain and Osei, at this moment the thought of Osei suddenly pierced his chest, erupting like a gushing water fountain.[29] (214–15)

In the Japanese orthography, foreign words like *illusion, elecriciteit* (from the Dutch), and *electrical machine* are rendered phonetically in the hiragana of native speech, suggesting the degree to which Bunzō has assimilated them to his own language. That in the midst of his obsession with Osei Bunzō suddenly recalls the word *illusion* is surely not the entirely *haphazard* thought of a randomly wandering mind. As the stream of associations indicates, the word *illusion* exists in Bunzō's mind as part of the Western lexicon of scientific *truth*, the subtext for the dissection procedure he applied to Osei's indifference. If the deeply reverberating sound of *Truth* was Osei's siren song, this sudden musing on *illusions* constitutes Bunzō's unsung refrain.

For Bunzō there is indeed a most profound connection between Osei and all of the associations attached to the word *illusion*. It is the unsettling proximity between truth and illusion that inhabits the space between languages—not only the ineffable difference-in-same-ness of *veritas*, truth and *shinri*, but also that of *shinri* and "shinri," *truth* and "truth." Bunzō's delusions and progressive paralysis constitute the quintessential afflictions of his era: a time of bewildering linguistic flux and interlingual mingling initiated by the shock of Western letters, leading to an urgent search for a national language amidst a heterogeneous mass of regional and class idioms, the sudden shift from a graphic to a phonocentric apprehension of language, and a profound devaluation of Chinese writing (kanbun) as the exclusive language of learning simultaneous to the rapid proliferation of Chinese words (kango) as the primary medium for translating Western concepts and cultural phenomena. What Gotō Meisei describes as the "relational discord" of *Ukigumo* can also be called linguistic discord; in fact, the only characters in the novel who actually share the same language are Omasa and Noboru. It is only when Bunzō has been completely forsaken by the world of spoken language and retreated to the quietude of his own room that he is finally allowed an epiphany of sorts; but in a world bereft of verbal exchange this epiphany can only underscore the pain of his isolation.

The language of *Ukigumo* directly reflects both the polyphony of heterogeneous class idioms and the complex polyglossia of Chinese, Western, and Japanese letters that constituted the original impetus for and the essential challenges to the vernacularization movement. It is this very linguistic heterogeneity that has enabled *Ukigumo* to remain at the beginning of modern Japanese literary history; it is what enables critics of essentially antagonistic positions to agree about the text's underlying modernity. Yet Futabatei's first novel is not just a reflection of the polyphonic and polyglossic conditions of his times; it is also a critical meditation on the same. Within the battle-field of written and spoken language—or foreign lingua francae and the native colloquial—represented by the struggle of Bunzō against Omasa and Noboru, what Osei personifies is the bewitching appeal of a language that can alchemically compound all these differences under the single sign of Truth.

If Bunzō's final paralysis can be traced to a fundamentally irresolv-able conflict between heterogeneous languages, then it seems quite fitting that Futabatei himself—as the person who both sensed and created this crisis in fiction—would meet the same fate as a novel-ist. By the time he was writing the final section of his debut novel,

Futabatei had already begun to harbor serious doubts about literature as a vehicle of truth. These doubts proved so consuming that Futabatei would not compose another novel of his own until 1906, and he even abandoned literary translation for almost an entire decade, until 1896. For him the language of Truth—that of Chinese writing, the criticism of Belinsky, and the fiction of Turgenev, Gogol, Goncharov, and Dostoevsky—had constituted an absolute value that demanded nothing less than a complete pledge of allegiance. In the context of modern literature it stems from the idealist stance that seeks meaning, rather than purely aesthetic value, in fiction. And, in the context of the Japanese vernacularization movement, it is a universal value that demands articulation in the colloquial tongue. This was the source of Futabatei's ambivalence as a writer, because it fostered an underlying sense of *betrayal* when he attempted to render this language in the form of Japanese vernacular fiction, which was also the only viable, if not already established, equivalent he could find.

Though the roots of Futabatei's growing skepticism toward literature were no doubt manifold, his disillusionment with the novel bears a striking resemblance to Bunzō's relationship with Osei. Just as Bunzō had idolized Osei as a bearer of Truth, Futabatei had embraced the novel as that which reveals the hidden ideas within the contingent forms of apparent phenomena. Yet, once he actually tried to achieve such a revelation in practice, he found himself confronted by a multitude of competing languages—in other words, the contingent forms of language itself. Futabatei may have discovered an idea in the forms of contemporary Japanese society worthy of revelation, but the narrative of *Ukigumo* shows that he had a much less certain relationship with the forms and ideas of language, despite his clear advocacy of the vernacular novel. Language being the very medium of the novel, Futabatei's profound loss of confidence in the ability of fiction to represent truth seems all but inevitable. We might say that, in intellectual terms, the vernacular novel was Futabatei's first love, but his early disillusionment with the genre—at least as it was written by himself and others in Japanese—prevented him from taking it on as a proper bride.

The next generation of radical vernacularists, the Naturalists, however, grew up with a significantly different set of linguistic contingencies, among which the language of Futabatei's translations would come to occupy a position of central importance. While Futabatei's claim that he could not take literature seriously ("Watakushi wa kaigi-ha da" and *Heibon*) would become one of the most prominent aspects of his intellectual legacy, the fruits of his labors as a literary translator would, ironically, nurture a generation of writers for whom the ideal literature was virtually synonymous with seriousness itself. What is uncanny about *Ukigumo* is that, in spite of its ostensible ideological implications as a vernacular novel, its narrative ultimately underscores the dilemma posed by the exotic appeal of the rhetoric of Western realism (Truth), and the phantasms fostered by its siren-like imitation in colloquial Japanese. It is almost as if Futabatei had unconsciously predicted the future of *Aibiki's* Naturalist progeny.

Part 2

TAYAMA KATAI AND THE SIREN OF VERNACULAR LETTERS

> The high collar in gold spectacles is
> a schoolgirl of the women's college
> at Mejirodai in the capital's west,
> poetry of Byron and Goethe in one hand,
> and praise of Naturalism on the lips.
> And so the rice shoots of Waseda rustle
> to the murmuring winds of demons and love.
>
> —"High-Collar Song"

In 1909 Kaminaga Ryogetsu gave the public a ditty that would crystallize its image of the era. In a few simple lines, the "High-Collar Song" provided a fairly complete inventory of the schoolgirl's cultural capital in the first decade of the twentieth century—the class privilege, intellectual status, and Westernesque cachet marked by her "gold spectacles," her love of modern literature, and the rather suggestive rustling all this inspired among "the rice shoots of Waseda," a school that had become a magnet for literary youth under Tsubouchi Shōyō's guidance. Ever since Kosugi Tengai's *Makaze koikaze* (Winds of demons and love) blew their way onto the pages of *Yomiuri Shinbun* in 1903, the figure of the schoolgirl increasingly came to signify the quintessence of the high collar, the provocative cutting edge of a rapidly advancing Japanese modernity. Moreover, her image had not only become the epitome of the Westernesque in the popular imagination but also a highly suggestive emblem for the most Westernesque brands of literature—romantic poetry and naturalism. (As antithetical as these categories may seem, we need only observe that most of naturalism's proponents in Japan had also been practitioners or supporters of romantic poetry to understand the assumed complementarity here.) The schoolgirl's relationship to modern literature—and hence to the rhetoric of love and sexuality—became an endless source of fascination for readers and writers alike.[1]

While many writers were attracted to this rich source of cultural capital, none had been so completely enthralled as Tayama Katai, an apparent victim of the affliction he called maidenitis ("Shōjobyō"). Katai's oeuvre and the personal life he so often made public in his writings attest time and again to his long-standing idolization of the educated young women of Meiji Japan and to the literary mediations that would fatefully direct the course of his "disease." For Katai, a personal identification with certain works of modern Western literature gave meaning to the chronic alienation he experienced as a lowly member of the Tokyo literary establishment. The schoolgirl figure, as a Westernesque woman of letters, would come to play a central role in this identification process. Moreover, Katai's personal stake in the intervention of modern Western letters into a hostile domestic literary scene would also lead him to idolize the radical vernacular style of Futabatei Shimei's translations from Russian fiction. Thus he may have been the perfect candidate to resuscitate the problematic relation first explored in *Ukigumo*—that of schoolgirls and the exotic appeal of Western letters.

As we shall see, Katai's advocacy of raw language in the landmark essay "Rokotsu naru byōsha" signaled a radical new vernacularism for the novel; in an age when the vernacular style had already become the lingua franca of Japanese fiction, Katai called for a revamping of the vernacular that would jettison its most writerly elements. Yet despite his profession of absolute faith in the technical ability, and even the moral and artistic necessity, of the "raw" vernacular to represent "nature," Katai made his name with a novel that, like *Ukigumo*, overlaid the pure image and promise of this ideal language of truth with the figure of a duplicitous Westernesque femme fatale. The fact that he unwittingly produced a variation on the *Ukigumo* theme of language and the Westernesque woman suggests an almost formal inevitability, as though new media simply could not be deployed in the absence of this figure.

A full two decades elapsed between Futabatei's debut novel and Katai's career-making publication of *Futon*. What transpired during these twenty years that would set the stage for the return of the Westernesque femme fatale as a siren of vernacular letters? Chapters 3 and 4 address this question from two angles: first, the evolution of Katai's relationship to literature and style and, second, his development of the Westernesque schoolgirl persona. Chapter 3 presents Katai's fraught relationship with the Japanese literary mainstream as the basis for his later stylistic rebellion and argues that his Naturalism ultimately consisted in the discovery of the self in the language of the other, a kind of exoticism that was enabled by Futabatei's vernacular translations. Chapter 4 charts the development of Westernesque women and the men who idolize them in Katai's fiction, showing how they register important changes in Katai's chronically frustrated relationship to changing ideals of love, marriage, and literature.

Katai's self-identification as a marginalized country boy with big city literary ambitions traces a path of gradually deepening alienation that would finally bear literary fruit in *Futon* by transforming the image of the Westernesque woman from a transparent metonym— first for social distinction (trophy wife), then for literary distinction (soulmate)—into an enigmatic siren who embodies the betrayal of language itself. How did Katai manage to arrive at such an articulation of the schoolgirl figure, one that would catapult him from an insignificant corner of Japanese literary circles to the forefront of the Naturalist movement and a permanent place in the annals of Japanese literary history? If it had not been for a feat of real literary invention, both Katai and *Futon* would have long since fallen into obscurity. By examining the radical breaks in style and the deployment of the Westernesque woman figure that occur in "Shojobyō" (Maidenitis, 1907) and *Futon*, chapter 5 outlines the process of stylistic experimentation that brought about modern Japanese literature's second fateful encounter with the siren of Western(esque) letters.

[3]

Portrait of the Naturalist as a Young Exote

Katai's relationship to the city of Tokyo was always heavily mediated by the written word, at first in a painfully material sense. In 1880, at the age of nine, Tayama Rokuya (Katai's given name) was sent to Tokyo to serve as an errand boy and aspiring apprentice to a bookseller in Kyōbashi. Thus his first experience of city life literally entailed carting heaps of books on his back. While the future novelist was running through the streets and alleys of Tokyo procuring and transporting book orders, his older brother Miyato was charged with the duty of actually reading books, as Katai recalls in one of the most poignant passages of *Tōkyō no sanjūnen* (Thirty years in Tokyo, 1917).

The Sound of Voices Reading Aloud

I walked over.

From the inside could be heard a gushing of voices reading aloud. The place was reminiscent of a daimyō's *nagaya*; and atop a latticed plaster wall, covered here and there with dust from the streets, could be seen a series of small windows burning in the hot rays of the westerly sun.

A large sign hung there, which read "Hōkō Gijuku."

On this side of the road was a large hackberry tree that created a cool shade from the summer sun, so pedicab drivers, vagabonds, and passersby were resting there.

The gushing sound of voices reading aloud!

I became wistful and pressed my slight figure to the window. In there is my older brother, who has come for training. Yet part of me felt pity at the thought of him having others see his younger brother looking like the errand boy I was, so I made no attempt to visit him openly. Such an artless, pitiful, trivial concern!

I thought it would be nice if my brother just happened to come out. And that it would be nice if he said, "Oh, it's you," and put his hand on my shoulder. With the fate of the entire family hanging on his shoulders, he is studying without resting his sleepy eyes. Without the money to buy *geta*, wearing the same old robes and threadbare *hakama*, he is studying with all his might. Even in the mind of a child, thinking of this made my own troubles seem hardly worth mentioning. Yet, in another way, my brother's studying like this also made me envious and sad.[1]

A bookseller's errand boy standing outside with the other menial laborers, timidly peering in on the windows of higher education, listening to the sound of voices reading aloud with a mixture of envy and sadness: here is an image that captures much of Katai's future relationship to the modern literary world, from its nearby emanation in Tokyo to its distant centers in Europe. As the above passage so clearly shows, Katai's position as an outsider vis-à-vis the cultural center was impressed upon him at a very young age; reconfirmed time and again, it would also form the core of his self-consciousness throughout his literary career.

Thus, almost from its very inception Katai's relationship with letters was shaped by the country-city divide, the gap between an increasingly central Tokyo and the increasingly peripheral provinces that emerged with Japan's transformation into a modern nation-state.[2] Though his first foray into the capital came to an abrupt end after less than two years, he returned to his hometown of Tatebayashi thoroughly enamored of Tokyo life. Sent back to school soon after his return home, Katai threw himself into the study of Chinese, which then provided a new way of participating in urban culture. In 1885 he began to submit Chinese poems and other compositions to the youth magazine *Eisai shinshi* (New magazine for the talented). Launched in 1877, *Eisai shinshi* was composed almost exclusively of reader submissions. As a significant number of its readers and submitters lived in the provinces, the Tokyo-based magazine promoted communication between provincial youth who would have otherwise remained isolated, while profitably stoking the fantasy of active participation in the cultural, economic, and social center of the nation's capital from which the magazine issued.[3] Convinced that the "building from which *Eisai shinshi* issued must be a splendid one indeed," Katai went to see it firsthand when he relocated to Tokyo with his family in 1886, only to find that the "half-Western-style building was a surprisingly tiny little affair."[4] This was the first in a series of illusions to be shattered by Katai's second experience of Tokyo life. Katai's gradual arrival in the city of his youthful dreams would ultimately lead him to dream of more distant places, the kinds of "there" that existed only in modern Western letters.

Already by the mid 1880s English was quickly becoming the lingua franca of higher education, diminishing the value of Katai's hard-won facility with Chinese. Not long after arriving in Tokyo, Katai began to study English with Nojima Kinpachirō, a family friend from Tatebayashi five years Katai's senior who was then attending Tokyo Daigaku Yobimon with the budding literary luminaries Yamada Bimyō, Ozaki Kōyō, Ishibashi Shian, and Kawakami Bizan. The wealthy and knowledgeable Nojima quickly took Katai under his wing, introducing him to the finer aspects of Tokyo's material and intellectual life.

I was the younger of the two, and there was no telling just how greatly I was influenced by this man's high-collar, literature-loving, straight-as-an-arrow temperament. In those days I wandered all over the streets of Tokyo with him. . . . At a small shop called Sankaku-dō on a corner in Ogawamachi, he would often buy ink, pens, and pencils. In that shop there was a plump young girl with luscious cheeks.

Even though he was extremely literary in temperament, and even though he was constantly perusing novels, history books, and biographies in English, he was not strong in Chinese learning, so he could not write well. In that area I at least wrote Chinese and Japanese poetry, so he always saw promise in me. "If only I could write a little better like you, I would do literature, you know. Because when all is said and done, the writer, the artist is the best and most elevated occupation." He had so much new knowledge about writers and novelists that one could only wonder where he could have gotten it from. Perhaps it was because he lived and breathed the same air as Kōyō, Shian, and Bizan. He criticized the study of [Shikitei] Samba that Kōyō was doing at Yobimon. "I'll tell you this. Nothing will come of studying Samba like those guys are doing now. In the West there are any number of great writers. There are great novels. From here on in, anyone who wants to do literature will never amount to anything unless they read things from abroad." Having said that, he would triumphantly list the names of great writers, counting on his fingers—"Dickens, Thackeray, Hugo, Dumas, Goethe."[5]

If the sound of voices reading aloud overheard through the dust-laden windows of Hōkō Gijuku had left the young Katai in awe of Chinese learning and the social advancement it seemed to promise for his older brother, Nojima's litany of foreign names would enthrall him all the more. Here was a fellow Tatebayashi man in Tokyo, "high-collar" yet familiar and straightforward, who more than made up for his weakness in Chinese learning with a cutting-edge knowledge of the West; a person who bought pens and pencils—the essential equipment of a Western education—and stated unequivocally that to be a literary artist was the "best and most elevated occupation." For Katai, Nojima's very existence was a literary education in itself. Nojima introduced Katai to the English and French fiction that was changing the face of the contemporary Japanese literary scene, and his well-stocked library of Western books gave Katai precious access to a type of knowledge that was far beyond the social and financial means of his family. Under Nojima's influence Katai established a personal relationship with "things from abroad," became an avid reader of contemporary Japanese fiction and literary translations, and began to experiment with the composition of his own novels, first in collaboration with an *Eisai shinshi* friend, then on his own.

Nojima's impact on Katai was twofold: first, he affirmed the occupation of writing as the most respectable of endeavors, an opinion that was not lost on the part of Katai that craved social distinction. Second, he impressed upon his young protégé the importance of foreign (i.e., Western) literature over and above the native literary tradition. Nojima actively encouraged Katai to pursue a dual career in law (i.e., politics) and literature, much like the English authors he favored. Yet, like so many other Meiji novelists, Katai began the study of English as part of his preprofessional training only to have his ambitions diverted to the new frontier of modern literature. After a case of typhoid and its attendant financial difficulties brought an end to his brief tenure at Nihon Hōritsu Gakkō (Japan School of Law) in 1890, Katai decided to pin his future solely on the literary side of the career path Nojima had proposed. On May 24, 1891, armed with nothing but a long-standing history of publication in *Eisai shinshi* and a newfound knowledge of Western fiction, Katai paid a visit to Ozaki Kōyō, one of the most commercially successful novelists of his day.

Kōyō's commercial success and the fact that he happened to live nearby certainly must have affected Katai's first choice of a literary mentor. Yet the aspiring young writer was also attracted to Kōyō's work, and particularly his style.

Kōyō's [*Ninin bikuni*] *Iro zange*, which came out as the first issue of the *Shincho hyakushu* series—this also moved me a great deal. At the least, in its style and in its narration *Iro zange* had enough power to enchant the youth of its day. And it also gave us the feeling that "something like this would not be impossible to write." It impressed us as something new and more familiar than distant kanbun and *kanshi,* or *waka,* or difficult English writing. And the fact that the writer was still young, only five or six years older than myself, lent me a certain strength and motivation.[6]

In *Ninin bikuni iro zange* (hereafter referred to as *Ninin bikuni*), Katai saw a style of writing that seemed new and yet infinitely more familiar than Chinese writing, Japanese poetry, or the Westernesque vernacular Bimyō had modeled after English. (Katai had emulated the latter in his first novel, *Aki no yū*, written in 1889 and never published.) He was just one of many readers in whom Kōyō's career-launching novel would produce this reaction.

We have already seen examples of the other literary styles, new and old, being practiced and developed in the late 1880s. Within that context, what was new, and what so familiar, about Kōyō's *Ninin bikuni* when it appeared in 1889? In response to the stylistic dilemma Western writing had inexorably posed for the composition of novels in Japanese, Kōyō wrote in the preface:

*not explaining the era, nor setting the place. among Japan's novels this type is rare.[. . .]

*as for style the inherited mixture of elegant and common diction pleases not. the vernacular style fails to agree so. after thoroughly agonizing over it all. the phoenix or the cock—the tiger or the cat. dreamt up this bizarre and unusual style that even oneself cannot judge. though not a story that favors humble talents. even so the author's pains how much. by taking that into account a bit. request honored appraisal

*as stated before. from the inherited writing of our world. the aspect differs though poorly executed so. readers at a glance say *hard*. the author finds not hard in the least. why must others call hard what one finds not hard. humbly beg the effort of a second reading that relies solely on the punctuation[7]

Let us first consider the more familiar stylistic elements of Kōyō's work. The literal translation above reflects what English readers will invariably assume to be an "abbreviation" of the subject—a characteristic of Japanese style that only appears as a "lack" in translation. Since the bulk of meaning in Japanese resides in the verb and its various inflections, rather than in a subject-verb predicate, the language rarely demands an explicit identification of subject. Thus, in the above passage, the first-person speaker only names himself as a grammatical subject when issuing a defiant challenge to his potentially hostile readers—"*sakusha wa* sukoshi mo tsurakarazu" (*the author* finds not hard in the least). This is a far cry from the language of Futabatei's *Aibiki*, wherein virtually each and every "I" of the original text is scrupulously—and, from the perspective of Japanese stylistic conventions, gratuitously—rendered as *jibun*.

The "abbreviation" of subject was an integral part of felicitous Japanese style. Indeed, abbreviation in itself constituted an important rhetorical device, one that *Ninin bikuni* rather enthusiastically exploited. For instance, let us consider the opening line of the novel:

miyako sae . . . sabishisa ikani katayamazato no shigure ato.
    even in the capital . . . how desolate in a remote mountain village after an autumn shower.[8]

Here, the use of ellipses to abbreviate what should read "it is desolate" brings English punctuation into the service of the native rhetorical devices of abbreviation and inversion, a move that injects a new, foreign element into the graphic landscape of Japanese writing without disturbing its basic rhetorical conventions. One might even say that Kōyō's use of punctuation actually reinforces a native rhetorical convention by lending it a graphically visible form. This is precisely the kind of linguistic adaptation that made the style of *Ninin bikuni* seem both new and yet familiar to contemporary readers.

As stated in his preface, Kōyō rejected both the mixture of elegant and common diction (*gazoku setchū*) developed in Edo fiction and the new vernacular style then being developed by Futabatei and Bimyō. The result of his search for another alternative was indeed "bizarre and unusual" if only for its idiosyncratic use of punctuation marks. Though Kōyō's use of white periods to set off distinct phrases was rather unusual at the time, it was presumably based upon the recently rediscovered work of Ihara Saikaku (1642–93).[9] What was truly strange was his abundant use of dashes and ellipses in the body of the text, which provoked one contemporary reviewer of *Ninin bikuni* to quip that all of the characters in the story must have been habitual stammerers.[10] According to Kitani Kimie, Kōyō's first attempt to develop a new literary style that would supersede the genbun-itchi model resulted in nothing more than a few simple innovations in Japanese punctuation.[11] In short, aside from its dashes and ellipses, almost every other stylistic aspect of the text was quite familiar to contemporary readers of Japanese fiction.

Such being the case, it is little wonder that Katai would mistake Kōyō as an easily imitable writer. If the stylistic requirements for modern fiction could be met with the addition of a few conspicuously new punctuation marks to the accepted conventions of Japanese rhetoric, it might very well seem that "something like this would not be impossible to write." Yet Katai's original initiation into the practice of writing had been based on kanbun, not gabun. Even the study of Japanese poetry had presented him with a level of difficulty that ranked with Chinese and English. In an age when a truly national language had yet to emerge and the practice of writing necessitated the acquisition of one or more languages that bore little resemblance to the conventions of the spoken tongue, the deceptively simple fact of "Japaneseness" did not necessarily make a written idiom more accommodating to a Japanese writer. Though Katai initially sensed an easy familiarity with Kōyō's use of Japanese, his personal encounters with the man would quickly destroy that illusion.

Indeed, any utopian images of the literary enterprise that may have been fostered in Katai under Nojima's tutelage were dispelled by the hierarchical order Kōyō had established in Ken'yūsha. The Ken'yūsha group happened to be planning the launch of a magazine to publish new talent when Katai sought Kōyō's literary and professional guidance in 1891, which may have been the only reason the literary luminary agreed to meet this complete unknown. Katai did all he could to impress the renowned writer with his knowledge of Western fiction.[12] But Kōyō was not the type to be particularly impressed by such knowledge, nor by a country boy's hard-earned facility with Chinese letters. He did not accept Katai as his own protégé, instead shunting him off to Emi Suiin, managing editor for the new Ken'yūsha magazine *Senshi bankō*. By joining the magazine under Suiin's tutelage, Katai became a minor satellite in the Ken'yūsha constellation. Shortly thereafter Kōyō frankly derided the first novel Katai had asked him to read, a stinging rejection the novice writer would never forget.

At the time I was writing something like this: The time is the beginning of spring, the snow on the mountains too gradually look warmer, so too the song-singing voices of firewood mongers quietly echo at and around the foot of the mountain. The flow of the stream makes its first sound, the village children too. . . .

This manuscript, which I still have today, was about forty pages long, written under the influence of *Ninin bikuni*. It is titled *Yukibotoke* (Snow Buddha). As I recall, I showed it to Kōyō and was laughed at. Even now, I still remember what Kōyō said to me then—"You know, even prose is worthless without a rhythm of its own. It can't be as obvious as the 7–5 syllabic pattern of Bakin, but something as lacking in rhythm as yours isn't even writing at all."[13]

This was the beginning of Katai's literary career, a lukewarm reception at best. In fact, Katai could only gain entrance into the Ken'yūsha by remaining on the buyer's side of the culture trade. *Senshi bankō* required a membership fee of 10 sen per month—five times the cover price of *Eisai shinshi*. No writer's fees applied in the event of publication, and the payment of dues only guaranteed the privilege of submitting one's work to the judgment of the editors and receiving a copy of each issue.[14] Essentially, it was an investment in one's professional future, more costly than participation in an amateur youth magazine, less expensive than academic tuition. Though it was a short-lived publication, *Senshi bankō* provides clear evidence of the novel's rise in social and economic status. Even for someone as financially strapped as Katai, the novelist's profession had become one worth investing in—particularly if, by a relatively small sum, one could gain entrance into the profession's only true guild.

Thus Katai became a paying member of *Senshi bankō* and established a teacher-disciple relationship with Emi Suiin. Suiin proved to be a sympathetic mentor whose lack of education in Western languages led him to admire Katai's reading knowledge of European fiction. Katai's relationship with Kōyō, on the other hand, remained ambivalent at best, distressing at worst. Unlike other young writers such as Izumi Kyōka, Oguri Fūyō, and Tokuda Shūsei, Katai remained a minor satellite on the periphery of the Ken'yūsha, never paying the full price of obeisance to its central authority, nor reaping the full benefits of membership in the guild.

In his literary memoirs Suiin recounts an episode that encapsulates the relationship between Kōyō and Katai. Suiin had arranged for Katai to publish a novel in the *Yomiuri shinbun*, a major Tokyo newspaper whose literary pages were virtually ruled by Ozaki Kōyō. An earlier version of the novel in question, *Yamagasui* (Mountain waters), had been published in the pages of *Senshi bankō*. Kōyō was enraged when he learned of this arrangement from a *Yomiuri* advertisement, feeling that Katai had not paid him due respect by calling on him personally with the news. In retaliation, he single-handedly rescinded the decision to publish Katai's story. Katai's professional debut in the vaunted literary pages of the *Yomiuri* was thus denied because of an unwitting social faux pas.[15]

Katai's experience with Kōyō's literary guild would become yet another false arrival on the long itinerary that finally led to Naturalism. So far, his odyssey had taken him all the way from the prospectless land of Tatebayashi to the virtual urban promise of *Eisai shinshi*, the city and educational facilities of Tokyo, the utopian Western library of Nojima Kinpachirō, and finally the very center of contemporary Japanese literary production that radiated from Ozaki Kōyō's study. But, to an awkward country boy, Kōyō's Ken'yūsha proved no more hospitable than the city of Tokyo itself. Instead of a literary promised land, Katai discovered a strictly hierarchical clique of urban sophisticates who closely guarded the tower of Japanese style. And, according to the undisputed king of contemporary Japanese fiction, this tower rose far too high to be scaled by the likes of Katai.

Katai clearly admired Kōyō's assiduous attention to stylistic detail, giving him the bulk of the credit for developing the modern vernacular style for Japanese fiction.[16] Yet his own experience as the abject member of the Ken'yūsha would leave him bitterly critical of the mainstream of Japanese fiction. Whatever may have initially led Tayama Katai to Ozaki Kōyō's door, the fundamental incompatibility of these two writers would leave indelible marks on the history of modern Japanese literature. It is no coincidence that "Rokotsu naru byōsha" adamantly announced Katai's liberation from stylistic enslavement within a year of Kōyō's death in October 1903.

Naturalism in and as Translation

The word *odyssey* is especially appropriate to describe Katai's experience because the final stop—his embrace of Naturalism—was also a homecoming, namely, a return to the literary ground first carved out in Japanese by Futabatei's *Aibiki*. Over the course of Katai's career as a writer, his intense desire to identify with the cultural vanguard of Tokyo combined with his chronic alienation from its most respected establishments to nurture a particular affinity for the semi-exotic language of translation. For this perpetual outsider the convention-defying example of Futabatei's vernacular translation would come to represent a powerful—and ultimately empowering—external intervention into the domestic landscape that had shunned him.[17] Once Katai embraced Naturalism, he would reject almost all that Ozaki Kōyō stood for, instead pointing to Futabatei Shimei as the essential Japanese model for his stylistic development.

The circumstances under which Katai pursued his literary career differed significantly from those that beset Futabatei's debut as a writer and translator. Because Futabatei started out with a well-defined concept of the modern novel derived from his readings in Russian, he found an inhibiting paucity of stylistic models from which to build a literary practice in Japanese. Katai grew up with precisely the opposite challenge: an overabundance of recently developed and still competing aesthetic ideologies, literary schools, and stylistic models from which to choose. Only seven years Futabatei's junior, Katai belonged to a distinctly different generation of Meiji writers—those who had come of age on the other side of the great divide marked by Tsubouchi Shōyō's *Shōsetsu shinzui*. By 1891, when the twenty-year-old Katai set his sights on a literary career and went knocking on Kōyō's door, critics were no longer decrying the paucity of new fiction, as had Shōyō just six years earlier. In resounding testimony to the impact of Shōyō's work, they instead found themselves wondering whether the plethora of novels and novelistic styles in their time signaled a brilliant golden age or a lamentably chaotic warring states period for literature.[18] According to Katai, it was a bewildering time to be a young writer.

> In that era of chaos, I had no idea how one should go about writing. Rohan's way of writing and Kōyō's way of writing were utterly different. Even for writing in the translation style, there was the difference between [Morita] Shiken and [Mori] Ōgai. Then again, there was also the free vernacular style of Futabatei's *Ukigumo*. And there was the historical novel of Bimyō, which took the vernacular for the narrative passages, and the written style for the spoken parts. As a literary apprentice in the midst of all this, I just wrote as much as I could while listening to the various theories of the great writers. . . . In that era, when my sensibilities were in constant flux, there was no clearly accepted view on writing, and I quickly fell under the influence of anyone who seemed interesting.[19]

Though the radical vernacular styles developed by Futabatei, Bimyō, and Saganoya Omuro had presented a provocative thesis for the creation of a new Japanese literature and wielded significant influence over other writers for a few years, the Saikaku revival initiated by Awashima Kangetsu and propagated by the neo-Saikaku styles of Kōda Rohan and Ozaki Kōyō presented an attractive antithesis to the Westernesque vernacular style, and Mori Ōgai would introduce yet a third alternative by deftly blending Chinese, Japanese, and Western rhetorical conventions in translation and composition. While *Shōsetsu shinzui* had clearly succeeded in elevating the intellectual and social status of the novel, the status of vernacular realism had yet to be determined.

Thus, while the novel's rise to prominence drew increasing numbers of young men and even a small number of young women to literary careers, most of Katai's generation of novelists experimented with a wide variety of styles and genres before turning to vernacular fiction as the ideal form of modern literature. During the first two decades of his own career, the range of styles and genres practiced by Katai was so broad as to virtually constitute a minihistory of Meiji literature—starting with the inherited forms of kanshi, kanbun, and waka and encompassing the various vernacular styles for the novel developed by Futabatei, Bimyō, and Omuro, the neo-Saikaku style of Kōyō, the Western-Japanese-Chinese blend of Ōgai, New Poetry, the subjective travelogue, the new and improved vernacular style perfected by Kōyō's later work, and, finally, the radically "raw" vernacular fiction of Katai's own making.

After the publication of *Futon* established Katai as a leading Naturalist, creating an increased demand for his personal observations on modern Japanese literature, he would return time and again to *Aibiki* as the formative reading experience of his youth. Upon Futabatei's death in 1909, Katai wrote of his 1888 translation:

That intricate description of nature—though we didn't understand it, we were thrilled at the thought that such a new form of writing existed. "Ah, it's autumn! Someone seemed to be passing by over there, and the sound of an empty carriage reverberated through the vacant air. . . . " Who knows how many times that single line reminded me of the plains of my country home, full of oak groves, or the alder-lined hills of Tokyo's suburbs. I am certain that the new way of seeing nature in Meiji literary circles truly owed much to this translation of *Aibiki*.[20]

As Katai's retrospective homage attests, the language of *Aibiki* had the stunning effect of altering its readers' very perception of nature. Oak and alder groves, features of the domestic landscape that stood firmly outside the realm of Japanese poetics, now presented themselves as viable subjects for literary writing. It was not so much that *Aibiki* had captured the intricacies of nature in language, but that its ineffably appealing style could give literary value to even the most mundane of natural phenomena. Moreover, the strange beauty of the language of *Aibiki* opened its readers' eyes to the *beauty of strange language*. In a later memoir Katai further elaborated:

Having been raised on the grandiose magnificence of the Confucian classics, as well as Chinese and Japanese writing, my mind and my mental cultivation were extraordinarily moved by this writing's intricate, strange manner of description. I was flustered by the thought that this was writing. Yet that intricate method of description was also a characteristic of foreign writing, and since I thought the writing of Japan would surely have to progress in that direction, from then on I began to pay attention to the magazines and newspapers.[21]

Katai's pronounced fascination with this kind of language reveals his Naturalism to be no less motivated by aesthetic interests than those writers he chastised for pursuing stylistic decorum at the expense of verisimilitude. What sets Katai apart is the fact that his vision of "nature" was not only mediated by literary language but particularly by the language of literary *translation*. As he himself claimed, "I read [*Aibiki*] enough to memorize it. And it would be impossible to say how much I used it as a reference in the writing of the vernacular style."[22]

As an art form whose primary goal is to bridge the gap between languages, literary translation is linguistic mediation par excellence. Thus, Japanese Naturalism is based upon a double mediation: not only the mediation of "nature" by language that necessarily occurs in any attempt at realistic representation, but, even before that, the mediation of one language by another. Yet the often-rehearsed rhetoric of Naturalist realism tends to obscure this defining feature. In what would become his most famous statement on the subject, "Rokotsu naru byōsha," Katai established a binary distinction between stylistic decorum and falsehood, on the one hand, and raw description and truth, on the other.

Everyone knows that falsehood should be despised. All people of discernment concur that letters in which the writing and the ideas do not correspond are worthless. Yet it seems that today's proponents of craftsmanship create writing that is not paired with thought, fill pages with falsehoods that do not come from the heart, and call this great writing, call it *bibun*. Writing is solely for the purpose of conveying meaning, so if one has written only what one thought, that is enough. Be it clumsy or deft, so long as one can believe to have written what one thought, then the purpose of writing has come to an excellent end. . . .

What about the literature of the West since the renovation of the nineteenth century? Gold-plated literature was utterly shattered to bits, cries that all must be raw, all must be true, all must be natural spread to every corner of continental literature, and this intellectual wave, with the force of a hurricane blowing away withered leaves, vigorously trampled over Romanticism, did it not? If not blood, then sweat; was this not the great call of the new revolutionaries?

Should you think it a lie, look at Ibsen, at Tolstoy, at Zola, at Dostoevsky, how astonishingly much blood and sweat has been poured into their works. Especially with a work like Dostoevsky's *Crime and Punishment*, which would shock the wits out of the craftsmanship contingent, there is a bold, raw description, hiding nothing whatsoever, that could never, even in one's dreams, be found in those craftsmen who look for the pretty in writing and aspire to gold-plated ideas.[23]

One might easily infer from this argument that Katai ascribed to the view that unadorned language could directly reflect reality and, further, that such language originated from the self—the "blood and sweat" of the individual writer. In fact, it is difficult to suppress the almost knee-jerk critical reaction to such apparent naïveté—the rejoinder that even the most naturalistic fiction is still a linguistic mediation, not a direct transcription, of reality. Yet to engage with Katai's argument according to such terms would only reconfirm the general truth that language always mediates, while failing to contend with a much more important truth particular to Japanese Naturalism: the fact that such literature was made possible by the linguistic mediation of *other languages*, not of some objective reality. Once we recall that the very rhetoric of Japanese Naturalism itself inhabited that ambiguous space *between languages*, we begin to sense a much more complex logic operating beneath the surface of Naturalist ideology as it was articulated in Japanese. For it is the space between languages that most powerfully challenges any assumption that language merely reflects, rather than mediates, reality or that language originates from, rather than engenders, the self.

Here the constant difficulty in finding a direct correspondence between the words of one language and another ultimately elicits a suspicion that certain realities can be articulated only in certain languages, and, vice versa, that only certain languages are capable of embodying, indeed creating, certain versions of reality. In *Kindai no shōsetsu* Katai recalls the following conversation with his close friend Kunikida Doppo (1871–1908):

We also talked about the future literary circles. At such times style was always a topic of discussion. He said that, before long, the foreign-style vernacular would surely take over. The style being used by Ichiyō and Rohan could never last for long, he said. And about the stiff travel writing of mine, he wondered why I would write in such a style.

Moreover, in his use of letters, he tried to be new, to use words that were like they had been translated from foreign writing. If it's going to be stiff anyway, the stiffness of having imitated foreign writing still has more to offer, he said.

"When I read foreign things, I always feel jealous, you know. There are great words that simply don't exist in Japanese, you know. For example, there is the phrase *sweet melancholy twilight*. It just cannot be translated into the words of Japan. *Sweet melancholy*—it just can't be said. How would you translate it, hm?"

"Well . . . if it were me," I thought, "if it were me, I might translate it as *mono omowashiki yūgure no hikari* [pensive light of dusk]." "*Mono omowashiki yūgure no hikari*—you just can't say that is a complete translation, hm. *Sweet melancholy twilight* is better, isn't it. In any case, there is a dearth of words in Japanese. In writing the style of the future, that will have to be taken into account, you know . . . "

"I suppose so . . . "[24]

Doppo's idealization of the English language demonstrates a thorough alienation from Japanese; for him the superiority of the vernacular style derived from its similarity to Western literary languages, not from its greater proximity to the native tongue. When Katai later adopted Naturalism, he often suggested that the superiority of the vernacular style lay in its transparency of meaning, yet he never strayed far from the underlying assumption that its value was rendered irrefutable by Western literary models. The Naturalist idealization of the vernacular style was based on two parallel notions: first, that its superiority would derive from its likeness to Western literary models and, second, that it would provide a transparent window onto nature. If indeed it is possible to discover a logic to this apparent contradiction within Japanese Naturalism, it can only be that "nature" was synonymous not with some objective reality but rather with a particular image of modern Western literature itself.

In fact, like literature, the modern Western concept of nature had no counterpart in Japanese until it was translated as *shizen* (also formerly read as *jinen*). As was often the case, this translation for a Western concept invested an old word with a new meaning. Yanabu Akira—a critic who specializes in the study of modern Japanese as a language of translation—proposes that the subtle disjunction between *shizen* and nature has been the source of confusion at numerous levels, from the deployment of *shizen* by Japanese Naturalists to later readings and interpretations of their texts. As an illuminating explanation for the difference between Katai's shizen and the objective reality of "nature," Yanabu's argument merits extended consideration here.

First, he points out that *shizen* was originally used in adjectival rather than nominal form, to describe that which becomes of itself spontaneously, without effort or human intervention. To the extent that it stands in a binary relationship to a notion of "artifice," shizen shared an important attribute with "nature." However, unlike the original meaning of *natura*, shizen did not refer to the "essence of things." Nor did it, like the post-Baconian understanding of *natura*, refer to the totality of things in the natural world. In Chinese and Japanese it was terms like *heaven and earth* (*tenchi*), *the myriad things* (*banbutsu*), and *mountains, rivers, and the great earth* (*sanga-daichi*) that named the multitude of external objects.[25] None of these nouns refer to anything constitutive or essential. Yanabu concludes that "*nature* belongs to the side of the object, in contradistinction to the side of the subject implied by artifice, but the inherited meaning of shizen belongs to a world in which subject and object are unified or have yet to be distinguished, so as to erase the subject-object opposition."[26]

Because the inherited meaning of shizen was never completely supplanted by the new meaning of *nature*, yet another meaning was created by writers like Katai and Doppo, unwittingly driven by the force of a verbal contradiction.

By being used as a translation word, *shizen* first came to be used in the same way as "nature." With its internal meaning left intact, it was used just like the word "nature," as an extension, in the same contexts. It was used as a word to discuss the material, objectified world. In semantic terms this is a contradiction. The semantic contradiction is not noticed by the word's users, but the sense of verbal contradiction is not lost. To the contrary, the verbal contradiction seeks out a new meaning and creates a new meaning. The users of the word *shizen* seek a meaning that will fill in the contradiction. Thus they arrive at the realm of [Doppo's] *shizenrashisa* (naturalness), *shizen no mama* (nature as is), *shokuchaku suru wo kanjitariki* (having felt contact [with nature]), and *butsuga yūkai shite shizen no zen'en wo genjikitaru* (in the fusion of self and object, the full circle of nature becomes manifest). The meaning of shizen is recovered, and a new meaning is born simultaneously.[27]

Yanabu also cites the following passage from *Katai bunwa* (Katai talks of literature, 1911) to support the argument that the Japanese Naturalist use of *shizen* recovers its former meaning by erasing the distinction between subject and object:

One could just as well say that aside from "naturalness," "coming close to nature," and "getting at the truth," art possesses nothing at all. Therefore, in praising a work of art, when people have felt it most they all say, "It is so natural. How natural it is. It is truly so" or "It gets at the truth."

Now then, when it comes to why we must value this naturalness, what is called nature, that is quite a difficult matter, of such depth that it cannot easily be explained even by religion or philosophy, so I won't go into it here, but it is crucial to know that this nature exists both internally and externally. One's own interior is also an instance of nature. Just as the cosmos of others is nature, we can say that the self is also an instance of nature. And the fact is that the same laws, the same rhythms flow through both self and other.

Because of this, that which is natural, that which is true, that which is close to a law, that which is close to a rhythm, is both the self, and the other. Therefore, that which is nature reverberates the most strongly with the other. Therein lies the life of art, its underlying foundations.

To talk about this from the angle of training, human beings want somehow to possess this naturalness. They want to be true. Though one has not yet been able to fully reach that frontier, one wants to cultivate oneself in order to reach it somehow. From the writer's angle this takes on primary significance. According to one's natural gifts and talents, one may reach this frontier sooner or later, or perhaps never be able to reach it at all, but, in any case, we writers spend our entire lives charging forward toward this "naturalness." On this point art and religion are quite similar. There is something like this in zen and meditation. There is a like promise of dedicated effort.[28]

As Yanabu observes, this concept of nature cannot be traced to the kind of Naturalism espoused in Zola's *Le Roman Expérimental*, wherein the writer-subject is conceived as a scientist—a detached observer of facts who designs experiments to demonstrate the laws of nature—not as a religious aspirant who strives to become a vehicle of nature.

Yanabu's comparative analysis of shizen and nature thus highlights an important aspect of Japanese Naturalism: the frequently repeated rhetoric of fusing subject and object. If we consider Japanese Naturalism only in relation to the "original" version of Zola, then we can only see this as a "mistake," a translation of Naturalism based on a misunderstanding. Yet Yanabu argues quite persuasively that the real "mistake" is to assume that *shizen* is always a semantically transparent window onto the Western concept of *natura*.[29] On the other hand, he also comes close to assuming an "essence" in the words *shizen* and *natura*, particularly when he personifies the "verbal contradiction" between them—it is the contradiction itself, and not the writers who use the word, that "seeks out a new meaning and creates a new meaning." There is a suggestion here that Japanese Naturalism was guided by an unconscious, linguistically—and even anthropologically—propelled desire to obliterate the differences between fundamentally incompatible Eastern and Western worldviews. From here it would be all too easy to create an image of Doppo and Katai as the unwitting embodiments of Chinese and Japanese religiophilosophical traditions.

Yet for writers like Katai the very advocacy of Naturalism qua *shizenshugi* was an eminently self-conscious attempt to identify with Western literary models over and against contemporary Japanese literary practices and aesthetic ideals. Katai invoked Naturalism as the vanguard of European literature, a higher authority that need not answer to the standards set by the Meiji literary establishment. In "Rokotsu naru byōsha" he enjoins the reader who might doubt the superiority of raw description to "look at Ibsen, at Tolstoy, at Zola, at Dostoevsky." The Naturalist ideal embodied by these writers then becomes a fulcrum to jettison the literature of the entire preceding generation of Meiji novelists, "the age of Kōyō, Rohan, Shōyō, and Ōgai."[30] The meaning of shizen developed by Katai was informed by a strategy of opposing the giants of Meiji literature by reference to a radical Western literary model. *That which is nature reverberates most strongly with the other.* This basic tenet of Katai's Naturalism does not harken back to a premodern, pre-Western world in which "subject and object are unified or have yet to be distinguished." Rather, it is the very means by which he identifies himself with European Naturalist literature, giving it the status of universal truth and himself the status of a person at least wise enough to recognize that truth. By recasting the literary landscape in the stark oppositions of nature/truth/contemporary Western literature versus artifice/falsehood/contemporary Japanese literature, Katai was able to clear out a space for himself that the Meiji literary establishment had denied him.

Katai's attack on literary craftsmanship was first and foremost a rejection of literature as it had been defined and practiced by Ozaki Kōyō. What, then, was the precise nature of Katai's critique? We have already seen the bold opposition he establishes between truth and falsehood in "Rokotsu naru byōsha." Yet, as we already know from our contemplation of the word *shizen*, the meanings of such abstract terms are slippery at best. For the moment, let us put aside the question of what Katai meant by truth and consider what he chastised as false.

Art appreciators—according to what these people say, writing must always be beautiful. Thought must always follow the direction set forth by aesthetics. . . .

Looking back on our own literary circles, the age of Kōyō, Rohan, Shōyō, and Ōgai was at the least an age of matured literature. As proof, debates on aesthetics flourished quite a bit, the agendas of the idealistic novel and the concept novel were frequently rehearsed, and not a single word or phrase was easily neglected in writing. Nay, most literati were known to the world for their writing skills, and appreciated by people for the excellence of their plot constructions. To say what kind of works we attained as a result of that, most are writings thickly covered in white facial powder, if not idealistic novels content with cowardly, petty description, if not gold-plated novels that command people's interest by purposely describing events so as to exaggerate their sensational qualities.[31]

In essence, Katai is attacking the kind of fiction that aims to please— whether its target be the "art appreciators" and aestheticians, or just "people" in general. To him, this was the essential problem with Kōyō's approach to the novel, as is clear from "Ozaki Kōyō to sono sakuhin" (Ozaki Kōyō and his works):

A brush that moves people's hearts—this is something Kōyō attained from a realm called the human passions, or sympathy, or some such. He always made his judgments from a place that did not stray a single step from the realm of the common, the ordinary, the horizontal.

Or rather, it even seemed that he always made an effort to remain within such common territory. . . .

It is said that Okume of *Kokoro no yami* (Darkness of the heart) is the best of the women this author wrote. And at the time the author was also said to be the best at depicting women. However, to say that he excelled in depicting women was something altogether different from the kind of description today's authors do. A woman the readers will like, a woman perfectly idealized—the critics of the day praised him for creating such women. . . .

The vernacular and his "realism" always seemed to progress in tandem. When writing in the vernacular, he usually took ordinary everyday life as his subject. *Ninin nyōbō* is like that. *Murasaki* is like that. *Tajō takon* is like that. And, when writing about ordinary everyday life, he apparently strived to make it interesting and colorful. That is where he differs from the earnestness of the author of *Ukigumo*, being that he was completely bound to the old theory "art must give people enjoyment."[32]

The moral impropriety of manipulating words to suit their recipient is a theme we have already encountered in *Ukigumo*. We should note that Katai's antipathy toward Kōyō's reader-oriented writing also resonates with the same class differences we observed in that context—Katai was the son of a low-ranking samurai, while Kōyō was the son of a well-known *netsuke* artisan and male geisha.[33] Moreover, the dismissive tone with which he refers to "human passions, or sympathy, or some such" as the guiding light of Kōyō's brush bears significantly upon his Naturalist tenet, "That which is nature reverberates most strongly with the other." Now we cannot fail to recognize that the "other" in this equation is not simply *someone other than myself*, as a literal reading would suggest, but a much more significant Other, one who did not belong to the generic category of people. Just as shizen might mean something other than the dictionary definition of nature, Katai's use of the terms *self* and *other* cannot necessarily be simply reduced to the generic subject and object.

For Katai, this Other could only have meant the Western writers to whom he allied himself as a Naturalist. This was another major point of contention between himself and Kōyō. Ironically enough, his first meeting with Kōyō had included a discussion of the very grandfather of Naturalism. In retrospect, Katai had this to say about Kōyō's appreciation of Zola:

Already, by the time he was writing *Yakitsugi chawan* (1891), he was reading the works of Zola. Using the folds of a fan to illustrate, he praised him for writing from every shade and angle of a thing. However, just as he thrilled to Saikaku but got nothing from him but his style of writing, in the case of Naturalism too, he seemed to be taken only by its manner of description, rather than its content.[34]

When Katai enjoined his readers to "look at Ibsen, at Tolstoy, at Zola, at Dostoevsky, how astonishingly much blood and sweat has been poured into their works," he was not only claiming the superiority of these writers over Japanese models but also issuing a challenge to take their works as seriously as life itself, as documents of "blood and sweat."

"Rokotsu naru byōsha" is not only the critique of a certain approach to writing but an implicit attack on ways of reading as well. At the heart of Katai's polemic against literary artifice lay an unremitting moral judgment against those writers who failed to be moved by the *content* of modern Western literature—or more precisely, its depth of meaning. Today, it may seem easy to dismiss Katai's hallmark essay as critically naive, logically flawed, or overly zealous in its adulation of Zola et al. But it also bears the seeds of a critical standard that has profoundly affected the category of modern Japanese literature. As a case in point, modern Japanese literary history has long since relegated Ozaki Kōyō to the realm of popular—as opposed to "pure" or intellectual—fiction, even while acknowledging his crucial role in elevating the status of the novel and perfecting the modern vernacular style. In large part, this fate can be ascribed to Kōyō's manner of relating to Western literature. A brief examination of Kōyō's relationship to Western letters will help us to understand the concept of literature proposed by the Naturalists and the critique of contemporary Meiji fiction set forth by Katai.

From fairly early on in his career, Ozaki Kōyō proudly proclaimed his affinity for the fiction of Ihara Saikaku, a fact that has often overshadowed his long-standing engagement with modern Western literature. As a result, he has frequently been contrasted with his archrival Yamada Bimyō, dubbed "the premature baby of Westernism" by Uchida Roan. When they were in school together, Bimyō and Kōyō cofounded the amateur literary circular *Garakuta bunko*. Like Bimyō, Kōyō was well-read in English literature, and the two clearly shared an enthusiasm for reading and writing fiction. But, as soon as Bimyō's career began to take off, he cut his ties to Kōyō and the circular, and it was with much resentment that Kōyō witnessed his former classmate's rise to literary stardom. In reaction, he quickly turned his back on the vernacular movement, going out of his way to lampoon his former colleague's stylistic taste in a piece titled "Contesting Favorites."

In this brief dialogue two young women argue vehemently over the relative merits of the genbun-itchi and *gazoku-setchū* styles. Once again, here we find the battle over style being waged in the words and images of women—both sides of the debate are argued by markedly feminine voices. After hurling a number of insults back and forth, the genbun-itchi proponent claims that if writing were likened to sculpture, then the gazoku-setchū style would be a dull awl and the vernacular style a sharp one. To this her opponent replies:

Is art only the depiction of real life? You keep talking about a sharp awl, but what I would like to ask you is this: just because that awl is capable of intricate workmanship, should one carve out a beautiful woman's nostrils and her nostril hairs, and where a single line would do for the eyebrows, mark out each single hair, and because a beauty must surely have hair on her shins, carve out the downy covering, finally ending up with a carving of a beauty that resembles a monster, and calling this the portrait of a highly wrought beauty? This may indeed look like a beauty or a goddess to the carver. To the onlooker, it is a monster.[35]

Thus Kōyō's resentment of Bimyō's professional success initially produced a staunch rejection of vernacular realism and an enthusiastic embrace of Saikaku that paralleled, in larger historical terms, the nationalist reaction to the excesses of the Rokumeikan era.

The stylistic rivalry between Bimyō and Kōyō has been viewed by many critics and scholars as the opposition of radical Westernist and conservative nativist. To be sure, Bimyō embraced the Western model of vernacular fiction while Kōyō initially rejected it; Bimyō gleefully plastered his pages with Westernesque literary ornaments while Kōyō sought to please his readers with just the right blend of the new and the familiar. Ultimately, it was Kōyō's genius for domesticating Western literary influences that gained broad acceptance for the vernacular style in Japanese fiction. Notwithstanding their divergent stylistic temperaments, however, Bimyō and Kōyō shared something in common at a much more fundamental level. Both writers related to Western fiction above all as novel stories told in new and interesting ways—in other words, as treasure troves of raw material for new plots and new expressions in Japanese fiction. Unlike Futabatei, neither of them were particularly concerned with literature as a sacred linguistic art for revealing truth (i.e., the idea hidden in the forms of phenomena).

In this sense both writers could be called adaptationists. And, indeed, at least thirty works of Kōyō's fiction can be categorized as adaptations of foreign works, the original sources ranging geographically from France, Russia, England, America, Germany, Italy, and China, historically from *Arabian Nights* and the *Decameron* to Zola and Dostoevsky.[36] Aside from his own readings in Western fiction, Kōyō also took advantage of his position as guild leader to commission translations of foreign works from his Ken'yūsha underlings, which he would then put to use in his own fiction. We know from Suiin's memoirs that Katai was one of the writers upon whom Kōyō relied for such translations (and that Katai complained of being poorly compensated for such work).[37] Thus Katai knew very well that Kōyō's fiction was often simply the product of rewriting, or, quite literally, *stylizing*, the translations provided by his underlings.

Ironically, the same critical criteria that Katai used to dismiss Kōyō as a fundamentally flawed novelist—i.e., an intrinsically flawed relationship with modern Western literature—would later be refined by Nakamura Mitsuo in order to denounce the literary precedent established by *Futon*. In an unwitting tribute to the language of Katai's "Rokotsu naru byōsha," Nakamura wrote in *Fūzoku shōsetsu ron*:

That this almost cruel gap emerged [between Oguri Fūyō's *Seishun* and Shimazaki Tōson's *Hakai*] is based, in essence, on the difference between their comprehension of modern literature and the difference in their approach to the self; more concretely, it is the difference between a writer who made the effort to truly make use of the concept of individuality— which forms the basis of modern literature—with his own sensibilities, and give it flesh and blood, and a writer who merely incorporated its surface techniques. . . .

In particular, after [Tōson] retreated to Komoro to "escape from the air of the city" in order to "make myself more new and concise," as he was painfully examining himself, he melded the various influences he had hitherto absorbed from foreign literature into his own flesh and blood, and the climate and environs of Japan, and engaged in several years of solitary experimentation toward producing a new image of literature that would be *something of his own*, as a result of which he bequeathed to us numerous studies, starting with *Chikumagawa no suketchi* (Chikuma River Sketches) . . .

In other words, he did not take the influences of foreign literature from his youth as just literature, and its effects first opened his eyes to a new dimension, while at the same time providing the means for giving form to the foment of that awakening.[38]

Like Katai, Nakamura's essential criteria for judgment is how a given writer responded to modern Western literature and what use he made of it—in other words, how a writer internalized, digested, and then externalized the foreign texts he read. Both Katai and Nakamura share the assumptions that modern Western literature should be taken as seriously as life itself—and that to do so constitutes the only proper way of life for a truly modern Japanese writer.

Based on this standard, Nakamura claims that Katai's *Futon* offered a "completely new"—but extremely problematic—approach to "making foreign literature one's own." If Kōyō and Fūyō had not been sufficiently "moved by the content" of Western literature, Katai had certainly been moved, but in the wrong way. Instead of emulating modern Western writers, Katai emulated the characters in their works and then became a character in his own novel. In Nakamura's view the result was a travesty of truth, another siren song that would lead countless other writers astray:

What is first clear from reading *Futon* . . . is that what moved Katai and what he emulated was Johannes of the play [*Einsame Menschen*], and not the author of the play, Hauptmann. . . .

To create a novel out of the author becoming a character in the novel and prancing about, and concordantly to see the guarantee of truth in such a work, is a way of thinking that consistently forms the background for the I-novel in our country, from Tayama Katai to Tanaka Hidemitsu. To write about oneself guarantees no mistakes. As long as it is fact, there is no lie about it. Such is the thinking.

... We can say that, as facile as it may be, here was a completely new approach to making foreign literature one's own possession, and the new sight of Katai's bold leap won out over *Hakai*.[39]

As Nakamura's critique suggests, *Futon* skirts the border between Fūyō's mode of superficial imitation (adaptation) and Tōson's mode of innovative emulation (translation). In his numerous disquisitions on style and composition, Katai never fully confronted the issues of adaptation, imitation, translation, and composition that his particular experience with the Ken'yūsha should have called into question. In fact, like Kōyō, he ultimately waged his battle in the arena of style. And, like Kōyō, he never completely extricated himself from the mode of adaptation. Yet, as Nakamura points out, he did come up with something "completely new." Significantly, he did so by writing about Westernesque women who could never quite be made "one's own."

Literary Desire and the Exotic Language of Love
From "Shōshijin" to Jokyōshi

Futabatei Shimei's first foray into the uncharted territory of vernacular Japanese fiction shook the literary radical's faith in literature to its very foundations, leading him to drop out of the literary scene altogether. By contrast, while Katai spent the first half of his literary career seemingly adrift in a sea of heterogeneous styles, he never questioned the essential value of the literary enterprise. Nakamura Mitsuo charged that Katai's critical mistake in *Futon* was to identify with the protagonist of Gerhardt Hauptmann's play *Einsame Menschen* rather than with the play's author. Indeed, Katai's desire to identify with the hero of a story was a predominant motivation for much of his work. Once he abandoned the prospect of a political career, his favorite would become the persona of the writer, the hero of the story of literature itself. And, for Katai, no drama of the modern literary artist seemed complete without a newly educated woman to play the supporting role. Whereas Futabatei's profound struggle with language had produced the first Westernesque femme fatale, Katai's interest in Westernesque women predated his attempt to revamp literary language by nearly fifteen years. The pairing of the modern writer with the modernly educated woman makes its first appearance in one of Katai's earliest works, "Shōshijin" (A minor poet, 1893); it is repeated exactly a decade later in *Jokyōshi* (The woman school-teacher, 1903), four years before the final, critical variation on the theme in *Futon*.

This examination of Katai's early maidenitis will trace the distinc-tively literary evolution of his Westernesque woman persona, setting the stage upon which *Futon* would resuscitate the metanarrative of linguistic betrayal embodied by the Westernesque femme fatale. As Saeki Junko has shown, the grand narrative of national progress spun by the Meiji ideology of "civilization and enlightenment" dethroned the woman of the pleasure quarters and installed the newly educated woman in her place as the heroine of choice. While Katai's images of the female educated elite certainly partake of this general trend, the narrative frame that lent them meaning in his texts would shift from a loosely sketched social realm ruled by external measures of educational pedigree, employment, and class status to a rarefied liter-ary realm ruled by internal measures of poetic sensitivity and spiri-tual depth, particularly in relation to the exotic language of love. It is in the movement toward purely literary values that the contours of Katai's feminine ideal gain greater definition and a conspicuously Westernesque aura.

At the bottom of Katai's maidenitis, however, we find an utterly commonplace Meiji romance. From early on, Katai associated the love of a beautiful woman with dreams of worldly success. As Kamei Hideo observes, this kind of fantasy was an integral element of the popular political novels of the 1870s and early 1880s "in which politi-cal aspirations were linked up to the dream of being loved by a beau-tiful woman."[1] By the late 1880s critics like Tokutomi Sohō began the work of discrediting this popular fairy tale, noting with disgust that "all the poor students cooped up in their second-floor boardinghouse rooms in Kanda wallow in this pleasant dream,"[2] and writers like Shōyō and Futabatei delivered the final blow, presenting narrators and protagonists who could no longer embrace such a naive vision of themselves or the world. Yet, as late as July 1906, Katai was still elaborating this motif as the main subject of a minor piece written for the youth magazine *Chūgaku sekai*. In "Kisu izen" (Ante-kiss), a first-person narrator reminiscing to a friend about his youthful innocence assumes a causal relationship between the adolescent awakening to the opposite sex, worldly ambition, and the will to study.

> When I would think a girl is pretty, I would just become helplessly infatu-ated, you know. . . . Whenever it happened I would always strive even harder, with the thought that I must become great no matter what, I must make a splendid success of myself as soon as possible, because I would want to be able just to make a promise with such a girl. You know, think-ing about it now, this fits with the order of life, so that at the age of around seventeen or eighteen, when boys become blindly amorous and infatu-ated with girls, ultimately, it is one of nature's ways to make them even more assiduous in their studies. . . .
>
> At the time, I was in my third year at a certain private high school, and for English I was reading Macaulay's biography of Clive or some such. The desire to achieve distinction seemed to burn, and when I heard the various success stories of people from the past and present, my breast was intolerably pained, and I felt unbearably agitated. And I can't tell you how much this burning desire to achieve distinction, together with the aspiration for love it stirred up, spurred me to devote myself to my studies.[3]

Today's parents are sure to find amusement in the idea that sex-ual awakening in boys is "nature's way" of making them study harder. Put differently, however, the general picture presented here becomes more familiar: bright and ambitious boy meets beauti-ful girl, burns with the desire to impress her, and then goes on to amaze the world with his talents. Although in Katai's telling it is not entirely clear whether the woman or the burning ambition comes first, we can easily connect this general outlook to the ideology of the self-made man that exhorted Katai's generation to "be ambi-tious" (W. S. Clark).

"Work hard, achieve distinction, and you can get the girl." To the young Katai, Ozaki Kōyō's marriage in March 1891 may very well have seemed like the real-life confirmation of this lesson. "At the time, rumors about Kōyō's marriage became the major gossip of the literary circles. Kabashima Kikuko. . . . Kiku [Chrysanthemum] and Kōyō [Autumn Leaves]; it was said that she was extremely beautiful, and that Kōyō was in love. . . . And to hear such gossip also gave me pain."[4] That Katai called on Kōyō just two months later may be nothing more than a fortuitous coincidence. But it is also entirely possible that the aura of success surrounding Kōyō—the implied bildungsroman of a young man who devoted himself to his studies, made a name for himself, and then reaped the rewards in a celebrated marriage—had a decisive impact on Katai's choice of career, allowing him to project his gendered fantasy of social distinction onto the persona of the modern novelist.

As Kamei felicitously puts it, the idealized self exemplified in the watershed political novel *Kajin no kigu* (Chance encounters with beautiful women, 1886) is "a heroic and benevolent self, appropriate to the adoration and respect showered on it by an idealized partner of the opposite sex."[5] Katai's response to Kōyō's marriage suggests that he was deeply affected by this literary formula, learning to judge a man's success by the type of woman he got. In his own fiction he took the formula one step further, deploying the female love interest as the measure of the interiority of the man who wanted but could not get her. The type of girl that Katai's protagonists wanted evolved from a simple beauty glimpsed in the moonlight—a mere sliver of sight and sound in "Shōshijin"—into a discerning poet with a voice of her own in *Jokyōshi*, and finally an aspiring young novelist and accomplished letter writer in *Futon*. While there are significant differences in how these women reflected upon the men who wanted them, there are also notable constants. In virtually all cases we will find an economy of desire in which the male subject's potential value is represented by the kind of woman he desires, and her value or desirability is in turn determined by the presence—actual or internalized—of a male rival. Both "Shōshijin" and *Jokyōshi* establish a clear connection between the Kataian protagonist's chronic sense of social alienation, his concomitant desire to identify with the figure of the solitary male artist, and his adulation of Meiji schoolgirls, three motifs that are reconfigured in the Naturalist fictions "Shōjobyō" and *Futon*.

Beauy is the Beast: Aesthetic Abstraction and Social Abjection in "Shōshijin"

As already noted, it was ultimately Katai's alienation from Kōyō that had the most profound impact on his literary career. First and foremost, he invested meaning in his alienation by embracing a romantic notion of the heroic, solitary artist. Needless to say, this image of the writer was diametrically opposed to the hierarchical structure and cliquish identity of Kōyō's literary guild. Within the Ken'yūsha Katai allied himself with Emi Suiin, Takase Bun'en, and Kawakami Bizan, a subgroup that launched their own literary magazine in 1892. United by their dissatisfaction with the standards set by Kōyō, they embraced a concept of the poet as consummate literary artist, in opposition to the figure of the urbane novelist that identified the Ken'yūsha. Takase Bun'en, a major influence on Katai and the de facto intellectual leader of the group, gave absolute priority to the poet over and above the professional novelist.[6] In one of the few pieces of literary criticism he left to posterity, Bun'en wrote: "For what is commonly called a novelist belongs to a certain profession, *but the poet is one who stands outside of the professions, transcending worldly affairs*."[7] (emphasis in original) In his deployment of the concept of poet Bun'en betrays a certain resentment against the worldliness (and worldly successes) of the Ken'yūsha mainstream, a feeling that was no doubt shared by Katai.

In "Shōshijin" this ostensibly transcendental poet becomes the privileged subject of fiction.[8] In a style that emulates the sentimental tone and elegant gabuntai sentence endings of Mori Ōgai's *Maihime*, the first-person narrator introduces himself as follows:

Forgetting both summer and the world as I momentarily paused in my tracks, my breast burned with the fever of never-ending reverie. Words like *writing, poetry*, and *master* traversed my breast countless times, and when I thought of the brilliance of the poetic visions I had put on paper today, and how brilliant would be the visions I should write on the morrow, quite unbearable did my happiness become. How joyous shall be the moment this work reaches completion, the moment when this work goes forth into the world![9]

Once again, we encounter a protagonist whose breast has been emblazoned with weighty written signs. While the petty bureaucrat Bunzō collapsed under the written sign of his own demise ("dismissal"), however, Katai's poet is visited by words that portend his imminent rise to greatness. The brand of "dismissal" on Bunzō's chest clearly referred back to the social sphere that measures individual worth according to the outer trappings of career prospects. By contrast, Katai's poet is preoccupied by written signs that seem to refer to nothing but themselves—"writing, poetry." It is this very autonomy from social referents that induces his euphoric state, his ability to imagine himself as a "master" in his own universe. And the story itself vigilantly guards the autonomy of that universe by refusing to offer any concrete examples of the "brilliance" that has inspired this poet's grand self-appraisal.

A crisis ensues when his happy soliloquy of metapoetic nothings is interrupted by an actual vision of beauty. During the brief walk inspired by his "never-ending reverie," he catches a glimpse of a young woman whose moonlit image becomes an overnight obsession.

In the shade of a nearby pine did I happen to notice someone standing still, a figure dressed in white. Then a child emerged from here and went over to the figure, seeming to be quite insistent about something.

You mustn't say such difficult things. So spoke the gentle voice of a woman. . . .

The young woman, still placating her fretful little brother, now stepped out from the dark shadow of the pine tree into the moonlight. Hidden in the darkness, I was able to view the young woman's entire figure.

From the disheveled *shimada* coiffure above to the hem of the white *kasuri* robe below, the figure standing bathed in moonlight was the very image of a moon goddess painting. (123–24)

Significantly, the goddess in white turns out to be the daughter of his family's former landlord. He fondly recalls having heard the sound of her "gentle voice reading aloud," and the voices of family members calling her name, "Okiku." (124) Given the subject matter of the narrative—a young writer's first steps on the road to literary acclaim—it is hard to ignore the fact that the love interest bears the same name as Ozaki Kōyō's wife. The image of her "gentle voice reading aloud" immediately associates her with the written word and modern education, while her identity as the landlord's daughter and her nominal resemblance to the prized wife of a celebrated novelist harken to the real social and literary hierarchies that propel the poet's dreams of transcendence.

Thoughts of Okiku interrupt the flow of his writing, "instantaneously severing the thread of imagination, making me feel as though heaven's horse had kicked me down to the world below" (131). Instead of inspiring the poetic effusions we might expect, this vision of feminine beauty occasions feelings of dejection. Okiku does not appear as the physical manifestation of lofty poetic ideals, but rather as the idealized embodiment of the elevated social status that the poet in fact covets. True to the logic of "Kisu izen," his obsession with Okiku is inextricably tied to a frustrated desire for social distinction he has sublimated into the higher pursuit of literature:

Watching her dear figure recede until it vanished from sight, I then turned at the intersection in the direction of Nijukki-chō. Violently did emotions of happiness, sadness, and indignation rise to pierce my breast. The desire to promptly send a masterpiece into the world and impress the world with the extent of my hidden talents filled my breast to the brim. In haste did I return home. (128)

In fact, the poet's struggle to both overcome and fulfill his worldly desires constitutes the main subject of "Shōshijin." His sense of indignation is further compounded when he receives a letter from a cousin who has just graduated from college, whose "account of the journey home and of his rejoicing parents was written with such pride as to painfully torment the breast of one such as myself, who had long since taken to contemptus mundi." (129) The pathetic contrast he makes with a cousin whose elite education promises a bright future precipitates a desperate attempt at self-legitimation:

But then did I reconsider my own case. At the least, am I not a poet who sings of the beauty of the universe? Compared to those who live out their entire lives looking into laws and regulations, do I not rank immensely far above? To think of such petty glories does not become a poet's wisdom, and, thinking of my work, I glanced at the manuscript disheveled on the desk and cried out in my heart, "See where this masterpiece will find its place!" (128–29)

Clearly, this transcendental poet's literary ambitions are fueled by an all-too-worldly resentment. His repeated attempts to reject socially sanctioned images of success give rise to a four-cornered world—"the figure of the young woman, cousin, wife, masterpiece" (130). These four terms translate into the almost oedipal literary romance that structures much of Katai's fiction: female object of desire, male rival, female sign of male social status, self-referential sign of male transcendence.

As with the women of letters who appear in *Jokyōshi* and *Futon*, Okiku serves as the foundation for a literary structure whose main function is to claim the torment of the solitary male artist. The extended monologue of "Shōshijin" never endows Okiku with more than the hazy outlines of an abstraction; her desirability essentially derives from the fact that she is beyond reach. Although she momentarily threatens to disrupt the poet's self-enclosed world of words, Okiku only serves as the catalyst for his self-conscious reinforcement of its boundaries. Finally, he decides to retreat to a country temple so that he can forget her and complete his "masterpiece." He returns to Tokyo, finished manuscript in hand, just in time to suffer through the celebration of Okiku's marriage to his ever enviable cousin. This final humiliation gives rise to the defiant song of self-consolation that ends the novella—a crescendo of five cries of "poet," culminating in a tear-soaked "masterpiece."

Thereupon I entered the study and sat before my desk. At this moment, my breast was violently pierced by an emotion of the effect, am I not a poet? I am a poet. At the least, I am a poet who sings of the beauty of the universe; I am distinct from those who take wives and live their entire lives within the bounds of regulations. Poet! Poet! So I vigorously cried in my heart. Even as I cried thus, my tears spouted forth like hail, soaking the entire manuscript of the masterpiece that lay on the desk. (167–68)

To the young Katai the figure of Okiku must have seemed like the perfect mechanism for aestheticizing the underlying tensions between his bright, worldly ambitions and his antiworldly literary practice. In a sense she provides fertile literary ground: the poet plants the seeds of his inferiority complex in her image and comes up with the roses of metapoetic agony. The result is either *bibun* (beautiful writing; poesy) or purple prose, depending on one's critical stance. It would take Katai more than a decade to come around to the latter view, and even then he looked back on this work as his true literary debut.

While the floating, abstract figure of Okiku is a far cry from her textually grounded and linguistically characterized Westernesque sisters in Katai's later fiction, her structural function presages Yoshiko's precipitous fall from the pedestal of the ideal Westernesque woman to the lowly status of a whore in the mind of *Futon*'s protagonist. Okiku is a Panlike two-way signifier, both a moon goddess and heaven's horse, with an upper body that points to the moon on high and an outstretched hoof that points (or rather, kicks) to the wretched earth below. She thus simultaneously serves as a sign for the enviable success of the man who "gets" her and a painful reminder of the abject status of the man who cannot. In its unabashedly straightforward expression of resentment, "Shōshijin" exposes to plain sight what most deployments of idealized femininity strive to conceal: that the goddess on high is none other than a monstrous inverse image of the male subject's sense of abjection. In other words, beauty *is* the beast. In this sense the transformation of the idolized Westernesque woman into a treacherous femme fatale in *Futon* seems like a foregone conclusion. By her very nature, Katai's female icon is destined to betray her idolater in the worst possible way: by exposing the sense of impotence that draws him to her in the first place.

Switching Idols Midstream: Competing Images of Love and Women in *Jokyōshi*

An important turning point in Katai's approach to love and the idealized woman it seeks, *Jokyōshi* marks the moment when he finally abandons the Enlightenment altar of love and marriage to join the esoteric cult of love and literature. Here Katai presents a protagonist who is torn between two fundamentally incompatible ideals: the monogamous ethic of mutual regard that was said to guarantee the sanctity of modern marriage and the mystical fantasy of total spiritual union that animated much of the hypothetical literary discourse on love. The impact this had on his depiction of the ideal woman is twofold: first, the figure of the wife comes to represent the disappointments of daily life, rather than the promise of the future embodied by the celebrated bride of the Meiji enlightenment. Second, the ideal of the beautiful female partner is transferred to a woman of letters, a figure who is no longer simply a passive object like Okiku, but rather an active participant in the literary language upon which the very concept of love is based. In "Shōshijin" the hint of a woman's modern education was little more than shorthand for the profile of the self-made man's ideal partner in the grand fairy tale of Meiji enlightenment. In *Jokyōshi* the depth of the educated woman's understanding, particularly in the field of literature, becomes the measure of her spiritual compatibility with the modern male writer.

These new developments can be traced to three major events in Katai's life: the literary friendship he struck up with Kunikida Doppo in 1896, his marriage to Itō Risa in 1899, and his discovery of Hauptmann's *Einsame Menschen* (Lonely lives) the following year. Katai was a virgin and Doppo a recent divorcé when they first met. According to Katai, the two twenty-six year olds often butted heads on the subject of love and literature, debating them in terms of the relationship between practice and ideal, and their often heated arguments appear to have had a lasting effect on him. The gap in sexual experience between them was narrowed by Katai's marriage to the younger sister of Ōta Gyokumei, a poet and friend of Katai's since their early days as *Eisai shinshi* contributors. By his own account this was a "love match"—meaning a marriage entered into willingly by both parties—rather than the traditional arrangement between families that members of the literati decried as "marriage by intimidation and threat" (*kyōhaku-kekkon*). But while Katai may have initially yearned for Risa as a goddess in white, he ultimately found modern marriage to be no less disappointing than the city of Tokyo itself. Just when the social roles of husband and father were making it increasingly difficult for Katai to identify himself with the figure of the transcendental poet, Hauptmann's play offered a new model for identification. While certainly not transcendent in the usual sense of the word, the portrait of the modern intellectual's loneliness in *Einsame Menschen* presented Katai with a chance to transcend an impoverished daily life by giving it universal meaning through identification with an image from modern Western literature. In place of the cries of "Poet!" in "Shōshijin," *Jokyōshi* thus serves up a Hauptmannian mantra of "lonely life" (*rōnrii raifu*).

For many Japanese writers the discourse of love was one of the most radical and exciting aspects of modern Western literature. As suggested in the title of an article by Yamaji Aizan—"Ren'ai no tetsugaku" (The philosophy of love)—the discourse of love in Meiji Japan constituted nothing less than a new body of knowledge. So alien were the religious, ethical, and literary ideas embedded in the Western sign of *love* as to require a new word in Japanese—*ren'ai*—to be distinguished from the native parlance of *iro* and *koi*. First appearing in the progressive journal *Meiroku zasshi* in July 1874, the meaning of this new term was initially elaborated in critical discourse, most prominently by the Christian intellectuals who wrote for *Jogaku zasshi*. As Yanabu points out, although the Western sign of *love* is not exclusively tied to the spiritual realm, its spiritual aspect was given primary emphasis in the process of translation into Japanese. Unlike Western literary images of love, pre-Meiji depictions of *iro* and *koi* do not assume a division between body and soul. As the concept of *ren'ai* became the dominant ideology, most writers, regardless of faith, would come to use the word *koi* as a more familiar synonym for the Chinese compound *ren'ai*; by contrast, the native term *iro* was reconfigured according to the Western concept of purely physical desire, "lust." In *Jokyōshi* the alchemy peculiar to the translation of the word *love* forges a dangerous liaison between eros and logos.

An interest in this new concept of the ideal relations between men and women formed the very basis for Katai's friendship with Doppo. Along with Kitamura Tōkoku, Romantic poet and author of several seminal essays on romantic love, Doppo's engagement with the new spiritual practice of romantic love earned him a special place in Meiji literary circles as one of its fallen heroes. Like Tōkoku, Doppo fell in love with the daughter of a wealthy Christian family, courting Sasaki Nobuko with a tenacity that earned him the ill-will of her parents. Defying their strict prohibition against seeing Doppo, the headstrong Nobuko moved in with him, and the two were officially married on November 12, 1895. However, this initial victory in the battle between young love and the authoritarian family system was soon overturned in April of the following year, when Nobuko abruptly deserted Doppo and returned to her parents' home. Doppo was unable to persuade her to come back and equally unable to fathom why she had left him. While Tōkoku's suicide at the age of twenty-five had left others to tell his story (e.g., Shimazaki Tōson's *Haru*), Doppo returned from the battlefield with his life intact, more than happy to tell the story himself. Indeed, it was Katai's desire to hear the well-known story from the horse's mouth that led him to Doppo's door.[10] Katai first met Doppo on November 12, 1896, the first anniversary of his failed marriage.[11] The impassioned eloquence with which he held forth on the subject of his disappointment in love virtually made it a literary event in itself, and the sexually inexperienced Katai quickly fell under his influence.

Although Katai himself never subscribed to the Christian faith, he so revered the altar of love and marriage that it brought to Japan that he preserved his virginity for his bride. Given that he did not marry until the age of twenty-eight, this was a significant act of devotion. "Kisu izen" suggests that, for a fervent believer in modern literature, the abstract ideal of romantic love could be as conceptually powerful and physically binding as the Christian ethic of chastity itself:

That's right, I was nineteen, and knew something about the meaning of love in the literary sense, so it seemed that the fickleness of my feelings until then was just too lacking in constancy, and I thought that if I am to fall in love again, this time I want to make it intense, the kind of love in which it just has to be that one person, and if that person becomes someone else's wife, I would spend the rest of my life unmarried. Of course, in my heart of hearts, I had doubts that such a thing could actually be done, though it was the sort of thing often written about in novels.[12]

As Saeki observes, few Meiji writers could resist the Christian ideal of romantic love; even one so completely unsympathetic to Christianity as Ozaki Kōyō made his breakthrough with a novel that projected the utterly foreign ideal of male chastity in marriage onto an unspecified Japanese past.[13] To the young Katai, who had been steeped in such romantic fictions, Doppo presented a living example of the intensity in love that he had only read about in books.

[T] had sympathy for K's sad love story, and he had also never experienced such a thing himself, so he always listened with a serious and thoughtful expression on his face. T did not yet understand the kind of love story that K had gone through. . . .

T had heard the story from K repeatedly. The story of Onobu—the woman with whom K fell violently in love, insisted upon marrying over the objections of her parents, and spent a honeylike half year living with on the G coast soon after his return from Hokkaidō—from this Onobu he had already separated, but, even so, even now, the details of that memory clung to K's mind and body, and he could not forget for so much as an instant. Not infrequently, K would sink back in his chair, put both hands behind his head, and spend half the day lost in thought.[14]

These displays of love's aftereffects—of a memory that clung to "mind and body"—left a vivid and lasting impression on Katai, and we can read their traces in the tormented protagonists of both *Jokyōshi* and *Futon*.

Whatever the reality of their relationship may have been, the Doppo of Katai's memoirs serves as a critique of Katai's pre-Naturalist past and as a harbinger of what would later come to pass. According to Katai's memoirs, Doppo frequently challenged his idolization of women, a tendency that would become the object of self-criticism in both "Shōjobyō" and *Futon*. In one reconstructed conversation Katai has Doppo saying that, with his failure to "understand women," it is a wonder that he can write novels at all—a notion that underwrites the portrait of the failed writer in "Shōjobyō"—and that his idolization of women is nothing but sexual desire, a proposition that forms the basis for the revelation of what Shimamura Hōgetsu called Tokio's "ugly thoughts" in *Futon*. While it seems highly likely that there was an element of projection in these retrospective portraits, the important point is that Doppo became a kind of internalized presence for Katai. This presence serves as the narrative foundation for *Jokyōshi*, which is written in the conversational vernacular and framed as a first-person account told to a close friend.

In a manner that illuminates the narrator's motivation to speak in *Jokyōshi*, Katai depicted the early days of his relationship with Doppo in terms of the friction between a pessimistic virgin's theories and a divorcee's bitter experience of love.

K did not like T's theories of contemptus mundi and virginity. Or, rather, instead of disliking them he believed that ideas that were full of such fantasy must be destroyed. For his part, T did not like the fact that K had already touched, if even only a little, the pollution of the world, the unsacred flesh of a woman. Even that would have been okay if K had not brandished his experience, which was nothing to boast about, but whenever T said something he would brandish it from on high, as though it was too much trouble to actually engage.[15]

Katai appears to have taken great pride in his identity as a "male virgin" (*otoko no baajin*), deploying it as a badge of moral superiority in his arguments with Doppo.[16] But it is clear from the image of Doppo in his memoirs that Katai ultimately felt his virginal ideology to be no match for his friend's depth of experience on the much touted battlefield of love. Indeed, after Doppo's death Katai would affirm his failure in love as the spiritual trial that had turned him into a great writer.[17] Against this background *Jokyōshi* can be read as a once belittled narrator's attempt to establish his credentials in the eyes of an internalized male rival by relating his own dramatic experience of the torment of love.

In both form and content *Jokyōshi* suggests that Katai's gradual conversion to Naturalism coincided with a progressive internalization of Doppo's critical views on love and literature. The novella can easily be read as the kind of love story by which Katai would have liked to represent himself to his friend, and much of its rhetoric resonates with the conversations reconstructed in Katai's memoirs. The opening address is particularly revealing:

At the time, you always criticized my feelings of contemptus mundi, constantly attacking me by asking why such false notes should come from a person living so pleasantly amid peace and happiness. I still remember it well—one hot summer day, as we opened our neckbands to let in the cool breeze coming from the pine-laden mountain in the back and shared a couple of bottles of beer with cold tofu or some such ordinary fare, I spewed an incessant stream of feverish talk. At the time, you were infuriated by my overly egotistic turn of thought and you said, "Don't be a fool. How can that possibly be? Give me proof, if you have any." I became all the more saddened and simply repeated the two words *lonely life, lonely life*—do you remember that?

Lonely life—to be sure, one facet of my life was that.[18] (Italics mark English words rendered in katakana transliteration.)

The rest of *Jokyōshi* serves as an elaborate retrospective defense of this "lonely life" mantra—the "proof," as it were. Like the debates between Katai and Doppo, the story of *Jokyōshi* is shaped by conflicting concepts of love. Specifically, the narrator-protagonist wavers between an ethical commitment to his "love wife" (*koi-nyōbō*) and an extramarital attraction to a beautiful woman of letters. These two poles reflect the puritanical ethic propounded by the young Katai, on the one hand, and the integral connections between literature and love, ideal and practice, spirit and body that he gleaned from Doppo, on the other. While Katai was not yet willing to completely abandon the ideals of his youth, he was beginning to internalize Doppo's critical voice. Thus, while the narrator complains about his wife's complete lack of interest in literature, he also nods to Doppo's beloved Wordsworth by praising her as nature incarnate.

Actually, I can say this now, but my wife had an element of true greatness. As you know, at a glance she was a woman who seemed utterly simple, childish, and rather slow of wit, but—no, even I myself did not think she had much depth of spirit or the power to affect others until after she died. There were even times when I compared her to other wives who were beautiful, wise, learned, and well-spoken and regretted that I had not married a woman who was a little more impressive, a little more versatile and sophisticated. But, thinking about it now, that was my mistake, and through to the end my wife had a great spirit that unconsciously resembled nature. (466)

Conversely, while he depicts the schoolteacher as an ideal partner—physically attractive and poetically sensitive—he is finally unable to choose her over his wife. In a strange twist on Hauptmann's play, Katai's schoolteacher is not "fatale" to the protagonist but rather to his wife, who dies in childbirth while agonizing over her husband's straying attentions. The protagonist, in a fit of remorse, abandons all thoughts of pursuing a relationship with the schoolteacher to devote himself completely to the duties of single fatherhood. *Jokyōshi* is the adaptation of a German play for which the spoken exchanges between Katai and Doppo may well have been the primary subtext.

One of many dramas from recently modernizing European countries to strike a chord among Japanese intellectuals by treating the individual's struggle against the family system and the concomitant conflicts between the new and the old, *Einsame Menschen* sets up an archetypal struggle between modern science and the religious tradition, individual and family, and new and old gender ideals. At the center of these struggles is Johannes Vockerat, a bright, young, and married scholar who lives with his wife and parents, frequently engaging in debates with his parents about the conflict between scientific and religious truth. His wife Käthe is a loving but uneducated woman who shows little interest in or understanding of his work. Enter Anna Mahr, a Russian university student who happens to visit his town and take up temporary residence in his home. Johannes and Anna quickly develop an intellectual rapport that blurs the boundaries between intellectual, emotional, and physical needs. Although both express their faith in the possibility of a Platonic relationship, their increasing intimacy torments the helpless Käthe and deeply troubles Johannes' parents. Realizing the gravity of the situation, Anna finally decides to leave town, whereupon Johannes commits suicide by drowning.

In the figure of Johannes Vockerat Katai could see himself. More precisely, he discovered a modern, Western, and literary image that he could easily project onto his own life. In typical Kataian fashion *Jokyōshi* replaces Hauptmann's scientist with a poet in the author's own image, transposing the source of alienation from the discourse of modern scientific truth to that of love and literature. Although a similar relationship ties the protagonist of *Futon* to the figure of Vockerat, the attempt at identification in *Jokyōshi* apparently did not impress the reviewers much. One particularly ascerbic review in *Teikoku bungaku* lumped the narrator-protagonist of *Jokyōshi* with all of Katai's protagonists, describing them in the most unflattering of terms: "Tayama's protagonists are all of the same mold. Namely, they are weak men, pathetic and effeminate, constantly uttering the word 'fate,' and treating the sanctity of love or some such as a personal talisman. He tries to draw the reader in with minor tensions and minor (but to the protagonist major) agonies that come from the deliberate forcing of emotion and will into conflict."[19] By contrast, the figure of the schoolteacher turned the reviewer's thoughts toward Hauptmann. The review neatly identifies the parallels with Hauptmann's play, offering a useful plot summary in the process:

[A] certain writer has engaged in a love marriage with a certain artless young woman, but she does not understand literature, so he had been passing his days in discontent because of the loneliness of the so-called literary life, yet when they retreated to a village to lead the pastoral life, he became acquainted with a woman schoolteacher of the village, a beauty possessed of literary tastes. The writer pays frequent visits to the woman schoolteacher in secret from his wife, and while they are in the process of enacting the so-called "embrace of two souls" or some such, rumors quickly spread throughout the entire village, and the rather discerning woman schoolteacher resolves to quit her job and leave the village, but the writer is wont to part with her, and he rushes to the train station to see her, but arrives too late. Just as he is in a half-crazed state, his pregnant wife, who has been worried about her own future and the relationship between her husband and the woman schoolteacher, suffers an agony so great that it is painful to behold and meets a tragic end. After the death of the wife he had originally loved, the writer decides to live alone and not remarry, and six years later he runs into the woman schoolteacher, at a beach in Chōshi, who is going to teach at a school in Taiwan, and the two finally part with her saying only, "Well, I guess it wasn't meant to be."

In this work the character of the woman schoolteacher is the most interesting. By this I do not mean that she is the most interestingly depicted. When we read this work we cannot but recall Hauptmann's *Einsame Menschen*—specifically, Johannes Vockerat is the writer in the present work, the wife Käthe who doesn't understand philosophy coincides with the artless wife who doesn't understand literature, and, finally, the woman scholar Anna Mahr takes the position of the woman schoolteacher. As for the fact that the schoolteacher has greater faculties of discernment than the writer, one could perhaps say that it is analogous to Anna Mahr having a clearer head and a stronger will than Vockerat.

Having so many points of similarity, however, when it comes to the question whether or not this work offers the same degree of interest as *Einsame Menschen*, such is not the case. Nothing can be done about it. Or, rather, it was a mistake to compare Katai to Hauptmann in the first place.[20]

This harsh characterization of Katai's work offers a vivid example of the kinds of critical attacks that his later writer-protagonists would lament in "Shōjobyō" and *Futon*. The reviewer's interest in the Anna Mahr figure also suggests the kind of exoticist gaze toward modern Western literature that would help to recreate the figure of the Westernesque femme fatale: in contrast to the punishing critique that precedes it, the final paragraph here has an almost wistful tone, as though lamenting Katai's lost opportunity to bring a Japanese Anna Mahr to life.

In its ability to set in motion so many of the characteristically modern conflicts—the clash of new and old, individual versus family, body versus spirit, scientific and philosophical truth versus religious belief and social convention, etc.—romantic love quickly established itself as an essential component of modern Japanese literature. This fact in itself virtually necessitated the presence of the Westernesque woman in works written by self-consciously modern male writers: male writers like Katai and Doppo could and did intellectualize about the meaning of love among themselves, but they were also compelled to seek out a female partner. At the very least, she had to be the kind of woman upon whom the ideal could be projected, as was more often the case given the narcissistic tendency for male writers to define the mutuality of "love" as the perfect reflection of oneself in another. To be more than a distant object of passive contemplation like Okiku, such a woman would have to be conversant in the semiforeign language of love; hence, she would have to be either Christian or familiar with modern literary and intellectual discourse or both. Almost by definition, therefore, she would have to be Westernesque.

In terms of physical appearance, the schoolteacher of *Jokyōshi* is indeed the very epitome of the Westernesque: "'[She wears her hair in] a large, English-style bun, her complexion is white, her nose is high, and though the contours of her face are a bit too large, the expression in her eyes is extremely powerful'" (482). While the "English" hairstyle is a conscious choice and the "white" complexion is certainly not an exclusively Western feature, the "high nose" may have been the ultimate in Westernesque physical attributes for a Meiji woman. To many Japanese the bridge of the nose commonly seen in Western physiognomy appears to be unusually high, by contrast to which Japanese physiognomy appears to be characterized by a "flat nose" or low bridge. By the early twentieth century significant numbers of fashion-conscious women (including Matsui Sumako and even Yosano Akiko) were submitting to the pain of paraffin injections to raise their nose bridges closer to the coveted Western "standard."

Among this preponderance of merely physical attributes, it is the final feature—"the expression in her eyes"—that connects the Westernesque woman of *Jokyōshi* to a specifically literary ideal. Well-known for his adulation of young women, Katai was interviewed on the subject for a special issue on feminine beauty in the magazine *Shumi* (July 1908). Just as raw description had become his ideal for literary language, self-expression uninhibited by inherited forms became his ideal for feminine beauty:

The eyes are the center of expression for the whole face, no, for virtually the whole woman, and I like eyes that are big and bright, full of expression, lively, eyes that talk, so to speak. Large, dark pupils with long eye-lashes are most splendid.

Her language should also be expressive. I have no interest in words that are cut to the mold. I like women who are lively when they talk, high-collar women, free women, women who have breathed new air.[21]

Katai was not the only Naturalist to embrace such an ideal. Both Tokuda Shūsei and Mizuno Yōshū shared his preference for high-collar women who were "full of expression," a phrase they repeated so often that it virtually constitutes a mold in itself.[22] The lively express-siveness Katai and his fellow Naturalists sought was still relatively new to the Japanese gender spectrum; just two decades earlier, Yamada Bimyō had described the schoolgirl heroines in *Fūkin no hitoshirabe* as being too lively, lamentably lacking the proper restraint expected of genteel women. Even Futabatei's depiction of Osei suggests a criti-cal view of unencumbered vivacity in young women.

Clearly, the cultural identity of the Meiji schoolgirl had changed significantly in the intervening years. Honda Masuko identifies a major shift in the public perception of schoolgirls after the Sino-Jap-anese war, when a certain amount of pride was taken in their sym-bolic representation of Japanese modernity. This period saw major government initiatives in women's education, culminating in the 1899 "Edict on Girls' Higher Schools," which required city and prefectural governments throughout Japan to establish and maintain girls' higher schools. By the turn of the century the image of this new gender type had begun to congeal around a distinct set of linguistic and fashion practices—the "schoolgirl's parlance" or *teyodawa kotoba* mentioned by Shōyō (see chapter 2), the simplified Western bun (*sokuhatsu*), the hair ribbons, the *ebicha-bakama* (maroon culottes), and the result-ing increase in freedom of movement that enabled young women to enjoy the Western imports of bicycle riding and lawn tennis.[23] At the same time, a fundamental shift was also taking place in the realm of literary aesthetics. With the rise of Naturalism, the rejection of stylistic restraints in literature would encompass a broader rebellion against convention in and of itself, especially the social forms that dictated proper feminine behavior.

In addition to an update in physical appearance, the Westernesque woman in *Jokyōshi* also acquires psychological depth, though largely at the wife's expense. While the wife, who remains nameless, is only distinguished by the precarious physical condition of pregnancy and her so-called nature (artlessness), the schoolteacher, Watanabe Kuniko, is well-endowed in both body and spirit. Unlike Okiku, Kuniko's voice is not just a distant phantom of the narrator's memory; she is a poet in her own right, a woman who reads, writes, and talks about New Poetry. The complex interiority suggested by her "expressiveness" is directly related to her personal engagement with modern literature. Kuniko's engagement with modern poetry enables her not only to discuss literature with the protagonist but also, and most crucially for this story, to partake in the discourse of love.

What did I talk about then? That's right, at first I took up a copy of [Yosano Akiko's] *Tangled Hair* that was laying on the desk and sang its praises, saying that its poetic visions far surpassed the old poets. The woman had marked in red the poems she always loved to recite, and pointing out a couple of these, she said, "When I read a poem like this, the tears flow. . . . " And how my heart trembled when I discovered that her tastes matched my own. What I had sought in vain from my beloved wife, the unfulfilled needs that left me lamenting alone over the *lonely life*, were now suddenly on the verge of being infinitely satisfied as I brushed up against her heart. (498)

Thus begins the "embrace of two souls" as sardonically named by the *Teikoku bungaku* reviewer. Critical commentary on Yosano Akiko's love poetry precipitates a quasi-philosophical meditation on love itself, whereupon the dangerous liaison of eros and logos gives rise to a veritable metalanguage of seduction.

Then I talked a great deal about love: Love is a mystery. Our trifling knowledge will never be able to comprehend it fully. Only *silence* and *silence* alone can even come close to it. Then I talked about various things, like the value of silence and the inner life, and as the talk reached its climax this woman just opened her eyes wide and listened intently, as though enchanted by a sound from somewhere far away.

This woman is certainly a spiritual human being.

Then I recall having also raised the topic of my usual theory of fate. In this universe there are three mysteries, namely, love, death, and fate. However, fate and death are *passive*, coming like the wind and going like the wind, having no connection at all with human beings, but love alone is *active*, making it extremely interesting. It's interesting because there is no faster way to arrive at the mysteries of the universe than to use the power of love. . . . Mutually moved by deep emotion, sharing silences, occasionally letting out long sighs—ah, how deeply did two earthly souls touch each other then. (498–500)

As a new ideal couched in a highly specialized language, the concept of romantic love fundamentally altered the language of courtship for its practitioners. In the narrator's semiforeign discourse, the term love remains so abstract that it becomes a subject in more than a merely grammatical sense; it is not simply the name of a human emotion, but rather a mystical force that motivates human action. In thus discussing love as a purely abstract proposition the narrator assumes a tacit understanding with his female listener that the topic has no immediate bearing on their relationship. But, at the same time, this abstract language has a particular aura that not only enchants the listener but even reproduces in her its very signs and symptoms—"deep emotion," "silences," and "long sighs." Indeed, Kuniko later compares the experience of talking about love with the narrator to an actual experience of the "mystery of love" from her youth.

Yanabu accounts for this aura as an effect of translation, quoting Aizan's "Ren'ai no tetsugaku" as a case in point.

Oh, love, which revolutionizes man's spirit and body!
Love, which cultivates a new frontier of taste and imagination!
Love, which creates a hero and a brave new being!
Love, which unites the family and the nation!
Love—may a great poet appear and astound those numerous writers
who have distorted you!

This rigid language, with its arms akimbo, crying "Love, which creates a hero and a brave being! Love, which unites the family and the nation!" is utterly abrupt, even comical. Obviously, the logic leaps. Just what does this person think "love" is, anyway?

But it isn't just him. In all probability the contemporary Japanese had been taught a "love" they could proudly affirm for the first time. And it came to them first in the form of a word. At any rate, it was a precious and splendid thing. Its meaning and content was still unclear. But, in any event, it was precious . . .

The popularity of "love" was first of all the popularity of the word "love."[24]

As a product of translation, the word *love* had a material value that preceded and even superseded its semantic value. In *Jokyōshi* the narrator's claim that "love is a mystery" takes this logic one step further: here, the profound import of love derives from the very fact of its inscrutability. Just as the exuberantly nationalist rhetoric of Aizan's disquisition on love inspires laughter in the contemporary reader, to the disinterested third party there is also something inherently comical about a stilted quasi-philosophical conversation that serves no other purpose than to provide an elaborate camouflage for carnal desire. In Katai's novella eros and logos join hands to produce the parody of desire parading as intelligence, ornamenting itself in the pretentious foreign diction of *sairensu* (a Japanese transliteration of *silence* that also, coincidentally, works as a transliteration of *sirens*). While Futabatei invited the reader to laugh by consciously exploiting this kind of parody in *Ukigumo*, in *Jokyōshi* both the author and the narrator-protagonist appear to be clowns in the parade.

[5]

Haunting the Laboratory of Vernacular Style
The Sirens of "Shōjobyō" and *Futon*

The 1907 publications of "Shōjobyō" (May, *Taiyō*) and *Futon* (September, *Shinshōsetsu*) marked a radical shift in Katai's deployment of the Westernesque woman, one that was specifically occasioned by his mid-career foray into the hard terrain of vernacular stylistic experimentation. Both works can be read as attempts to fulfill Katai's earlier call for "raw description" in a way that would decisively dissociate him from the long line of sentimental fiction already attached to his name. Their experimentality is evident not only in the sharp contrast they make with his earlier work but also with each other. Indeed, the differences in style, tone, and narrative effect are so striking that they could as well have been written by two different authors: if "Shōjobyō" reads as a slightly acerbic send-up of the author's own worst foibles, *Futon* reads as a self-involved representation of inner turmoil by a writer constitutionally incapable of humor. Critics and scholars have generally positioned "Shōjobyō" as an important prelude to *Futon*, and the portrait of the marginalized, middle-aged writer's attraction to the schoolgirl figure does provide a clear topical connection between the two works. But we should be wary of the temptation to read this short story as a step forward on some inevitable path of Naturalist evolution paved by Katai's personal life and literary convictions. To the contrary, it could be said that many aspects of *Futon* represent a retrogressive retreat from the new ground opened up by "Shōjobyō," a work best characterized as an exploratory first step on a path ultimately not taken. In spite of the fact that *Futon* resuscitated precisely the kind of narrowly subjective viewpoint that critics had long since dismissed as only capable of representing "minor (but to the protagonist major) agonies,"[1] which Katai had just gone to great lengths to radically relativize in "Shōjobyō," it was *Futon* that made literary history, while "Shōjobyō" languished on the outer edges of the literary critical radar. This comparative reading of the two texts is motivated by a key critical question: what exactly was it about the configuration of vernacular style and gender representation in *Futon* that finally managed to produce a version of Katai's personal fetishes that would profoundly affect the critical readership of his day and even fundamentally alter the literary landscape for future generations?

The following discussion of "Shōjobyō" and *Futon* will examine how each work configured the relationships between narrator, protagonist, reader, literary style, and Westernesque women, and to what effect. What I have named the Westernesque femme fatale was a siren who haunted the gap between languages, a place that was both acknowledged and traversed in the most critical way by the language of vernacular translation. The Westernesque women of "Shōjobyō" are sirens of a different sort: they inhabit the private fantasy world of a hopelessly outmoded writer, a place where the prettified language of imaginary maidens reigns supreme. Although one of these sirens ultimately leads the protagonist to his death, none of them can be described as a femme fatale, as none are invested with interiority or intention. It was not until *Futon* that Katai's Westernesque woman would take on the role of a duplicitous femme fatale. Just as significantly, it was not until *Futon* that Katai would directly tap into the innovative potential of the language of vernacular translation. This chapter aims to reveal the integral connection between these two developments, which worked together to forge a new relationship between author, narrator, protagonist, and reader for modern Japanese fiction.

Pretty Women, Pretty Writing, and Literary Emasculation

Far from the no-man's-land between languages, the Westernesque sirens of "Shōjobyō" haunt an in-between space that is densely populated and socially grounded: the route that takes the modern commuter from home to the office and back. In a manner that interestingly presages the train perverts who became symptomatic emblems of urban alienation in late twentieth-century Japan, the protagonist here finds the opportunity to gaze upon and fantasize about beautiful young women (mostly schoolgirls) in the train and its immediate environs to be the only source of solace in a daily life that otherwise merely shuttles back and forth between domesticity and a dreary desk job.

The Sotobori train arrived, so he got on. Sharp eyes immediately searched for the colors of a beautiful kimono, but unfortunately there was no one aboard who could meet his wish. But simply having gotten on the train calmed the spirit, and from here on, at least to the point of reaching home, was like his own paradise, and [he] felt at ease. Stores and signs along the road passed before the eyes like images on a shadow lamp, calling to mind a host of beautiful memories, so that was a good feeling. [2]

In stark contrast to *Jokyōshi* and *Futon*, "Shōjobyō" leaves the private realm of literature behind, instead focusing on the kind of desire that can only be mobilized by public space.

A beautiful young woman in the middle of a crowded train—to him, nothing could afford such feelings of happiness and profound aesthetic pleasure as this, and until now he had already experienced this happiness several times. The soft kimono touches the skin. The untouchable perfume releases its scent. The texture of warm flesh invites an ineffable yearning. Above all, the smell of a woman's hair gives rise to a kind of intense desire in the man, and that gave him a pleasure that cannot be captured in words. (69)

Upon transferring to the Kōbu line from Ochanomizu, the train was practically full to capacity due to the ongoing exposition, so he forced his way into the conductor's area, managed to get a foothold outside of the right-side door, and held on tight to the brass bars. As his gaze wandered inside the car, he got a jolt. There, just on the other side of the glass window, is the beautiful young lady with whom he had once boarded the train at Shinano-machi, the one whom he had been wishing by all means to meet, to see once again, practically being crushed by fedoras, university caps, and Invernesses, aboard the train just like a dove ringed in by a flock of crows. (70–71)

It is the palpable tension between public and private gazes, external appearances and internal visions, that lends "Shōjobyō" its basic structure and source of interest; its narrator is distinguished, within Katai's oeuvre, by a singular ability to animate both gazes at once.

The train left Yoyogi.

The spring morning is pleasant. The sun spreads its gentle rays, and the air is unusually crisp and clear. Beneath a beautifully haze-enshrouded Mount Fuji, a dark line of trees from a large oak grove and chaotic rows of newly built houses in the lowland of Sendagaya pass by quickly, like the images of a shadow lamp. But even better than this silent nature are the beautiful figures of maidens, so the man was practically pouring his entire soul into the faces and figures of the two girls opposite him. But it is more difficult to gaze upon living beings than to look at silent nature, since there is the worry of being caught if one looks too hard, so [he] pretends to be looking to the side, and then casts sidelong glances, quick and sharp as a flash of lightning. Someone once said that when looking at women on the train, it is too glaring to look straight on, and yet people will also find it suspiciously noticeable if one stands far away, so it is most convenient to take a seat diagonally opposite, at a rather oblique angle. What with a yearning for maidens that amounts to nothing less than a sickness, the man of course need not be taught this little secret by others, having a natural sense of the timing, and he never fails to grasp a felicitous opportunity. (68)

By inviting the reader to watch the man as he expertly steals glimpses of women from under the public gaze—that is to say, at precisely the moment when he is both hyperconscious of the eyes of others and yet completely unguarded, assured that he has mastered the "secret" of averting their detection—this narrator exposes the psychological profile of the protagonist in a way that cannot be found elsewhere in Katai's works.

The main character of "Shōjobyō" is not characterized by his self-proclaimed love for a single woman, but rather by his pathologized yearning for an entire category of women. The protocinematic deployment of the train as a site of moving images, repeatedly compared to a "shadow lamp," gives way to a composite image of Westernesque women that the protagonist carries around like a secret stash of opium: "Finding the dark, gloomy room unbearably lonely no matter how one looks at it, [he] puffs on a cigarette, from which a long wisp of bluish-purple smoke drifts upward. As he stares at it, the girl from Yoyogi, the schoolgirl, the beautiful figure from Yotsuya, and others all get mixed up together, intertwined, and seem to be the figure of one person. While the foolishness of it does occur [to him], yet [he] apparently does not find it unpleasant." (684) It is worth noting that this is the only work by Katai to connect the image of the Westernesque woman with the experience of *pleasure*, as opposed to the kind of resentment-driven desire that usually characterizes his fiction. If anyone can be said to have inherited this legacy, it would have to be the distinctly anti-Naturalist Tanizaki Jun'ichirō, whose tales of heady desire in "Aguri" (1922) and *Chijin no ai* practically luxuriate in the "foolish" adulation of Westernesque women. On the balance, however, the narrator of "Shōjobyō" casts these intoxicating sirens as little more than telltale signs of the protagonist's diseased mind.

Katai's own idolatry of young women had left him open to the charge of parading his idiosyncratic fetish as literature, a criticism that undoubtedly formed the basis for the anomalous self-caricature of "Shōjobyō." In a sudden shift into a merciless mode of self-satire that was neither foreshadowed by earlier writings nor ventured again in later works, "Shōjobyō" replaces the poet who "sings of the beauty of the universe" and the one who theorizes about "the power of love" with a "literary man" who writes puerile "novels of yearning," "coquettish poems," and "New Poetry."

The name of this protagonist is Sugita Kōjō, a literary man needless to say. When young, his name was fairly well known, and two or three of his works had even been rather acclaimed. Indeed, it surely never occurred to him, nor to others, that by the time he reached the age of thirty-seven he would be part of the staff for a trifling magazine publishing house, commuting to work every single day, even proofreading copy for trifling magazines, and finally submerging below the horizon line of the literary circles without further ado. But there is a reason things turned out this way. This man, having been this way for a long time now, seems to have a bad habit of fawning over young women. Upon seeing a young, beautiful woman, his eye for observation, which is normally rather sharp, utterly loses its authority. In his youth, he enthusiastically wrote so-called maiden novels, which for a time quite enchanted young men, but novels of yearning that lack observation and ideas cannot hold people's interest forever. Eventually, the notion of this man and young women became the butt of laughter in the literary circles, and all of the novels and other pieces he wrote were dismissed among peals of laughter. (67)

The close resemblance of this character to its author should be evident from the previous chapters. For the first and last time in his long career, Katai's narrator joined the ranks of his harshest critics in deploring his fetishistic attachment to young women as a mark of literary failure, rather than a medal of distinction for the literary persona.

"Shōjobyō" draws a direct parallel between the protagonist's chronic maidenitis and his penchant for prettified writing.

And the editor in chief, being a sarcastic and unpleasant man, thinks nothing of taunting people. When he goes to great pains to write something beautiful (*bibun*), the editor in chief responds with a jibe—*Hey Sugita, there you go again getting all soft on girls.* No matter what he might say, he is laughed at on account of young women. So on occasion he gets miffed, spouting off to himself—*I am not a child, I am thirty-seven years old, making a fool of a person like this goes beyond the pale.* But that soon fades away, and undeterred, he composes coquettish poems and New Poetry. (69)

The use of the term *bibun* here, which may have originated as a translation for belles lettres, requires some explanation. As we can see from the passage above, Katai used the word in a rather loose sense that included not only flowery prose but poetry as well. In *Bibun sahō* (A guide to *bibun*, 1906) Katai defines *bibun* as the expression of beauty—i.e., artistic ornamentation—in any style or genre of writing.[3] By suggesting a pathological connection between the attachment to stylistic ornamentation and Sugita's fatal weakness for young women, "Shōjobyō" gives rise to an image of bibun as a symptom of effeminacy. At the very least, it leads to Sugita's constant emasculation at the office.

The editor in chief called out to him, "Hey Sugita."

"Huh?" He looked over.

"You know, I read your recent work," he said, laughing.

"Is that so?"

"As usual, it certainly is beautiful. How is it that you can write so prettily, hm? It's no wonder that some people think you must be a handsome guy. I mean, I heard that some journalist or other was quite surprised to see that you have a large build, contrary to all expectation."

"Is that so?" said Sugita, with a resigned laugh.

"I say, long live young women," chimed in another editor, taunting him. (70)

Among his friends Sugita's idolization of young women also becomes the source of speculation about his sexuality. Indeed, the following passage may have been intended as the kind of bold revelation of a hidden truth that would "shock the wits out of the craftsmanship contingent."

"It's so strange. It might be some kind of illness, you know. I mean, his thing is just adoration alone. He just thinks they are beautiful, nothing more. If it were one of us, at such times the power of instinct would quickly rear its head, and we could not be content just to look with adoration."

"That's right, there must be something biologically *lost*," someone said.

"Isn't it probably more temperamental than biological?"

"No, I don't think so. I think that when he was young, he over indulged himself."

"What do you mean by indulged?"

"I don't have to spell it out for you to know what I'm talking about. . . . I mean that he damaged his body all by himself. When such a habit lasts for a long time, apparently a certain biological element gets *lost*, and the body and spirit do not come together." (67; italics mark English words rendered in katakana)

In sharp contrast to "Shōshijin," *Jokyōshi*, and *Futon*, which all lay claim to an overblown image of the tormented, solitary male artist, "Shōjobyō" deploys eroticized images of Westernesque women to signal the protagonist's loss of authority, of properly-functioning libido—in short, of masculine identity.

The self-portrait of the failed writer in "Shōjobyō" reminds us that Katai's relationship to pretty writing was much more complex than that suggested by the polemic of "Rokotsu naru byōsha." While he may have attacked the giants of Meiji literature for advocating stylistic decorum, he himself had not only tried to follow their lead, but failed miserably in the attempt. For Katai bibun was a former aspiration that had turned into a sign of his own degradation. Even two years after he had loudly proclaimed the superiority of raw description, Katai still had a young readership who associated his name with the more florid elements of literary style, enough for him to publish a book-length guide on how to write beautifully targeted at young writers. In fact, like Sugita, Katai himself was still writing what we might call "maiden" poetry, which he must have intended as bibun in its most easily accessible form. The following is an abbreviated example from the popular magazine *Shōjo sekai* (Maiden's world), written shortly before "Shōjobyō."

To a Certain Maiden

Maiden, what troubles you?
Forlorn figure lingering in step,

head hanging so sadly,
upon lashes a clinging dew.

Maiden, what pains you?
Coming from a life of innocence,
into the world now, into the sullied world,
be it the loneliness of that change?[4]

Aside from his sentimental fiction, it was surely this kind of precious schlock from which Katai hoped to dissociate himself by means of self-caricature. The sharp focus on the schoolgirl's allure in *Futon* shows that he did not entirely succeed in curing his own maidenitis through the writing of "Shōjobyō," but he did manage to create a narrative voice that bore no traces of the pretty language he had renounced in his Naturalist theories of literary style.

From First- to Third-Person and Back

Both "Shōjobyō" and *Futon* maintain the close resemblance between author and protagonist that characterizes so much of Katai's fiction. What immediately sets them apart from Katai's earlier works, and from each other, is their distinct uses of third-person narration. "Shōshijin" and *Jokyōshi* are both representative of Katai's marked preference for first-person narration, or what critics in his day called the "autobiographical style" (*jijotai*).[5] "Shōjobyō" abandons this mode entirely. Here the use of third-person narration creates a critical distance between narrator and protagonist that was virtually unprecedented in Katai's fiction. While this narrative style may have constituted a personal revolution for Katai, it was certainly not an innovation in itself. In *Futon*, however, the narration hovers ambiguously between subjective first-person enunciation and objective third-person description, forging an entirely new relationship between narrator and protagonist for Japanese fiction. The critical difference between these two narrative strategies is easily gauged by the yawning gap in the reception of the two texts, particularly in relation to their "raw" manifestation of sexual repression. Both works put the spotlight on the protagonist's tormented sexuality in a way that could potentially qualify them as bold revelations of the author's personal secrets. The discussion of Sugita's sex life did draw the curiosity and interest of contemporary critics, but the short story certainly did not cause a sensation. By contrast, *Futon* was immediately hailed by Shimamura Hōgetsu as the "bold confession of a person of the flesh, the human being stripped naked."[6] The impact of *Futon* had as much to do with its narrative style as with its presumably autobiographical sexual content.

Let us begin by considering the narrative style of "Shōjobyō." If the protagonist of "Shōjobyō" is a caricature of the author, the voice of the narrator bears so little resemblance to anything Katai had written before that we can only characterize him as the internalized presence of Katai's harshest critics unleashed.

When the 7:20 A.M. Yamanote-line train into the city passes through Yoyogi Station shaking the ground beneath the cliff, there is a man trudging through the rice paddies of Sendagaya. There being no day when this man does not pass through, on rainy days dragging an old pair of boots through the deep mud of the rice paddy paths, and on windy mornings passing through with a hat pulled down over the eyes trying to avoid the dust, the people in the houses along the way recognize the figure from a distance—there's even a military wife who rouses a husband from bedraggled spring sleep with a "that person has already passed by, so you'll be late for work."

The figure of this man began to appear on the rice paddy paths about two months ago, when the suburb opened up, a new house was built on the corner of this forest and the top of that hill, and large structures like the mansion of Major So-and-so and the mansion of an executive for Such-and-such Company could be seen, picturelike, among the great rows of zelkova trees that were what remained of the Musashi Plains, and since there seem to be five or six rental houses on the other side of that row of zelkova trees, well, he must have moved in over there—so goes the chief rumor.

Now just because a person passes by gives no cause for starting rumors, but the countryside is a lonely place with few people and, what's more, the appearance of this man is most distinctive, cutting a strange figure with a ducklike gait, an indescribable incongruity—and this incongruity came to attract the idle eyes of people along the way. (64)

There is no "poet" in this opening passage—just a funny-looking man on his way to work, described by a narrator whose vernacular idiom is anything but lyrical. Three basic rhetorical devices establish the sardonic tone of the narrator's voice here: the identification of the protagonist by the generic noun *man,* the present tense, and the nominal sentence ending (a technique known as *taigen-dome* which defies representation in English). As the story unfolds, we also notice another defining characteristic of this narrative voice: a marked preference for the casual form of the sentence-final copula, *da.*

By introducing the protagonist with the objectifying marker *the man,* rather than his proper name or a personal pronoun, the narrator immediately proclaims critical distance from his subject. While this strategy may have been new to Katai's writing, it was anything but new to Japanese narrative convention, tracing as far back as the tenth century poetic tale *Ise monogatari.* This is not to say that the effects of the technique remained the same over the centuries, only that it was a familiar narrative idiom. We should also note that personal pronouns are completely absent in the above passage—and only rarely used in the rest of the text (where absolutely necessary, I have supplemented them in my translations for the sake of clarity). The use of third-person pronouns in Japanese (*kare* and *kanojo*) derives from the translation of Western grammatical conventions, and *Futon* will employ them strategically from the very first line.

Significantly, most of the few minor lapses into the simple past tense in "Shōjobyō" occur in direct representations of the protagonist's thoughts. Particularly in the case of third-person narration, the use of the present tense creates an immediate distance between narrator and narratee by implying the simultaneous and separate presences of an observer and an observed party. By contrast, the past tense can link the observer to the observed within an implicitly shared space of memory. As Mitani Kuniaki has pointed out, the use of the sentence-final particle *ta,* which marks the past tense, was neither part of pre-Meiji literary convention, nor is it used in spoken Japanese to describe past thoughts or feelings that do not belong to the speaker. To describe another person's past thoughts or feelings in Japanese requires the attachment of a conjectural form such as *darō*. In this sense the combination of the past tense sentence-final *ta* with third-person narration played a significant role in bridging first- and third-person perspectives.[7] In *Futon* the simple past will become the dominant mode of representation.

As for the nominal sentence-ending, this translation-defying technique owes its particular effect to the fact that the Japanese language locates the main verb at the end of a clause. In part, its use can be explained by the same premium on linguistic variation and distaste for repetitive use of the copula that defines stylistic felicity in English. In addition, the effect of clipping a sentence with what we might call a hanging nominal encourages the reader to fill in the blank with more than a simple connecting verb. Depending on context, this can either result in the suggestion of an ineffable emotion or the raised eyebrow of a critical narrator.[8]

The use of the casual spoken declension of the final copula *da* is the most idiosyncratic aspect of narrative style in "Shōjobyō" and the most puzzling.[9] By 1907 Kōyō's efforts to refine the vernacular had long since made the expository declension *de aru* the final copula of choice for the overwhelming majority of vernacular novels. The choice of politeness level and tense in the final verb declension was fraught with difficult narratological issues, forcing the author to establish a new relationship between narrator, reader, and narratee. The only prominent example of a third-person narrative I have been able to identify that may have influenced Katai's decision of *da* is Uchida Roan's translation of Dostoevsky's *Crime and Punishment* (*Tsumi to batsu*, November 1892–February 1893). Like Katai's "Shōjobyō," Roan's translation is written mainly in the key of *da*, with occasional uses of *de aru*. Yet there is no conclusive evidence of an intertextual relationship. In the end, it seems most reasonable to surmise that Katai's use of *da* in "Shōjobyō" was an idiosyncratic experiment in "raw description," soon to be eclipsed by the stylistic and narratorial innovations of *Futon*.

We can best understand the "raw" impact of *da* by first looking at the refined version of the final copula developed by Katai's literary bane, Ozaki Kōyō. After years of struggling to mold the vernacular to his own sense of literary aesthetics, Kōyō succeeded in domesticating this strange wild bird of translation and even making it sing. In *Tajō takon* (Full of tears and regrets, 1896), the sentence-ending copula not only attained just the right degree of neutrality vis-à-vis the reader, but finally overcame its abject status as the ugly duckling of vernacular style to become an organic, rhythmic element for each sentence to which it lent closure. Here is a brief example from *Tajō takon* in which the final *de aru* could easily have been clipped from the sentence in a *taigen-dome*:

Kono wabishii yoru wo [9] kono wabishii zashiki ni [10], kono wabishii hito ga [9] kou neshizumatte iru [9] sono wabishisa no [7], sara ni ika bakari ka wa [10] shiru mono mo naku [7],—tada ame ga futte [7], yoru no fukeyuku [7] bakari de aru [6]. (brackets contain syllable count)

This lonely man sleeping away this lonely night in this lonely room, such loneliness utterly unbeknownst to even a soul, —there is only the falling rain, and a deepening night.[10]

Instead of ending with a suggestive verbal lacuna that would direct the reader's attention to an unspoken sentiment floating somewhere beyond the field of the printed page, Kōyō chose instead to enclose a lacuna of dashes with a final declarative copula. Moreover, the articulation of the copula brings this sentence to a rhythmic full circle, with the final phrases providing a 7/7/6 refrain to the opening 9/10/9 syllabic pattern. Though the effect of the final *de aru* here can only be roughly approximated in English, we might compare it to the subtle difference between "there is only the falling rain and a deepening night," and "only a falling rain, and a deepening night." Both formulations are poignant in different ways. Kōyō's sensitivity to the felicitous rhythms of Japanese prose endowed an awkward syntactical necessity of literal translation with a subtle nuance and rhythmic function of its own.

The *de aru* style established in *Tajō takon* quickly seduced other novelists, including Katai himself.[11] Yet in 1907, when this decisive refinement of the vernacular style had already firmly entrenched itself in Japanese fiction, Katai momentarily switched to the coarse tone of *da* in "Shōjobyō." This may well have been a conscious rejection of Kōyō's highly crafted *de aru*, meant to provide a model for the kind of "raw" language Katai had proposed in his hallmark essay. Yet no one embraced it as a revolutionary new style of description. If Katai's chronically sentimental narrator had already been rejected by critics, the third-person narrator with a penchant for running critical commentary was a voice familiar from gesaku fiction, a stigma that perhaps only the ironic feline narrator of Natsume Sōseki's *Wagahai wa neko de aru* (I am a cat, 1905) could overcome.[12] Katai himself was well aware of this problem. In *Bibun sahō* he writes: "In the novel, no matter what happens, one should never use words of criticism. Quite often description turns into explanation, but to make critical comments immediately gives rise to the specter of petty subjectivity, rendering the work devoid of interest."[13] The third-person narrator of "Shōjobyō" manages to achieve the effect of critical commentary without resorting to "explanation" by enlisting the coarse, subtly sardonic tone of *da*.

Of the eleven cases of the *da* sentence-ending in the narrative passages of "Shōjobyō," seven present information about Sugita that is rather unflattering and at times even comical.[14] For instance, the second sentence of the novel, ending with "*there's* even a military wife who rouses a husband from bedraggled spring sleep," emphasizes the mechanical precision of Sugita's daily commute. Another *da*-final sentence introduces an amusing anecdote about Sugita's encounter with a young woman on his way to work. The last three instances come closest to implying the narrator's personal critique of the protagonist. One is the statement, quoted above, "While the foolishness of it did occur [to him], yet [he] apparently does not find it unpleasant." Here are the other two examples.

sunawachi kare no tanoshimi to iu no wa densha no naka no utsukushii sugata to, bibun shintaishi o tsukuru koto de, sha ni iru aida wa, yōji sae nai to, genkōshi o nobete, isshōkenmei ni utsukushii bun o kaite iru. shōjo ni kansuru kansō no ooi no wa muron no koto da.

In other words, his pleasure being the beautiful figures in the train, and writing bibun New Poetry, when at the office, as long as there is nothing else to do, [he] will spread out manuscript paper and throw [himself] into the writing of beautiful words. It's a matter of course that impressions of young women abound. (69)

sabishisa, sabishisa, kono sabishisa o sukutte kureru mono wa nai ka, utsukushii sugata no tada hitotsu de ii kara, shiroi ude ni kono mi o maite kureru mono wa nai ka. sō shitara, kitto kaifuku suru. kibō, funtō, kanarazu soko ni seimei o hakken suru. kono nigotta chi ga atarashiku nareru to omou. keredo kono otoko wa jissai sore ni yotte, atarashii yūki o kaifuku suru koto ga dekiru ka dō ka wa mochiron gimon da.

Loneliness, loneliness, is there no one who will save [me] from this loneliness? just one beautiful figure will do—is there none who will wrap this body in white arms? Then [I] would surely recover. Hope, fighting strength would certainly discover life in that. This cloudy blood could become new again, [he] thinks. But of course, it's doubtful whether or not this man can in fact revive a renewed courage on that basis. (70)

Whereas the distant, expository tone of *de aru* enables neutral statements of fact by a self-effacing third-person narrator, the unmistakably spoken derivation of *da* has an almost emphatic tone similar in English to "let me tell you," ensuring that any narrator who uses it will be characterized to some degree by his own "subjectivity." At issue is whether or not that subjectivity will necessarily be seen as "petty."

While the spoken *da* sets the overall tone for "Shōjobyō," Katai also makes discrete use of *de aru* and its past-tense declension *de atta*, allowing us to examine the distinct effects of the two copular forms. Although it is impossible to clearly demonstrate in English the inherent connection between the final *da* and the critical stance of the narrator vis-à-vis his subject, the following instances of *de aru* and the past-tense *de atta* in the same text should help to illuminate this connection by contrast.

koto ni, onna no kami no nioi to iu mono wa, isshu no hageshii nozomi o otoko ni okosaseru mono de, sore ga nan tomo meijō serarenu yūkai o kare ni ataeru no de atta.

Above all, the smell of a woman's hair gives rise to a kind of intense desire in the man, and *that gave him a pleasure that cannot be captured in words*. (69)

henshūchō no tsukue ga mannaka ni atte, sono fukin ni henshūin no tsukue ga gokyaku hodo naraberarete aru ga, kare no tsukue wa sono mottomo kabe ni chikai kurai tokoro de, ame no furu hi nado wa, ranpu ga hoshii kurai de aru.

The editor in chief's desk is in the middle, with about five editor's desks lined up around it, but his desk sits closest to the wall, in a place so dark that on rainy days, *a lamp is wanted*. (69)

michibata no samazama no shōten yara kanban yara ga sōmatō no yō ni me no mae o tōru ga, sore ga samazama no utsukushii kioku o omoiokosaseru no de ii kokochi ga suru no de atta.

The various shops and signs on the roadside passed before his eyes like the projections of a shadow lamp, which called to mind many beautiful memories, so *that was a good feeling*. (70)

All three examples are verbally constructed as statements of objective fact, rather than opinions or observations that could only belong to the narrator. Since they are also objective statements of the protagonist's own feelings, they can imply the narrator's sympathy, or at least concurrence, with his subject. Here, we see the potential of the ostensibly neutral expository copular ending to blur the distinction between the protagonist's subjectivity and the narrator's "objectivity"—or, more precisely, the narrator's status as a detached observer. While the final *da* binds statements directly to the narrator as a speaking subject with a distinct personality, the expository *de aru* here does not bear any kind of vocal imprint at all, instead representing the protagonist's feelings as transcendental verbal facts. It is precisely this potential to fuse subject and object in the expository form of the copula that Katai will exploit in *Futon*.

The Novelty of Personal Pronouns

While *Futon* is generally regarded as the fountainhead of the I-novel (*watakushi-shōsetsu*), one of its peculiarities as a confessional work is the fact that it is written in the third-person. Among the various possibilities for writing in third-person Japanese, Katai chose to begin the novel with *kare,* the Japanese translation for "he." If the narrators of Katai's earlier works each had their own distinct voice, with its own distinct problems, the narrative voice of *Futon* effaces itself to achieve an impression of neutral transparency. This is not the transparency provided by an omniscient narrator, but rather that of a sympathetic witness who has complete access to the thoughts and feelings of the protagonist alone. All that stands between this narrator and the object of his sympathy is the immeasurable distance—an equally immeasurable proximity—between the first-person pronoun of *I* and the third-person *he.* The boundary between the two is most significantly blurred in the opening passage:

Descending the gentle slope of the road that leads from Koishikawa's Kirishitan-zaka to Gokurakusui, he thought. "With this, the relationship between me and her has been settled. How ridiculous to have had such thoughts at thirty-six, with a wife and three children. Yet . . . yet . . . can it really be true? All that affection showered upon me—was it simply affection and not love?"

Numerous emotion-laden letters—the relationship between the two simply was not of the customary order. What with a wife, children, public opinion, and a student-teacher relationship, didn't dare to fall deeply in love, but a tremendous storm certainly lurked in the depths of the throb of hearts in shared conversation, the sparkle of meeting eyes. It seemed that if only the opportunity had presented itself, the storm at the very depths would suddenly gain force, and wife, children, public opinion, and the teacher-student relationship would be shattered in one fell swoop. At least, this is what the man had believed. In spite of that, now thinking back over the events of the past two or three days, the clear fact was that the woman had made a false sale of her affection. Deceived me, thought the man countless times. And yet, being a literary man, this man had enough wherewithal to take an objective view of his own psychology. The psychology of a young woman is not a matter easily judged; it may be that that warm, welcome affection was simply a development of the nature particular to women, and the expression of the eyes that looked so beautiful as well as the behavior that felt so kind were all simply unconscious, just as a flower of nature provides a kind of solace to the onlooker. To concede a point, even if the woman had loved me, myself being a teacher, she being the student, myself being a person with a wife and children, she being a beautiful flower of youth, nothing could possibly come of any mutually sensed feelings. But even if another point is conceded, when that feverish letter, making direct and indirect allusions to the writhing of the heart, imparted the last emotions, it seemed as though the force of nature were bearing down hard on this one, yet this one did not solve the riddle for her. Women being of a modest nature, how could possibly go beyond this to make any more obvious an approach? Following this line of psychology, she may have caused the incident at hand out of disappointment.

"At any rate, the time has passed. She already belongs to another!"

He yelled this aloud as he walked, pulling at his hair.[15]

Strictly speaking, should we call this a "third-person" narrative? Here, third- and first-person perspectives are seamlessly intermingled. Until reading the line "At least, this is what the man believed," we are not sure whose thought is being represented in the second paragraph—that of the narrator, the protagonist, or the author as narrator as protagonist. Only one other sentence in this paragraph interrupts the steady stream of indirect discourse: "And yet, being a literary man, this man had enough wherewithal to take an objective view of his own psychology." The narrator's statement is then immediately corroborated by a retreat into free indirect discourse, leaving us again to wonder just who believes this view to be "objective"—the narrator, or the protagonist, or both? Or is it a self-reflexive comment by the author, borrowing the "objective" authority of a third-person narrator to legitimate his own self-analysis? Why should the mere fact of "being a literary man" guarantee an objective view of one's own psychology? This was certainly not the case in "Shōjobyō," whose protagonist was also "a literary man, needless to say." It is this kind of authoritative self-assertion of the writer's identity that makes it impossible to see the "literary man" of *Futon* as a character being observed by a completely autonomous narrator and/or author.

This confusion of perspectives—or felicitous fusion, depending on one's critical stance—begins with the very first line of *Futon*. This novel *begins* with an unspecified "he," who is only introduced by his tormented thoughts about an unspecified "she." If this does not seem odd in contemporary English, it is only because a similar style of personal narration has already become fairly commonplace in our language as well. Yet we would be hard-pressed to find examples of fiction in English—or any other Western language—contemporaneous to or predating *Futon* that actually *begin* with a third-person pronoun. *Kare* and *kanojo* immediately mark Katai's text with the strange language of translation. At the same time, his use of these translation words departs significantly from the conventional Western *he* and *she* to create a radically new language for Japanese fiction.

Beginning with Dutch in the eighteenth century, *kare* was used to translate the third-person masculine pronouns of Western languages. Yanabu reminds us that not only was its original function markedly different from the Western convention it was meant to represent in Japanese, but it continued to differ in crucial ways even after the historical intervention of translation.

In the first place, *he* is a third-person pronoun, but *kare* was originally a demonstrative pronoun. In Japanese there was no third-person pronoun to begin with, and I believe that, even today, we should say that it does not exist. . . .

As a rule, the third-person pronoun is used in place of a noun that preceded it, in the place of repeatedly enunciating that noun. In such a case the semantic content of the third-person pronoun is exactly the same as the previous noun. If one first says *Robert* . . . and in the next sentence says *he . . . he* means the same thing as *Robert*.

But in the case of *kare*, it was used in the same way as the *are* form of the Japanese trio of pronominal prefixes *ko/so/a* that become *kore/sore/ are*. . . . *Kore* and *kochira* (*this* and *here*) refer to something close to the speaker, *sore* and *sochira* (*that* and *there*) refer to something close to the listener, *are* and *achira* (*that* and *over there*) refer to something that lies beyond both of their spheres of influence.

In other words, *kare* originally referred to something external and distant to both speaker and listener. Conversely, *kare* is connected to the position of the speaker. By contrast, the third-person pronoun of English and other such languages has nothing to do with the position of the speaker, but objectively refers to something that has already been said. For instance, if we see something for the first time, we could call it *are* or *kare*, but as a rule we could not call it *he*.[16]

The meaning of *kare* was transformed by its use in the translation of Western languages. This first affected the Japanese language in the composition of fiction and then entered the spoken idiom. However, even when *kare* did finally enter the spoken idiom, it was not as a personal pronoun, but rather as a novel way to say "boyfriend" in Japanese. In the written language of vernacular fiction, *kare* could not become a true equivalent for *he* because, unlike proper names, it did not refer back to anything that existed in Japanese social reality.

The proper name exists within the world of people. Even if it is a name created by the author, so long as he created it to seem like a real person, then it cannot distance itself from the contractual conditions of existence. . . .

Kare does not exist in the world of people. For the daily language of Japanese that lives in the world of people does not have a *kare*.[17]

In Japanese, when it is necessary to refer directly to a specific person, the proper name is the preferred form of identification; pronouns are only rarely used, and carry very specific information about the relationship between the speaker and the person being referred to. Moreover, the Japanese language does not require the explicit articulation of grammatical subject or object, much less the use of a third-person pronoun. Hence, the word *kare* qua *he* entered the Japanese lexicon as a "superfluous" element.[18]

Significantly, Yanabu identifies *Futon* as the original site for the new meanings that accrued to the superfluous *kare*. Contrary to Katai's insistence that "writing is solely for the purpose of conveying meaning," Yanabu argues that he used translation pronouns in *Futon* for the sake of the exotic words themselves—a thesis that is certainly supported by Katai's homages to the beauty of strange language in *Aibiki*.

I believe that Katai used such a *kare* and *kanojo* in an extremely conscious manner, as a venture. By this, I do not mean that he was conscious of the meaning of the words, but rather that he consciously used them, or tried them out, fully knowing that they seemed strange within the rhetorical context of Japanese writing. For instance, there are the lines "'At any rate, the time has passed. *She* already belongs to another!' *He* yelled this aloud as he walked, pulling at his hair." Even today, the words *kare* and *kanojo* only rarely appear in the conversational passages of novels. At the time, this kind of expression surely did not exist. It is the word *kanojo* that made Katai choose this expression.

At any rate, Katai wanted to use the words *kare* and *kanojo*. It is not because they were missing from Japanese writing. Nor is it because Katai's way of thinking demanded it. He was seduced by *kare* and *kanojo* as words of translation. In the Western novels that Katai avidly read at the time, *he* and *she* were used all over the place. The third-person narrative style for the novel had already been achieved and was sufficiently mature. But there was nothing at all special about *he* and *she* in Western writing. When sideways writing was translated into Japanese, *kare* and *kanojo* would appear. It was an age in which they were just beginning to emerge.

Katai was enchanted by these words that were apparently necessary yet superfluous to Japanese writing. Because he was enchanted, he endowed these words with an important function they had never before known.[19]

As we have already noted, *Futon* begins with an unspecified "he" who is thinking about an unspecified "she." Such a use is certainly more in keeping with the originally demonstrative *kare* than with the personal pronouns of Western languages. In fact, the grammatical functions of proper noun and pronoun are reversed in *Futon*: we do not find out what "he" is called until the beginning of chapter 2, which reads, "He called his name Takenaka Tokio." ("Kare wa na o Takenaka Tokio to itta," 73) This movement from personal pronoun to proper name effectively reverses the function of each, so that "Takenaka Tokio" becomes the substitute for *kare,* rather than vice versa. Thus the Japanese translations for *he* and *she* take on a much greater specificity and rhetorical weight than their common usage as pronouns in European languages would assume. In Katai's hands, *kare* and *kanojo* virtually become proper nouns in themselves. They are not translations of the generic *he* and *she,* but rather Katai's personal appellations for Hero and Heroine—the eminent Others who populate his fetishistic image of literature.

Not surprisingly, "he" associates himself and his "she" with other prominent literary figures—

By some sudden association, recalled Hauptmann's *Lonely Lives.* Before things came to this, had thought of teaching this play as part of her daily curriculum. Wanted to teach the agony and mental state of Johannes Vockerat. It was three years ago when he read this play, at a time when couldn't even imagine that she existed in this world, but from that time he was a lonely person. Didn't go so far as to compare himself to Johannes, but personally sympathized—if there were a woman like Anna, it would be natural to fall into such a tragedy. Now, sighed at the thought of being someone who could not even become that Johannes.

Of course, didn't go so far as to teach her *Lonely Lives,* but had taught Turgenev's short story *Faust.* In the four-and-a-half-mat study, brightly lit by lamp, her youthful heart brimmed with adulation for the colorful love story, expressive eyes sparkled with even deeper meaning. The high-collar pompadour, combs, ribbon, a line of lamplight illuminating half the body, and when pressed face closer to the single volume of the book, the indescribable scent of perfume, the scent of flesh, the scent of a woman—when explicating the passage in which the protagonist in the book read *Faust* aloud to an old lover, the man's voice violently trembled.[20] (72–73)

Before "he" or "she" are given their own proper names, they are associated with proper names from Western literature that were quite well-known to Katai's audience. This attempt to establish parity also affects the language of the text at a more subtle level: the explicit demarcation of the "protagonist *in the book*" implies the existence of another protagonist, the *he* who is not "in the book," as though the two might be easily confused.

As shown in the previous chapters, Katai's literary career skirted the border between adaptation and translation, or vulgar parody and high exoticism, in numerous senses. In terms of *Futon*'s critical reception, however, the tacit guidelines provided by Futabatei's style of literary translation guaranteed that the scales would not be weighted entirely against Katai's favor. The appeal of Futabatei's translations lay above all in the exotic aura of his vernacular style (to which, of course, the narrative content is inextricably tied). Because the Naturalist idealization of transparent language was also an implicit valorization of this aura, the kind of stylistic innovation displayed in *Futon* would inevitably affect its critical reception. In fact, the one contemporary reviewer to express strong disapproval of Katai's literary name-dropping in *Futon* also implied that his main reason for reading the novella was its intriguing new style:

"He" thought such things as this upon descending the gentle slope that leads from Koishikawa's Kirishitan-zaka to Gokurakusui. "With this, the relationship between me and her has been settled." Finding interest in this opening line, I read on, and the traces of the great pains Mr. Tayama took in the writing made me exclaim "what hard work it must have been," but I thought the frequent pulling out of the names of Western writers and the summaries of their works to indirectly describe the protagonist's agony and private thoughts, boring the reader at any rate, was a very bad idea and even a dereliction of duty.[21]

If Katai's stylistic slight of hand could not erase the impression of vulgar parody from the minds of all readers, it was more than sufficient to generate an enthusiastic response from Japanese proponents of Naturalism and to garner many emulators in the field of autobiographical fiction. The lasting historical impact of Futabatei's translations derives from the radical stylistic strategy by which he externalized his reading of Russian literature in the language of Japanese. By contrasting analogy, *Futon*'s critical success derives in large part from its invention of a new method for internalizing European literature, as Nakamura points out: "What moved Katai and what he imitated was the character of Johannes delineated in the play and not the author Hauptmann who wrote the play."[22] That Katai was able to carry off this feat of literary imitation without tripping the critical alarm of vulgar parody owes entirely to his use of language.

Unlike the earlier Kataian protagonists we examined, the "he" of *Futon* can dress in the fancy clothes of other literary figures and yet project a compelling image of psychological depth. Katai's first-person protagonists cried out to the reader, loudly proclaiming their identities with refrains of key words like *Poet!* and *lonely life.* Such acts of self-narration might be compared to inscribing a self-portrait "Like Vincent van Gogh, I too am a painter"—a gesture that paradoxically points to the knowledge that one's brushstrokes are not, in fact, painterly enough to convey the resemblance. The more vigorously these characters proclaim their own identities, the more ridiculous they seem. In "Shōjobyō," by contrast, the portrait of a literary man emerges from multiple perspectives—the idle speculation of neighbors and colleagues, the jibes at the office, the laughter of the literary circles—all brought into focus by the roving eyes and ears of a third-person narrator. This narrator strips his protagonist down to a pathetically unliterary pathology of chronic alienation, emasculation, and autoerotism. If the narrators of "Shōshijin" and *Jokyōshi* were overly self-conscious, Sugita is not self-conscious enough: increasingly submerged in a fantasy world, he has no use for the knowledge that the literary costume he wears—the decorum of "beautiful letters" and New Poetry—has become ridiculously outmoded. The "he" of *Futon* suffers from neither of these extremes. This protagonist is conveyed to the reader not by his own vocal assertions, nor by the objectifying gaze of a roving third-person narrator, but by a magic linguistic window onto the thoughts of an unnamed man. As Yanabu puts it, *Futon* "does not simply narrate the 'I' of the author. It entrusts the 'I' of the author to 'kare.' And thus does the 'I' get created as an issue, an exposed existence."[23]

By means of this deceptively simple device, Katai endowed his usually pathetic protagonist with an impression of psychological depth that critics were eager to embrace.

If the agony of life that comes from the pain of self-consciousness and the discordance of taste and ideology seen in Hauptmann's *Lonely Lives* is depicted in its outlines in the older work *Jokyōshi*, then we should see that *Futon* has depicted its contents. If the agony that characterizes an age of strong self-consciousness was manifested spiritually in the sad love of a man past middle-age in *Rudin,* then we should see that in *Futon,* the same agony, by means of the same direction, is manifested psychologically or biologically.[24]

Yet the critically acclaimed Naturalism of *Futon* consists neither in the true-to-life realism of its representations, nor in its bold confession of the "facts" of the author's private life.[25] As Yanabu observes, "*Kare* does not exist in the world of people." Katai's use of "superfluous" pronominal appellations renders his protagonists categorically *incapable* of representing reality "just as it is," because it suspends them in a world that only exists between languages—specifically, between the spoken Japanese vernacular and the written vernaculars of the West. In fact, the revolutionary Naturalism of *Futon* must be located in this stylistic innovation itself, which magically transports both protagonists and readers from the paltry realities of daily life to an interlingual utopia. Of course, this is what most compelling modern literature does—manipulate language to endow the familiar with unexpected meanings, thereby stimulating the reader's imagination in new and exciting ways.

In *Futon* Katai invented a transcendental third-person subject that, in its very lack of ties to the social world of spoken language, could overcome many of the most divisive differences between author, narrator, protagonist, reader, text, and subtext. As Sōma Gyofū commented, "What makes me especially happy is that in confronting a literary coterie full of people who confuse Naturalism with realism and believe that its sole defining quality is the cold, objective description of phenomena, this work shows what Naturalism is really capable of—distancing by means of intellect and fusing by means of the emotions."[26] Finally, after two decades of experimentation in the laboratory of Japanese style, Katai had hit upon a formula for converting foreign letters into literary gold. Katai's *kare* exists somewhere outside the bounds of language, prior to the social construct of the proper name. "He" is not only the Protagonist of the unfurling story, but may also be the narrator as well as the author. And, finally, "he" is also the protagonist who is not "in the book," a Japanese subject who recognizes his own image in the universal truth of modern Western literature. By means of this invention, "contemporary Japanese life" becomes that which profoundly reverberates with "Western literature." The anxiety that inheres to the parodic condition can give way to the elation of discovering felicitous parities that bridge the gap between emulating self and eminent other. *That which is nature reverberates most strongly with the Other.* Thus Katai invites the reader not only to identify the protagonist with the author and other literary figures but also to include himself in the circle of identification.

The Westernesque Femme Fatale as Vernacular Text

Having duly acknowledged the import of Katai's innovative use of third-person pronouns in *Futon*, we must now attend to the fact that such innovation alone would not have been capable of inducing the broad sense of literary epiphany that this novella apparently afforded its first readers. In order to have the kind of impact that it did, as the long-awaited arrival of Japanese Naturalism *in practice*, it had to carry a narrative content that could make its style seem not only new but also necessary and inevitable. Although many critics have already noted the integral relation between the narrative style of *Futon* and its production of interiority, I would add that its deployment of the Westernesque femme fatale was an equally crucial element of its success. What enabled *Futon* to marshal sympathy from a readership that had been largely dismissive of Katai's maidenitis was its unprecedented representation of modern female interiority as enigma.

In *Futon* "that which is nature" finally boils down to the lowest common denominator of sex.[27] *Kare* is introduced by way of his obsession with a certain *kanojo*, and the questions that drive him throughout the narrative all revolve around the hidden "truth" of her sexualized interiority: did "she" want me? and did "she" have "impure" relations with that man? In search of the answers, "he" turns time and again to "her" letters. *Kare's* attempt to analyze "his Anna" begins with her "numerous emotion-laden letters" and "that feverish letter," later progressing to an invasive search through her desk for letters from her boyfriend. The vernacular siren of *Ukigumo* here takes the form of a written cipher, while the smitten male protagonist remains the doubt-ridden interpreter of her signs. And it is in the problematic relationship between writing and the "truth" of sexual desire that *Futon* reveals its own anxieties about language, gender, and cultural difference.

The amateur poet and teacher of *Jokyōshi* was also a "woman of letters." But she was neither siren nor cipher. Kuniko communicates in a language that is completely transparent, requiring no interpretive work on the part of her admirer; she simply loves him as he loves her. It is the Westernesque quality of her physical appearance that first impresses the protagonist and the reader. By contrast, the protagonist of *Futon* first comes to know his "Anna" through her writing.

It was around that time, received a letter, full of adoration, from a woman named Yokoyama Yoshiko, a student of the Women's College in Kobe, born in Bichū's Niimi-chō, a fan of his writing. The name Takenaka Kojō was somewhat known in the world for writing bibun-style novels, and until now quite a few letters had come from fans and idolizers in the provinces. It was "please correct my writing" or "please take me on as a disciple"—impossible to respond to each one. So, upon receiving that woman's letter too, curiosity was not stirred enough to think of writing back. But having received three impassioned letters from the same person, even Tokio could not fail to take notice. Said to be nineteen years old, judging from the phrases in the letters [her] expressions were surprisingly deft, an earnest plea to become Sensei's disciple and devote a lifetime to literature, no matter what may come. With the writing in an effortless cursive, seems to be an utterly high-collar woman. (73)

Here, high-collar aspect literally becomes a function of letters: the personal résumé conveyed in them, their "expressive" style, and even the effortless cursive of the handwriting. Fascinated by the image that emerges in her writing, the protagonist pulls out a map of Okayama,

Yoshiko's home prefecture, to look up Niimi-chō. He then examines the details of the map as though it might be a geographical representation of her body.

> The thought that such a high-collar woman existed in the middle of these mountains, ten *li* into the depths of the Takayanagawa valley from the San'yō line, made it seem somehow warmly familiar, and Tokio looked at every detail of the area, its topography, mountains, and rivers. (73)

Long before she becomes a physical presence in Tokio's life, he has already developed a physical attraction to the textual materials from which he constitutes her. It is not only the message conveyed in her letters but also the Westernesque beauty of their material form that appeals to him:

> Then, just when thought this would be sure to prevent a reply, to the contrary, four days later an even thicker envelope arrived, three sheets of blue-lined Western paper covered in small letters with violet ink, repeating over and over the plea to become a future disciple and not be abandoned, writing that wanted to study literature properly. Tokio could not but be moved by the woman's ambition. Even in Tokyo—even those who graduated from girls' schools didn't understand the value of literature, but from the phrases of the letter seemed to know everything so well, immediately sent a reply and established a mentor-disciple relationship. (73–74)

In essence, the protagonist of *Futon* falls in love with a woman who is quite literally a text. In fact, letters are Yoshiko's preferred means of self-expression, and they serve as the catalyst for all of the main "events" in *Futon*.

As we have already seen, Katai's rebellion against conventional decorum transformed not only his stylistic values but also his concept of the ideal woman. A hint of this new gender value can be found in the rhetoric of "Rokotsu naru byōsha" itself, wherein the phrase "writings thickly covered in white facial powder" strikes an uncanny resonance with the preface to *Ukigumo*. Just as Futabatei had invoked the images of Westernesque women's fashion—"roses blooming on heads"—to underscore the need for literary language to catch up with social reality, Katai likened stylistic decorum to the traditional cosmetic for Japanese women. We can easily infer the intended opposite here: the simile of raw description and the "natural look" of a woman wearing little or no makeup. Already, by the time of *Ukigumo*, schoolgirls had begun to look down on the traditional thick coats of white powder as a sign of "poor taste."[28]

In *Futon* the dichotomy of old and new in literary styles is neatly paralleled by a pronounced generation gap. In a passage often cited as evidence of the *Futon*'s status as a "social novel," the narrator describes the changes that characterize late Meiji Tokyo:

Society moves forward with each passing day. The trains changed the face of transportation in the city of Tokyo. Schoolgirls became an influential force, and one could no longer see any of the old-style girls of the days when he had fallen in love. And the youth held their own, taking a completely different attitude in everything, whether discoursing on love, discussing literature, or talking about politics, so that one felt it had become permanently impossible to connect with them. (72)

This distinction is given a gender slant, made particularly manifest in the two types of women represented by Tokio's wife and disciple. Here, the outmoded yet deeply ingrained body language of the "ducklike gait" does not mark the frustrated writer, as in "Shōjobyō," but rather his old-fashioned wife.

Former beloved—now wife. At one time, was certainly beloved, but now the times have changed. The rise of women's education in the last four or five years, the founding of women's college, the pompadour, the maroon culottes, there was no longer a single one embarrassed to walk side by side with a man. In such a world nothing was more pathetic to Tokio than to resign oneself to a wife who possessed nothing but docility and chastity, with the old-fashioned coiffure of the married woman and a ducklike gait. (74)

By contrast, Yoshiko's generation of Meiji schoolgirls have not only broken the mold of traditional decorum, they have also developed a new vernacular for the face, making it a transparent window onto a broader range of emotional states.[29]

[Yoshiko's] face is not so much beautiful as expressive, if it is extremely beautiful at times, there are also times when it can be somewhat ugly. There was a light in the eyes that was extremely active. The women of four or five years ago were utterly simple in the emotions they displayed and were only capable of displaying three or four types of emotion, such as the face of anger or the face of laughter, but by now there were many women who deftly displayed emotions in their faces. Tokio was always aware that Yoshiko was one of them. (76)

Just as Katai casts style as a critical measure of modern literary value, Tokio sees women as the measures of a man's worth. To Tokio, Yoshiko's generation of Meiji schoolgirls appears more liberated, more complex, more expressive, and infinitely more qualified for intimacy with the opposite sex based on mutual understanding, and all these qualities reflect extremely well on the men with whom they associate.

Going out on the streets, there are those on intimate walks with a beautiful, modern wife; upon visiting a friend, there is the young wife who joins the husband's party and eloquently enlivens the conversation; and then facing one's own wife, who doesn't even try to read the novels this one took such pains to write, turns a deaf ear and a blind eye to a husband's suffering and anguish, and simply wants to raise the children well—just could not help crying out loneliness. Could not help feeling, along with Johannes of *Lonely Lives*, the meaninglessness of the housewife. This— this loneliness was shattered by Yoshiko. Who could keep a still heart with a high-collar, up-to-date, beautiful woman disciple calling him *Sensei! Sensei!* with the admiration due to a person of actual consequence in the world? (74)

With her cutting-edge Westernesque appearance, language, and literary interests, Yoshiko, by merely calling him "Sensei," confers upon Tokio an honorary membership in the exclusive modern vanguard from which he had felt permanently alienated. Finally, we should note the facility with which Katai's ambiguously personed narrator can command the reader's sympathy without resorting to the narrow subjectivity of a first-person claim. The rhetorical question that closes the above quote, as enunciated by an objective third party, signals the reader to either identify with Tokio and affirm the universality of his emotions or be branded as a self-deceiving hypocrite.

In order to safeguard his newfound status as the "Sensei" to a high-collar beauty, Tokio goes to great lengths to maintain the illusion that he and Yoshiko speak the same language and share the same ideals. For instance, when his wife comments on Yoshiko's behavior, he is all too eager to demonstrate his superior understanding of her new-fangled ways. In the merchant-class neighborhood of central Tokyo where Tokio's sister-in-law lives, Yoshiko's sumptuous dress is enough to raise eyebrows. Even worse, from the perspective of the older generation of women, she is in the habit of taking late night walks with her male friends, stirring up neighborhood gossip. Tokio takes such complaints from his wife as a perfect opportunity to embrace the new woman and chastise the old. "Old-fashioned people like you just can't understand what Yoshiko does. If a man and woman should so much as walk or talk together, you immediately think it suspicious or strange, but that way of thinking and talking is in itself old-fashioned. Today, women also have self-awareness, so if there's something they want to do, they just do it." (75)

In front of Yoshiko herself, Tokio assumes the stance of an expert in new womanhood. Like Bunzō with Osei, he uses his private lessons to teach his protégée the literary language of the new woman according to his interpretation of key Western literary examples.

"Women must also be self-aware. It won't do to be dependent-minded like the women of old. As Sudermann's Magda said, there's no good in being the spineless type who just moves from a father's control straight to a husband's. As a new woman of Japan, one must think and act on one's own." Having said this, would talk about Ibsen's Nora, Turgenev's Elena, and the fact that the women of Russia and Germany were well endowed with both emotion and strength of will. "But being self-aware includes self-reflection, you know, so you can't just arbitrarily brandish your will and ego. You must be prepared to accept complete responsibility for your own actions." (75–76)

In a rare—and thereby suspect—moment of access to Yoshiko's thoughts, the narrator claims her to be a highly receptive, eager, and admiring student. "To Yoshiko, these lessons of Tokio's seemed more meaningful than anything, and admiration grew all the more. Thought they were more free, and had greater authority, than the teachings of Christianity" (76). As a reflection of the "man of literature" he sees himself to be, the composite image of Western literature, freedom, and the high-collar Yoshiko's admiring gaze powerfully appeals to Tokio's vanity. When that image is threatened by Yoshiko's newfound love, Tokio holds it together by offering Yoshiko his understanding—though barely able to contain his jealousy, he promises to act as the "protector" of her love. As Yoshiko's love affair develops against the staunch opposition of her parents, she increasingly frames her situation as the heroic struggle of new against old, a storyline that she has learned from Tokio himself, and one whose merits he cannot openly question without revealing his own hypocrisy.

Thus trapped in an ill-fitting mold of his own making—the high-minded literary mentor, enlightened in the ways of modern love—Tokio engages in the mental, emotional, and at times even physical contortions that constitute the main source of narrative interest in *Futon*. Much as he strives to maintain his image of Yoshiko as the Japanese embodiment of his pristine Western literary ideal, however, a more vulgar, popular image of the schoolgirl always lurks just beneath the surface of *Futon*. "Compared to other girls' schools, the Christian girls' schools are completely free with respect to literature. By that time there was a prohibition against reading books like *Makaze koikaze* and *Konjiki yasha*,[30] but, before the Ministry of Education's intervention, students could read anything so long as it wasn't at school" (74). Special mention of the forbidden novels *Makaze koikaze* and *Konjiki yasha*, both stories of failed love featuring schoolgirls, invokes the common media image of an integral connection between modern women's education, novel reading, and sexual desire, as captured in Kaminaga Ryogetsu's "High-Collar Song." The Ministry of

Education officially forbade schoolgirls from reading these novels on the claim that young women were particularly susceptible to the pernicious influences of reading, a notion that was further reinforced by newspaper reports of the scandalous sexual conduct of schoolgirls. Indeed, the public's interest in the seamier side of schoolgirl life was such that these best-selling newspaper novels were followed up by journalistic feature stories purporting to expose the real lives of schoolgirls, including a thirty-five-part series in the *Mainichi Shinbun* titled "Tales of Fallen Schoolgirls." According to the anonymous author of this series, a person who claims to have had years of experience in women's education, it had become common schoolgirl practice to use novels about romantic love as love letters, underlining the climactic love scenes of a novel in colored pencil and sending the book to a man to indicate one's own wishes.[31]

Tokio initially resists this popular sexualized image of female literary consumption by agreeing to act as Yoshiko's literary mentor. In addition to projecting his own pristine image of the Western new woman onto her, he thereby acknowledges her as a future *producer* of novels. Ironically, however, it is her very ability to produce texts that reinvigorates the sexualized image of the schoolgirl that Tokio invests so much energy in denying. The talent for self-expression that originally forged her bond with Tokio is also what makes Yoshiko a sexually suspect provocateur. In a rare moment of sardonic commentary, the narrator of *Futon* suggests that the accoutrements of the woman novelist are little more than an attractive front for an altogether different kind of trade.

Yoshiko's study, the eight-mat guest parlor, is noisy from the racket of people and children passing on the heavily trafficked road in front. By the Ikkan lacquer desk is a bookcase that looks like a miniature version of the Western-style bookcase in Tokio's study, on top of which there is a mirror, a rouge dish, a bottle of white face powder, and another large bottle full of potassium bromide. This, apparently, is taken when the head hurts something awful from nervousness. In the bookcase the collected works of Kōyō, the *jōruri* librettoes of Chikamatsu, an English textbook, and a recently purchased collected works of Turgenev that particularly stands out. And, when the future woman writer comes back from school and sits at the desk, does not just write, but rather writes many letters, so male friends are numerous indeed. Letters in the man's hand come in quite the numbers too. Among them one a student at the Higher Normal, and one a student at Waseda University, and that one had occasionally come to visit, apparently. (75)

If an "old-fashioned" public regarded women as passive consumers of literature who were thereby susceptible to adverse sexual influence, *Futon* ultimately casts suspicion on the modern Japanese woman as a self-conscious producer of texts: Yoshiko's free exchange of letters with many men leads to a forbidden exchange of passion with one, the manipulation and betrayal of another, and, finally, the early termination of her own budding literary career.

Tokio's obsessive scrutiny of Yoshiko's writing and sexuality constitutes a main motif throughout *Futon*, beginning with the opening chapter. As we eventually learn, at this point he has just discovered that Yoshiko has a boyfriend, a twenty-one-year-old Christian student of theology from Kyoto named Tanaka Hideo. Their affair began with a secret rendezvous in Kyoto on Yoshiko's way back to Tokyo from her parents' home. Although we are not privy to the details of how they first met, it is clear that the two must have been carrying on a correspondence for some time before their first tryst. An exchange of letters between Tokio and her parents quickly reveals the gap in Yoshiko's itinerary, whereupon she confesses to Tokio, swearing that her love is "sacred" (i.e., not carnal). With each new development in Yoshiko's love affair, Tokio's jealousy and nagging doubts escalate. As Fujimori Kiyoshi points out, it is Yoshiko's letters themselves, which contain the "secret" of her sex life, that constitute the true object of Tokio's fetishistic desire.[32]

First, the mere use of the plural first-person pronoun *we* in one of Yoshiko's letters sets off a storm of suspicion: "We have not only passion, but reason! What is this *we*! Why not write *I*, why use the plural!" (79) Like the tiny little *but* that tormented Bunzō, this single word sows a seed of doubt that continues to gnaw at Tokio's idealized image of "his Anna."

Among Yoshiko's words, Tokio found distasteful the use of the plural "we," and the way of talking as though an official promise of engagement had already been made. Found suspicious that such words would come from the mouth of a maiden in the flower of youth, still only nineteen or twenty. Tokio felt all the more keenly the changing of the times. Thought of how much today's schoolgirl ways differed from the maiden ways of the times when they had fallen in love. Needless to say, it is a fact that, from the standpoint of ideals and tastes, Tokio had looked upon these schoolgirl ways with pleasure. Having received an education from the olden days would never permit one to keep up as the wife of the Meiji man of today. It is his pet theory that women too must stand up, must fully cultivate the power of the will. He also, on not a few occasions, advocated this pet theory to Yoshiko. But upon seeing these newfangled, high-collar ideas in action, simply could not help knitting the brow. (84)

Tokio's idea of the new woman precluded the very notion of her sexual freedom. To the contrary, he tells Yoshiko that a woman's freedom could only be guaranteed by her virginity: "once the body is relinquished to a man, the woman's freedom is completely destroyed" (88). In the discursive terms of *Futon*, premarital sex for a woman is thus cast as retrograde behavior, much as Bimyō's narrator saw Okaku's infatuation as a throwback to the Tempo era.[33] Tokio has already lost Yoshiko's heart to another man; now the only important question is whether or not he has also lost her body, the foundation apparently necessary for his precious image of the Japanese new woman. Increasingly suspicious that the real meaning of Yoshiko's "we" is "we've had sex," Tokio searches for concrete evidence, this time turning to Tanaka's letters.

A passion between the two that could not be exhausted by any amount of writing—so frequent was the exchange of letters that Tokio, using the excuse of supervision, suppressed the conscience and looked through desk drawers and writing box when Yoshiko was out of the house. Ferreted out two or three letters from the man and quickly read over them.

The sweet words typical of a lover flowed everywhere. But Tokio labored to search out a greater secret. The traces of a kiss, the traces of sexual desire—might not these be apparent somewhere? Might not the relationship between the two have progressed beyond a sacred love? But what could not be grasped from the letters either was the true circumstances of that love. (85)

Just as Tokio had examined the map of Okayama as though it might be an extension of Yoshiko herself, his search for the traces of sexual experience in her love letters treats them as proxies for her body. As this virtually pornographic invasion of Yoshiko's privacy shows, Tokio's pursuit of the "true circumstances of that love" is nothing less than a desire to strip Yoshiko naked, to discover what really lies beneath the surface of her seemingly "effortless" and straightforward expressions. The underlying violence of this desire becomes yet more apparent when Tokio demands that Yoshiko produce Tanaka's love letters for her father to see, in spite of her own father's reluctance to press the point.

"And what view do you take of the relationship between the two?" Tokio asked the father.

"Well, we probably have to assume that they have had relations."

"At this point, I think it necessary to make certain, so should I have Yoshiko explain her trip to Saga [Kyoto]? She said that she first felt this love after her trip to Saga, and there must be letters to prove it."

"Now, now, there's no need to go so far . . . "

The father, while believing there to be a relationship, apparently fears this becoming a fact.

Unfortunately, Yoshiko just then came in bringing tea.

Tokio called [her] over to press for a show of letters from before and after that time in order to prove innocence, saying that there must be some letters that would give proof.

Upon hearing this, Yoshiko's face suddenly turned red. A considerable degree of distress made itself plainly evident in both face and demeanor.

"But recently, I burned all the letters from that time." The voice was low.

"Burned?"

"Yes."

Yoshiko's face dropped.

"Burned? That can't be."

Yoshiko's face reddened all the more. Tokio could not but be furious. The fact stabbed his chest with frightening force. (97)

Considering that Tokio has been searching for concrete textual evidence of the truth of Yoshiko's affair, it is extremely curious that "the fact" finally "stabbed his chest" only when he is denied access to her love letters. Ostensibly, the cause for his rage is the belated realization that Yoshiko has been deceiving him, that she must have already "had relations" with Tanaka. But it is also possible that his rage is sparked by the burning of the letters themselves: now he has been deprived of the primary object of his fetish, Yoshiko as text.

In fact, once he has been permanently shut out of the textual history of Yoshiko's love, Tokio sexualizes her completely, his rage quickly turning into an ugly rape fantasy.

Tokio's anguish that night was extreme. So vexing, the thought of having been deceived. No, infuriating, the thought of having earnestly done as much as possible for their love, while being robbed of Yoshiko's spirit and flesh—[her] all—by a mere student. If that's how it was—if the body had already been relinquished to that man, there was no point in valuing the virgin's chastity. I should have made a bold move and gotten sexual satisfaction. With this thought, the beautiful Yoshiko, who until now had been placed in the upper reaches of the heavens, seemed no better than the likes of a harlot, and felt like denigrating not just that body but also the beautiful attitudes and the expressions. And, writhing and writhing that night, got almost no sleep. Various emotions traversed the breast like black clouds. Tokio thought with a hand on [his] breast. Thought, maybe I should go ahead and have it this way. The body is sullied, already relinquished to a man anyway. Thought, at this point, perhaps send the man back to Kyoto, exploit that weakness, and have my own way. (97)

At long last the idol worship of the "maiden," so characteristic to the Kataian protagonist, has been shattered. The beauty Tokio had seen in Yoshiko—in her language, her attitudes, and her body—is rendered cheap by the profound shock of her deceit and the loss of virginity it attempted to conceal. If the physical purity of the virgin had offered a blank slate just waiting to be inscribed with the letters of the male imagination, Yoshiko's acquisition of her own sexual history expels her from the protagonist's imaginary world, where she once rubbed shoulders with Anna, Vera, Elena, and Magda, the eminent female Others of Western literature. Bereft of literary meaning, now she is just so much flesh, and Tokio's longstanding desire for her is reduced to the same level. In thus exposing the raw sexual desire that lies beneath the literary trappings of Tokio's love, *Futon* appears to fulfill the Naturalist objective of "revealing truth." As Suzuki points out, it is this revelation of "the ugly mind" (Hōgetsu) that contemporary critics embraced as a triumph for Japanese Naturalism.[34]

As we have seen, the narration of *Futon* primarily focuses on presenting Tokio's psychological responses to Yoshiko—how she became the object of his desire, how he felt about and responded to the news that she had fallen in love, and so on. The narrator is so closely tied to his protagonist that one could even argue that every description of Yoshiko has already been filtered through Tokio's consciousness. On the basis of the narrator's words alone, then, one might hypothesize that *Futon* draws no conclusions about the character of Yoshiko, but only about Tokio himself. However, the text takes a different approach, presenting the verbatim quotation of three of Yoshiko's letters and the partial quotation of a fourth. These texts stand out as the only undeniably direct representations of Yoshiko herself, in her own words. The first two relate new developments in her relationship with Tanaka, the third is an apology to Tokio for lying about this relationship, and the fourth is a formal greeting from Okayama after Yoshiko has been forced to return home with her father. Tokio's obsession with Yoshiko's letters and her sexualized interiority is paralleled by the text's insistence upon quoting her letters in full, only to expose their duplicity in the end. It is no coincidence that the first three are written in the vernacular, while the last one reverts to the formal epistolary style. Through the use of her own letters, *Futon* represents the Westernesque femme fatale as not only a retrograde Japanese parody of a new Western gender ideal but a stylistic traitor to boot.

The Japanese epistolary style was characterized by a set of rhetorical conventions and social formalities that were even more rigid than the rules for writing fiction in gabuntai or kanbun-chō. Seasonal greetings, polite inquiries into the addressee's health and wellbeing, use of the antiquated humble verb *sōrō*, and a high degree of circumlocution (particularly in references to oneself) are some of the trademarks of the formal epistolary style. To write a letter in the "vernacular" rather than the formal *sōrō-bun* was to abandon all of these conventions in favor of a style of communication that could imitate face-to-face contact. The letters to Katai from Okada Michiyo, the real-life model for Yoshiko, offer relevant examples of each style. Michiyo first wrote to Katai shortly after he published *Jokyōshi*, sending him two letters in the formal epistolary style requesting the favor of his tutelage. When these failed to produce a response, she resorted to the unorthodox approach of making an appeal in the colloquial. In thus flaunting stylistic conventions, she managed to create a linguistic self-portrait that may have struck Katai as the very embodiment of his literary ideals.

The particular effect of Michiyo's spoken style emerges most vividly in contrast to her epistolary style. As a point of comparison, here is an unmodified literal translation of the opening passage of her first letter:

in these most dreary days as rain brings ruination to the deutzia flowers how honorably passing time respectfully imagine taking up brush or perusing books near placid round window and from far far away offer humble admiration to sensei who knows not even whether or not such as one exists to suddenly thus offer letter must surely seem most suspect indeed but woman-child since entering age of discernment has been fortunate to know of sensei's great name and privately feels endearment and admiration and upon respectfully reading *no no hana* and *furusato* at last was overcome with admiration offering many humble apologies for undecorous behavior woman-child in humble prostration begs of sensei generous forgiveness and favor of reading letter offered from the depths of the heart[35]

This letter closely adheres to formal conventions, opening with a seasonal greeting, inquiring into the current conditions of the addressee, and offering apologies for the impropriety of sending a letter to a stranger. Particularly in its avoidance of personal pronouns, Michiyo's circumspect language pays respect not only to the addressee but also to the proper distance between strangers.

Compared to this stiff formality, the language of Michiyo's third letter verges on the flirtatious. Although Katai had yet to respond to her earlier letters, Michiyo takes full advantage of writing in the colloquial here to insinuate a certain kind of intimacy in their relationship. "Sensei, surely will kindly accede to the humble request made, right? with the intention of helping out a lone woman right, Sensei?"[36] The familiar tone of Michiyo's third letter—most conspicuously marked in the Japanese with the expression "nee sensei" (translated rather ineffectually as "right, Sensei?"), an intimate and casual form of address—completely ignores the fact that no actual relationship exists between the speaker and the addressee. While the man she calls "Sensei" has yet to acknowledge her letters with a reply, she refuses to acknowledge the actual distance between them. "Sensei" is no longer a respectful way of referring to Katai by title instead of name, but rather a second-person appellation that directly engages him in a virtual conversation. She further abandons the conventional humility of the circumspect self-referent "woman-child" to voice a direct emotional appeal in the feminine first-person I (*watakushi*). In order to capture the tone of the spoken interjections *nee, yo,* and *wa,* I have used first- and second-person English interjections in brackets below. All other uses of *I* reflect the use of *watakushi* in the original.

But [I mean] if Sensei still pronounces that this is no good, well I honestly don't know what to do [you know] things don't in the least go the way I want, so so frustrated that just want to die [I tell you] the world is after all called samsara, so it is only natural to be sad, but I just can't help from crying [I tell you] Sensei, please, please find it in your heart to save this pitiable woman. . . . (ellipses in the original)[37]

Even without the advantage of a face-to-face meeting with her chosen mentor, Michiyo seemed to have an intuitive grasp of just which feminine wiles would appeal to him. We can easily imagine that her daring use of the spoken idiom impressed Katai as a powerful example of direct self-expression uninhibited by the bounds of conventional decorum. Here Michiyo abandons an epistolary style that entrusts the relationship between strangers to a set of established linguistic conventions, instead creating a relationship on her own terms. Surely, we can hear the intimate feminine call of *nee sensei* echoing in the background of *Futon* 's claim that no one "could keep a still heart with a high-collar, up-to-date, beautiful woman disciple calling him *Sensei*! Sensei! with the admiration due to a person of actual consequence in the world." By means of this direct appeal, Okada Michiyo was finally able to entice Katai to step into the role she had already carved out for him. The seductive appeal of Michiyo's vernacular style thus provided Katai with the inspiration for Yoshiko, the consummate siren of vernacular letters.

Yoshiko's first quoted letter to Tokio—written "in the vernacular by an utterly graceful hand" (78)—conveys the news of Tanaka's unexpected arrival in Tokyo. Here, Yoshiko's writing does indeed closely mimic speech, opening with a disarmingly familiar tone. Toward preserving her image as the model student, she also invokes her mentor's own words repeatedly, almost as though to mollify him in advance.

Sensei—

Actually, had wanted to ask advice in person, but it was so sudden that acted on independent judgment.

Really, at four o'clock yesterday a telegram arrived from Tanaka saying that would arrive at the Shinbashi station at 6, so there's no saying how surprised I was.

Believing that not such a frivolous man as to come for no reason, was all the more distressed. Sensei, please forgive. I went to meet at the scheduled time . . .

. . . And then, I related everything already told to Sensei, and Sensei's deeply compassionate words, offering to become the witness and guardian of our sacred, sincere love into the future as well, whereupon [he] was deeply moved, and wept tears of gratitude.

. . . That one must not get involved in actual problems midway through one's studies, this precept of Sensei's [I] have completely absorbed and intend to uphold, but after getting [him] settled at the inn, since had made the trip all the way out here, ended up suggesting seeing the sights for just a day. Sensei, please kindly forgive this. (78–79)

The remainder of the letter appeals to Tokio's sympathy, explains the rationale for Tanaka's visit as a desire to protect Yoshiko from the wrath of her parents, and repeats the assertion that their love is "sacred" and their relations "unsullied." The second letter, written several months later, announces Yoshiko's bold decision to live with Tanaka as man and wife, in spite of her parents' continuing opposition. Here, she appeals to Tokio's sympathy by placing his judgment and understanding above that of her own parents.

As guardian, it is only natural that [you] should worry. But even after Sensei was so kind as to explain everything about us to [my] parents at home that time, [they] still do nothing but get meaninglessly angry and refuse to deal with [me], and this is simply too cruel; if disinherited, it just can't be helped. Fallen, fallen, [they] say practically in unison, but is our love something so frivolous? And [they] talk about the family face, but I am sure Sensei will permit that I am not such an old-fashioned woman as to fall in love according to parents' convenience.

    Sensei,

    I have made up my mind. Yesterday, there was an ad for a female intern at the Ueno library, and plan to apply for it. If the two of us work tirelessly, surely won't starve. (91)

Again, Yoshiko strives to use the language that she has learned from Tokio—that of the new, independent woman. Both letters proclaim her innocence directly and indirectly, framing her dilemma in terms that Tokio cannot easily reject. In the end, however, they become the indelible proof of Yoshiko's duplicity.

The clincher is the third letter, which Tokio receives the day after he has finally confronted "the fact" of Yoshiko's sexual maturity. The context in which Yoshiko writes and "sends" this letter demonstrates an extreme, even suspect, reliance on the written word—what does it mean to write in a language that mimics speech while actually refusing to speak? As for content, its frank admission of guilt casts a long shadow over her previous letters.

Claiming no desire to eat, Yoshiko would take neither lunch nor dinner. A depressing atmosphere filled the house. . . . The wife went upstairs to press the case for eating at least one bowlful to stave off hunger. Tokio was drinking saké with a bitter face to the desolate dusk. Shortly, the wife came back downstairs. When Tokio asked what [she] was doing, it turned out that in the dark room, without even turning on a lamp, [she] had been draped over a letter half written and left on the desk. Letter? Letter to whom? Tokio was furious. Pounded up the stairs with the intention of announcing that it was no good writing such a letter.

"Sensei, I beg of you . . . " heard an imploring voice. Still draped over the desk. "Sensei, I beg of you, please wait a little longer. I will write it in a letter to present to you."

Tokio went back downstairs. After a while, the maid was called by the wife to go upstairs to light a lamp, and [she] came back down with a letter for Tokio.

Tokio read with a thirsting heart.

Sensei,

I am a fallen schoolgirl. I used Sensei's good will, and deceived Sensei. Believe that offense is too great to be forgiven, no matter how many apologies are made. Sensei, please have pity on a weak person. The duties of the new Meiji woman Sensei taught, I was not putting into practice. In the end, I am still an old woman, without the courage to put new ideas into practice. I discussed it with Tanaka, and decided that no matter what might happen, this at least would never be divulged to another person. Nothing can be done about what has already passed, but made a promise to maintain a pristine love from now on. But, Sensei, when thinking that all of Sensei's agony has been caused by my own shortcomings, just cannot sit by and watch. All day today, this tormented the heart. Please, Sensei, kindly have pity on this pitiful woman. There is nothing left but for me to humbly implore Sensei. (98)

Surely, this must be the only epistle in the history of Japanese literature to begin with the fantastically "raw" statement, "I am a fallen schoolgirl." In the space of a few lines, Yoshiko has confounded the ideological assumptions that underpin Katai's Naturalist stylistic ideals. Her admission of guilt, of being an old-fashioned woman who lacks the "courage to put new ideas into practice," is articulated in the straightforward vernacular style that he has idealized as the best possible medium for representing truth. At the same time, the apparent lack of artifice in Yoshiko's previous letters is thereby exposed as a calculated effort to conceal the truth from Tokio. While Futabatei openly exposed the comical aspect of Bunzō's operations by characterizing Osei as a natural-born mimic, the text of *Futon* follows Tokio in his pursuit of the "truth," while leaving the character and interiority of Yoshiko open to question. If Osei's siren song of Truth rose up from the phantasmic space between languages in a profoundly multilingual world, Yoshiko's vernacular letters have emerged in a nearly monologic text from within the depths of a new phantasm for modern Japanese literature: that of female consciousness itself.

As Fujimori points out, "Yoshiko was fully conscious of the semantic effects of epistolary form, and excelled in presenting herself as a written sign (in this case, the sign of the high-collar schoolgirl)."[38] According to the terms of the text, Yoshiko's ability to express herself is directly related to her ability to both seduce and deceive others— or at least those who, like Tokio, have a personal interest in reading her uninhibited expressions as transparent windows onto her inner thoughts. Paradoxically, it seems that a woman's self-conscious use of transparent language and expression is actually *less* legible than the emotional signals that come from the old-fashioned woman who strives to repress her feelings.

But in less than a month Tokio realized the impossibility of keeping this lovable female disciple in his home. Docile wife made no effort to express discontent or show any signs of it, but humor gradually grew worse. An endless anxiety permeated the endlessly laughing voice. (75)

While Tokio has no trouble interpreting his wife's nervous laughter as an intense discomfort with Yoshiko's presence, it is Yoshiko's "emotion-laden letters" and other vernacular expressions that send him into paroxysms of doubt and desire.

Futon exposes the hypocrisy of Yoshiko and Tokio alike, but it is only Yoshiko who is so thoroughly defined by her use of language. The fact that Katai identified this ultimately stereotypical "fallen schoolgirl" with the very language he idealized as a Naturalist manifests his own complex relationship to language, without having it reflect poorly upon the idealized identity of the male writer. In "Shōjobyō" Katai employed a distinctly spoken form of the Japanese vernacular to establish the protagonist's fetishistic attachment to an idealized fantasy of the opposite sex and an increasingly anachronistic form of writing (bibun). The result was a story that exposed the writer-protagonist's loss of authority without successfully establishing a new form of authority for the author himself. By contrast, Futon marshals the exotic magnetism of the written language of vernacular translation to establish the disjunction between a male writer's idealization of vernacular style qua modern Western literature and the unanticipated opacities of a new Japanese gender icon that has taken on a life of its own. In so doing, Katai managed to affirm the transcendental value of the "raw" vernacular even while producing a text that undoubtedly relativizes that language's claim to represent the "truth." Thus, through a process of vernacular experimentation, a modern Japanese writer's anxiety about the instability of language was transformed from a portrait of the failed writer into a representation of the most conspicuously modern type of Japanese woman: the Westernesque femme fatale. The repeated claim by contemporary reviewers that the protagonist of Futon was deserving of the reader's "sympathy" is surely not unrelated to this innovative construction of the male Meiji writer's alienation. Although even Katai's most sympathetic readers were quick to point out that the character of Yoshiko was left vague at best, it is by means of her very opacity—more specifically, the underlying assumption of a female vernacular interiority that both demands and defies hermeneutic analysis—that Tokio himself attains an interiority akin to subjecthood.

The underlying importance of this new twist in the relationship between the male protagonist and the female object of his desire is suggested by the contrast between the critical reception of *Futon* and Oguri Fūyō's *Seishun*. Hōgetsu, who would champion *Futon* as the "bold confession of the human being stripped naked," had this to say about *Seishun*:

> If the description from start to finish cleaves to an awareness of [the protagonist's] faults and weak points, isn't that the descriptive method for creating a comic rather than a tragic protagonist? This suspicion is not inapplicable to the protagonist of *Seishun*. With a slight alteration he could become the protagonist of a comedy. Because [the author] was determined to treat him with seriousness, he was saved from comedy, but the result is that the work overall is unable to elicit deep sympathy from the reader. As one reads one is made to feel that the protagonist is a dislikable man, a cowardly man, and a pretentious man, but one is not made to feel that he is a pitiable man. . . . Upon reflection, it seems that there was insufficient wherewithal to turn people's thoughts directly from the protagonist's character to a broader fate through the realization that a person under such circumstances in such an age must debase his character in such a way. In other words, for the protagonist of such a major setting there was an insufficient depth of character.[39]

As Hōgetsu's reaction shows, Fūyō had served up an emblematic example of the pseudo-Western man in his male protagonist, Seki Kin'ya (see the introduction). At the same time, *Seishun* is also arguably the birthplace of modern Japanese literature's first truly new woman, though the term *atarashii onna* plays no part in this text. As Oka Yasuo points out, the character of Ono Shigeru was quickly overshadowed by the critical interest in Kin'ya himself, in spite of the fact that the novel's title must certainly refer to her own "youth" as well and that Shigeru is actually the one who matures over the course of the story.[40] Midway through the novel her relationship with Kin'ya results in an illegal abortion, a plot twist that certainly resonates with the popular notion of the fallen schoolgirl. Contrary to the kind of narrative expectations such a term sets up, however, Shigeru's disillusioning love affair does not bring about her downfall, but rather strengthens her determination to establish her own independence. As the novel comes to a close, she is preparing to set off for Manchuria to take up a teaching position at a school for Chinese women, having concluded that Kin'ya will never be more than the sum of his passionately spoken yet empty words. But Shigeru did not seduce Fūyō's critical readership in the same way that Yoshiko helped to seduce Katai's. In the end, her main narrative function was to underscore the pathetic hypocrisy of a man of many words rather than to represent a new model for Japanese womanhood. In spite of his own sympathy for women's struggles to achieve independence, Hōgetsu did not even seem to register the radically new character type that Fūyō had created in Shigeru. As the object of a desire that is finally revealed to be carnal at base, Yoshiko also serves to highlight the pathetic hypocrisy of a literary man, yet her status as a linguistic enigma within an otherwise seemingly transparent text simultaneously coalesces an image of his hidden psychological struggles that was capable of eliciting the reader's sympathy and self-identification. Thus the exoticism of the Westernesque femme fatale, rather than the domesticated realism of the Westernesque woman, helped to lay the foundation for Japanese Naturalism.

Futon ushered in the golden age of Japanese Naturalism that accompanied the last five years of the Meiji period. As critics and scholars have pointed out, Naturalist fiction only dominated the literary scene for a couple of years before new writers began to move out in other directions. Yet studies of Japanese Naturalism have consistently ignored its most spectacular achievement: the development of a completely new paradigm for the Japanese stage. The next chapter will explore this branch of Naturalism, in which the connection between new languages and the Westernesque femme fatale had literally fatal consequences.

Part 3

STAGING THE NEW WOMAN
The Spectacular Embodiment of "Nature" in Translation

From the maroon *hakama* culottes, the crested *haori* jacket, the *hifu* coat, the shawl, the *momoware* coiffeur, the English bun, and the ribbon, to the positioning of the hips, the posture of the body, the manner of sitting in the bicycle saddle, the turn of the head, the look in the eyes—it seems that all these elements have been planned out with extreme care. . . . In this manner the lady who has received the new education seems to cry out her desire to step up onto the new stage of the twentieth century.

—"Young Ladies' Bicycle Troupe Appears at Plum-Blossoming
Mukōjima," *Yomiuri shinbun*, February 2, 1901

As a commemoration of the resolution of the actress question, as a commemoration of the first liberation of women onto the stage, this woman's Nora should be remembered for many years to come.

—Kusuyama Masao's review of Matsui Sumako in
A Doll's House, Yomiuri Shinbun, November 30, 1911

On November 28, 1911, at the Imperial Theater, the Literary Arts Society (Bungei Kyōkai) headed by Tsubouchi Shōyō and his prize disciple Shimamura Hōgetsu staged the first public Japanese performance of Ibsen's *A Doll's House*,[1] translated into Japanese as *Ningyō no ie* by Hōgetsu and starring Matsui Sumako in the role of Nora. An overnight sensation, this performance established the actress as an absolutely indispensable element of modern theater for the first time in Japan. If Futabatei Shimei and Tayama Katai had distinguished their practice of radical vernacularist fiction with female characters who stood on the ambiguous cutting edge of Japanese modernity, the radical vernacularization of the stage literally employed the body of a woman as part and parcel of its project. Offstage, Sumako would also become Hōgetsu's extramarital lover, a scandalous liaison that could easily be read as an extension of the narrative line developed in *Futon*.

For Hōgetsu the Literary Arts Society's production of Ibsen marked the critic's determination to cross the divide separating literary ideals from actual practice. Three years before the Literary Arts Society began to train actors and actresses, Hōgetsu had already expressed his dissatisfaction with traditional Japanese theater and called for a return to "nature" in the manifestation of human emotions on the stage.

If we break down these three elements [of dance, nature, and exaggeration], then the element that must obviously be overthrown is the third one, namely, the exaggerated gestures, facial expressions, and the taste for the grotesque in kabuki. . . . The same can be said for all the performing arts that remain close to puppet art. As long as human beings are performing, then what necessity could there be for imitating puppets, which don't move by means of muscle? Despite the fact that this should obviously be replaced by naturalistic facial expressions, the stupidity of this exaggerated style of performance is that it has fallen to the level of exaggeration under the impetus of being more artistic, embracing the traditions of history, and whatnot. In a past age, when taste had not yet risen above puppets hanging on strings and that line, perhaps people could be content with this, but it can no longer suit the taste of Japan after our passage through the current of realistic, naturalist nineteenth-century European literary arts.[2]

It was this concept of a more naturalistic theater that he attempted to realize in his work with the Literary Arts Society, and the rave reviews of *A Doll's House* seem to offer ample testimony to his success. Above all, Matsui Sumako enjoyed critical acclaim for her "natural performance" of Nora.[3] Yet what could possibly be natural about a Japanese woman in the early twentieth century dressing the part of a Norwegian housewife, speaking in Japanese, and dancing the tarantella?

The Literary Arts Society enactment of a Norwegian domestic drama hovers somewhere between modern theatrical realism and the kind of exotic spectacle popularized in Europe by Gilbert and Sullivan's *The Mikado*. That contemporary audiences had so little trouble suspending so many layers of disbelief to embrace this radically exotic theatrical event as the arrival of "realistic" gender representation on the Japanese stage provides resounding testimony to the alchemical properties of translation. Indeed, the fact that Sumako was representing a woman from a modern European play translated into the Japanese vernacular formed the very basis for her acclaim, as I will show in the following pages.

Despite the all-too-apparent unnaturalness of Matsui Sumako's Western drag, however, little inquiry has been made into the reasons *why* her performance of a Norwegian housewife was immediately hailed by critics as the triumph of the modern Japanese actress and as a stunning example of natural gender representation. For instance, the seminal study of Matsui Sumako in English—Ayako Kano's *Acting Like a Woman in Modern Japan: Theater, Gender, and Nationalism*—sheds light on shifts in gender and theater paradigms that attended the emergence of the modern actress, but it also implies that Sumako's audiences would have assumed "a natural and transparent relationship between the signifier (Japanese woman's body) and the signified (the Western woman)."[4] Surely, it would be either naive or condescending to assume that Sumako's audiences saw her performance of Nora as the natural representation of a *Norwegian* woman. The striking visual incongruity of a Japanese woman performing the role of a Norwegian housewife serves as a clear reminder that there is no universal "woman." At the same time, the fact that contemporary audiences perceived Sumako's performance as a stunning feat of realistic gender representation reveals the emergence of a new concept of "woman" that could subsume even the most conspicuous of differences between individuals. Kano identifies this new phenomenon as a shift to an essentialist and expressivist definition of woman wherein "a certain essence of womanhood was thought to reside in the physical body, and this essence was thought to be expressed outwardly in appearance and behavior."[5] What I would like to suggest is that such an essentialist and universalist view of woman in Japanese theater was in fact enabled *by* Matsui Sumako's performances of modern Western drama, rather than the other way around. The fact is that prior to her performance in *A Doll's House*, there were very few among the theatergoing public who actually believed that a Japanese woman of her generation could convincingly play the role of a Western woman on the stage. To put it in another way, whatever essence was supposed to dwell in and be expressed outwardly by the physical body of woman, the majority of male theater pundits apparently believed that it had yet to take up residence in the body of a Japanese woman or that the bodies of Japanese women were not up to the task of "expressing" it. It was Matsui Sumako who would change their minds.

By the time that Sumako rose to the challenge of playing Nora in 1911, the idea that the new era was most provocatively figured by a new type of woman had long since prepared the way for the spectacular fusion of Japanese female body and Western literary image. Japanese intellectuals were already familiar with the New Women of Ibsen and Hauptmann as well as Hermann Sudermann's Magda (*Heimat*, 1893) and the defiantly single mother of Grant Allen's novel *The Woman Who Did* (adapted by Shimamura Hōgetsu as *Sono onna* in 1895). In *Futon* Tayama Katai rendered the first Japanese fictional incarnation of the New Woman in the figure of Yokoyama Yoshiko. His pathbreaking identification of the new generation of Meiji schoolgirls with the heroines of late nineteenth-century Western literature was soon echoed in Morita Sōhei's *Baien* (1909). This novel, even more sensationally autobiographical than *Futon*, presented a fictionalized account of the author's failed double suicide attempt with Hiratsuka Raichō, the future leader of the women's literary movement *Seitō*. Like Takenaka Tokio, the protagonist of *Baien* repeatedly interprets the heroine's words and actions according to his favorite works of Western literature, especially Gabriele d'Annunzio's *The Triumph of Death*. Even Sōhei's mentor Natsume Sōseki could not resist joining in the fray, creating his own portrait of the Meiji schoolgirl in *Sanshirō* as an example of the "unconscious hypocrite" from Hermann Sudermann's novel *Es War* (The Undying Past).[6]

In all these novels the male protagonists are drawn to an alluring female intellect whose underlying intentions defy their dogged attempts at interpretation. The new women of *Futon, Baien,* and *Sanshirō* are eternally enigmatic, distinguished by a conspicuous form of self-consciousness that not only attracts self-consciously modern men but also confounds them by expressing itself in a new language whose rhetorical conventions have yet to be established. Through the new idioms of "schoolgirl parlance," schoolgirl fashion, and convention-defying body language, the female educated elite of the late Meiji period established a new gender identity that seemed eminently self-conscious not only to novelists like Katai, Sōhei, and Sōseki, but even to the journalist who reported on the bicycle-riding young women at Mukōjima and concluded that the "extreme care" they seemed to invest in every facet of their appearance must signify their "desire to step up onto the new stage of the twentieth century." His metaphor unwittingly reveals an important connection between the incipient notion of modern femininity as a self-conscious performance and the birth of the modern actress. For several years before Matsui Sumako debuted on the stage of the Imperial Theater, the seed idea for the modern Japanese actress had already been germinated through increasing literary attention to the enigma of modern female self-consciousness and the new literary ideologies of Naturalism.

In this day and age it does seem entirely natural for an actress to perform the role of a woman. As a result, the story of Matsui Sumako easily lends itself to a larger narrative in which the advent of the modern actress in Japan was merely one more inevitable step forward in the march of modern progress—in this case, the development of theatrical realism and women's liberation from the yoke of tradition. Indeed, the fact that Sumako made her name in the performance of a Naturalist drama about one woman's awakening to the crippling effects of conventional attitudes toward family and gender seems the perfect emblem for such a narrative. Yet we have already become aware that the much vaunted nature of Japanese Naturalism was not a simple matter of realism. Moreover, as Kano reminds us, feminist critics and scholars have already debunked the view that there is something inherently natural about a woman "acting like a woman." The striking images of Sumako in conspicuous whiteface as Ibsen's Nora clearly demand a more complex narrative, particularly if we are to make sense of the claims of natural gender representation that were attached to her performances.

In fact, Sumako's stage performances of Hōgetsu's translations offered a stunning resolution to a problem that had confounded radical vernacularists like Futabatei and Katai: not the proper literary representation of women, but rather the proper literary deployment of the Westernesque in and as language. While the fictional characters of Osei and Yoshiko ultimately suggest the impossibility of reconciling the differences between the multiplicity of written and spoken languages that the vernacular was supposed to achieve, Matsui Sumako actually embodied and spoke the very language of vernacular translation, at least while she was performing on stage. If the protagonists of *Ukigumo* and *Futon* delighted to hear the songs their own language made when sung by Japanese women of the new generation, we can well imagine the heady effect Sumako's embodiment of "nature" in translation must have had on her audiences, not to mention the translator-director himself. Not surprisingly, her life as an actress—both onstage and off—would be powerfully circumscribed by a narrative pattern that had already been firmly established in vernacular fiction: the movement from New Woman to femme fatale. If, as Kano argues, this trajectory in Sumako's career was a function of the sexualized and commodified female body exceeding the limits of transparent expression placed upon it by the theater of logos, it can also be said that language itself also always exceeds the bounds of transparent expression. This is especially apparent when language is performative. And in modern Japanese literature the Westernesque woman qua femme fatale had personified the treacherous excesses of linguistic performance well before Matsui Sumako lent her body to the expression of Western texts on the Japanese stage. Thus the fact that contemporary audiences perceived Sumako's performance as a stunning feat of realistic gender representation would be best understood within the broader context of the longstanding literary relationship between the vernacular, translation, and the Westernesque femme fatale. What follows is an account of how this relationship unfolded on the modern Japanese stage.

[6]

Setting the Stage for Translation

Everything in Japan has enjoyed the benefits of Western civilization, except for drama, which runs around in circles trying to avoid these benefits.

—Osanai Kaoru's opening speech for the Free Theater's performance of *Lonely Lives*, Imperial Theater, October 1911

What most obviously and incontrovertibly set New Theater apart from all other forms of theater in Japan was its insistence upon translation. Osanai Kaoru, the leader of the Free Theater (modeled after André Antoine's Théâtre Libre and Otto Brahm's Freie Bühne), sought to bring about "a true era of translation in the theater circles of Japan."[1] Shōyō and Hōgetsu also believed in the power of and need for translation to transform the Japanese stage. But in contrast to the novel, which saw its first translation boom in the Meiji teens, the theater proved hostile to translation for nearly half a century. Long before the New Theater movement was launched in Japan, the influx of Western culture had spawned numerous attempts to revamp the Japanese stage. Yet the multiplicity of sign systems that converge to create the total sensory experience of the theater created an imposing, multilayered barrier of cultural difference. Unlike the novel, this barrier could not be dismantled by the verbal magic of literary translation alone. Virtually every aspect of Japanese theater posed a stark contrast to its Western counterpart—from the physical structure of the theater itself, the props and stage settings, the dress and makeup of the players, to the multiple languages of music, dance, gestures, and words and their particular combinations in performance, not to mention the underlying assumptions and sensibilities that dictated theatrical forms and endowed the plays themselves with meaning, emotional impact, and entertainment value. Such being the case, it is no surprise that the most successful early attempts at Westernizing the Japanese stage relate to the physical structure and material culture of the theater itself—the installation of tables, chairs, mezzanines and lobbies, and the replacement of candles with gas lighting.[2] A long and complex process with many twists and turns, the transformation of the Meiji stage did not progress in a straight, evolutionary line toward New Theater. Theater histories have often painted the picture of a slow but steady march toward modern realism, beginning with changes in Kabuki performance style and content and moving through the tawdry verisimilitude of Kawakami Otojirō's New School (*shinpa*) before arriving at truly Western-style realism, represented of course by the productions of Osanai's Free Theater and Shōyō and Hōgetsu's Literary Arts Society. However, it may be more accurate to describe the process not as a gradual accretion of increasingly realistic elements that culminated in full-fledged realism, but rather as a gradual dismantling of the many layers of resistance to new and exotic elements on the stage, one that finally made way for the most exotic elements of all: the translated text and the modern actress.

Snubbing Conventions: Stripping the Face, Speaking the Lines

To briefly catalogue some of the key developments in this dismantling process, we should look to the innovations of Ichikawa Danjūrō IX (1838–1903) on the Kabuki stage and those of Kawakami Otojirō's New School. With an illustrious career spanning the gap between late Tokugawa and Meiji Japan, Ichikawa Danjūrō IX has been described as perhaps the most famous of all actors in the history of Kabuki. He was particularly known for privileging his own sense of realism above the well-established conventions of Kabuki performance, appearing on the stage without the customary thick makeup, using language that sounded more like speech than dramatic line, and employing subtle dramatic pauses (*hara-gei*) at moments when the audience would otherwise expect a dramatic utterance or grand pose.[3] While his iconoclastic methods were not well-received by longstanding fans of Kabuki, they helped to draw a new audience of educated elites to a theater that the Tokugawa Shogunate had only tolerated as a necessary evil for the commoner classes. In Itō Sei's words, "All [Danjūrō's] efforts were in perfect accordance with the philosophy for the reform of drama developed later by Morita Kan'ya. The new intelligentsia of the Meiji period gradually became acclimatized to the realist, humanistic appeal of Danjūrō's techniques, accepted him, and came to see him as the foremost actor of the day."[4]

Kojin Karatani has described Danjūrō's acting techniques as a form of genbun-itchi, providing an incisive account of the latent paradigm shift that gradually transformed the Japanese stage:

With its origins in puppet theater, Kabuki began with the substitution of humans for puppets. In order to dehumanize the actors on the stage and make them more puppetlike, it was necessary to apply powder "in an exaggerated manner" and perform spectacular actions which "involved ridiculously grandiose movements of the body." The heavily made-up, boldly patterned face of the Kabuki actor was nothing other than a mask. What Danjūrō brought to Kabuki, and what can be seen even more clearly in later Shingeki performance, was the naked face.

Perhaps we may say that before Danjūrō's time it was the face decorated with makeup that conveyed a sense of reality to the audience. For them, the *face as concept* could be apprehended sensuously, in the same manner they found satisfaction in landscape as concept.... As Levi-Strauss has observed in *Structuralist Anthropology*, in primitive tribes ornamentation *is* the face or produces the face. It is through ornamentation that the face is endowed with its social existence, its human dignity, and its spiritual meaning. In other words, the human face was originally a figure, something like kanji, and it was only through a process of inversion that the "face as face" came into view.... It was only through such an inversion that the naked face—the naked face as a kind of landscape, took on meaning in and of itself and what had been insignificant became profoundly significant.[5]

On the stage, this incipient "vernacularization" of the body necessarily preceded the transformation of language that defined the modernity of the Japanese novel. As Karatani rightly points out, certain aspects of early Meiji theater foreshadowed later developments in the field of Japanese fiction. Yet the complexity of the performance art and the primacy of performance over text in Kabuki theater ensured that the vernacularization process would be completed in the written arts long before it could thoroughly transform the stage.

As we have already seen, the use of colloquial diction in the vernacular novel could only attain the status of writing through the process of translation, which infused ordinary words with the exotic aura of the foreign. On the stage, too, language had to be more than just ordinary, everyday "talk." Like the written arts, the theatrical enunciations presented on the Japanese stage were quite distinct from those of daily speech, employing rhythmic elocution that often followed the 7–5 syllabic pattern that forms the basis for Japanese poetry. Danjūrō attempted to break free of this convention, claiming a preference for imitating "speech" (*hanashi*) in his lines. But rather than a more colloquial style of talking, he apparently used difficult Chinese diction and even began his longer monologues by informing the audience, "I will now proffer a speech" (*tadaima enzetsu itasu de gozarō*). As a result he alienated many in his audience, who complained that his lines were "incomprehensible."[6] His attempt to anchor his lines in the weighty language of the educated elite reminds us that in the arts, even those which value performance over written text, the development of a vernacular style is not a simple matter of imitating "speech." In fact, the very lack of interest in written texts in Kabuki may have actually impeded the development of a vernacular language for the stage, since it rendered translation both unnecessary and unwelcome. If Ishibashi Shian was alienated by the descriptive language of Futabatei's vernacular *Aibiki*, we can easily imagine how his contemporaries would have reacted to a theatrical production in which all the players spoke a vernacular Japanese that sounded so strange. It took nearly two decades for Japanese readers to accept and appreciate this kind of literary language in the novel, and it would take nearly four decades for a significant number of Japanese theatergoers to appreciate its actual enunciation on the stage. Even in 1904 there was still a tremendous gap between Japanese stage language and the translated vernacular of literature, as Matsumoto Shinko points out with respect to Osanai's translation-adaptation of *Romeo and Juliet*.

The criticism of Osanai's translation mostly centered on the dialogue between Kumeo and Yurie. For instance, in those days in Japan, lovers would never say "I love you" to each other. In traditional dramas, girls are often more forward than boys in the love scenes; however, they do not reveal their thoughts so directly. Furthermore, Osanai's use of the word *kekkon* (marriage), which at that time was merely a legal term, contributed to the foreign and unnatural feeling to the words spoken by the actors of the Masago-za production.[7]

As we recall from Osei's pronouncement of "truth," in the performative context, speech that imitates translation easily spills over into the realm of the absurd. Without the intervention of nearly thirty years' worth of *written* texts, in which the novel played a central role, the vernacularization of the Japanese stage could not have been completed.

What Conventions? or, New School as Blank Theater

If the longstanding conventions of Kabuki theater proved highly resistant to change, the new era of Meiji did clear enough space for a few upstarts to thrive in the field of entertainment. Ultimately, it was the New School—a mongrel brand of theater that in many respects imitated Kabuki, but did not adhere to any consistent set of theatrical conventions—that made the greatest contribution to clearing the stage for translation. On the one hand, the rise of the New School showed that it was possible to develop a commercially viable theater outside the confines of the Kabuki world; on the other hand, its appropriation of Western drama—especially Shakespeare—also convinced the literati that only translation could produce a truly new theater.

Originally known as *sōshi shibai* or politicians' plays, New School theater traces its roots back to 1888, when Freedom Party politician Sudō Sadanori hit upon the idea of performing contemporary political novels on the stage as part of the party's propaganda efforts.[8] A few years later his lead was followed in Yokohama and Tokyo by fellow Freedom Party member Kawakami Otojirō, who was to become the greatest impresario of the New School. Kawakami had no formal training whatsoever in the art of acting. What he did have was an uncanny ability to anticipate and satisfy the desires of his audience, whether it was a Japanese public hungry for vivid representations of the Sino-Japanese war (1894–95), Americans and Europeans eager to see exotic representations of Japanese manhood and womanhood (1899–1902), or again Japanese audiences curious to see what Kawakami had brought home from his tours of America and Europe (1903). If there is anything that unifies his work from these three very different periods, it would seem to be the great flexibility afforded to a live performance art that does not adhere to any particular set of theatrical standards or literary conventions.

The first sign of Kawakami's genius as an impresario could be seen in 1894, with the onset of the Sino-Japanese war. In August he produced *Sōzetsu kaizetsu nisshin sensō* (The wondrous and magnificent Sino-Japanese War), and its immediate success inspired a trip to Korea to witness the war in person. Upon his return to Japan, Kawakami then staged a reenactment of what he had purportedly "seen and heard on the battlefield."[9] Like the newspapers, whose circulations skyrocketed from 1894–95, Kawakami's theater troupe reaped the full benefits of the war. The fact that he was not trained in the longstanding conventions and artistic traditions of Kabuki enabled him to create a spectacle that boldly laid claim to journalistic realism, shrewdly capitalizing on the public's hunger for representations of the war abroad. Kawakami's play took its raw material not only from the war itself but also from battle scenes in two French plays.[10] Its claim to journalistic realism was thus only a claim; of greater importance was its manner of representing the war through live action scenes. In November 1894

Danjūrō also tried his hand at a war play, but it was a flop. "Danjūrō dressed up as a sailor and used sticks of dried fish to demonstrate the movements of the navy battleships. He tried, in other words, to portray the war by *talking* about it."[11]

This phase in the development of Kawakami's New School theater lasted only as long as the war itself—once hostilities were over, the fickle public lost interest in this brand of "realism" and his troupe was beset by severe financial difficulties. The next major development was a tour of the West that began in the United States in 1899. It was during this tour that Kawakami's wife Sadayakko, a former geisha, became an actress.[12] For their first show in San Francisco, he performed *Kojima Takanori* and she performed the dance of *Dōjōji*. Both of these plays belong to the standard repertoire of Japanese theater. As we have already noted, Kawakami himself had no formal training in any tradition of Japanese acting. As a professional geisha, Sadayakko was well trained in the art of dance, but she was not one of the scant handful of women trained in Kabuki performance. The Kawakamis' idiosyncratic performances of Kabuki standards would no doubt have met with an icy reception on the Japanese stage. But the matter of professional training had little meaning for American audiences, whose primary interest lay in the exotic spectacle of Sadayakko's dance and Kawakami's use of judō moves. Once Kawakami figured out what the American public wanted to see, he made up his own play combining the dance of *Dōjōji* with the sword fighting of another Kabuki standard, *Saya ate*. Titled *Geisha and the Knight*, this was a representation of Japan and the Japanese theater that many critics consider to be a national disgrace.[13] Through Henry Irving's introduction the Kawakami troupe gained entrance to the hallowed halls of the Coronet Theater, where his production of *Geisha and the Knight* provoked such an enthusiastic response that Kawakami's troupe was invited to perform at Buckingham Palace. When he brought this production to the World Exposition in Paris, he and Sadayakko also enjoyed the critical acclaim of such cultural luminaries as Paul Valéry, André Gide, Paul Klee, and Isadora Duncan, and a fascinated young Picasso even made several sketches of "Madame Yakko" on stage.

If Kawakami had presumed upon the ill-informed, exoticist curiosity of European audiences in his productions of "Japanese theater," after his return to Japan he would exploit the same kind of curiosity in domestic audiences by producing a series of Shakespeare adaptations in Japanese. In 1903 his troupe performed *Othello* (February, Meiji-za), *The Merchant of Venice* (June, Meiji-za), and *Hamlet* (November, Hongō-za). Kawakami's troupe was not the first to perform Shakespeare on the Japanese stage. In 1883 Inoue Tsutomu published a free rendition of *Merchant of Venice* titled *Seiyō chinbun jinniku shichiire saiban* (A strange story from the West: The trial of pawned human flesh). The sensational nature of the story made it a bestseller, and two years later it was adapted for performance on the Kabuki stage as *Sakuradoki zeni no yononaka* (A time of cherry blossoms and a world of money).[14] But Kawakami was the first to model his performance of Shakespeare after the stylistic mode of Western theater. He called this new venture *Seigeki,* a term first used by Ōgai to distinguish spoken drama from opera. In Kawakami's usage, the term also took on the connotation of "correct performance of Western drama."[15] Essentially, this was an attempt to physically reproduce the kind of stage he had seen during his overseas tours: using large props and lighting, removing the *hanamichi* entrance ramp from the stage, and performing plays based solely on spoken lines and gestures.

Bound to neither theatrical nor textual tradition, Kawakami was able to respond very quickly to his latest audience and to his audience's latest interests. As one of the few Japanese of his day to have seen a Shakespeare performance on the Western stage, he laid claim to a certain kind of cultural authenticity for his Seigeki movement. But for members of the literati that claim was severely limited by the fact that Kawakami showed little interest in Western drama as literature. When Kawakami's troupe first arrived in Boston, Henry Irving and Ellen Terry happened to be in town performing Shakespeare's *Merchant of Venice.* Possibly one of Kawakami's first experiences of a play performed solely on the basis of spoken lines and gestures, without the accompaniment of music, dance, and narration, it may have struck him as an easy feat compared to the Japanese theatrical standards to which he was accustomed. After seeing the production, he decided to present his own version in Japanese, which consisted of simply imitating the gestures of Irving and Terry and mouthing gibberish to suit the action.[16] In this sense, he followed in the Kabuki tradition of valuing live performance far above written text. Thus while Kawakami's work liberated the stage from the tight grip of many theatrical conventions—replacing carefully patterned movements with live action, presenting an actress as a main attraction, and getting rid of the dance, musical accompaniment, and narration customary to virtually all forms of Japanese theater—it left the most important one intact: the treatment of the written text as nothing more than a loose guideline for performance.

As a case in point, Kawakami commissioned Emi Suiin to adapt *Othello* for his stage. We recall from the previous chapter that Katai's mentor could not read any Western languages; he based his adaptation on a translation by Tozawa Koya. As Kano's reading shows, the Suiin adaptation had a logic all its own:

The hero of the Japanese version is called not Othello but Muro Washirō. He is described as a "new commoner" (*shin heimin*), a term for former outcasts newly incorporated into the status of commoner under the Meiji government. He is a Japanese from the lowest caste who has been struggling to gain the status of a full-fledged national subject through his military conquests. While a "*shin heimin*" may be the closest thing corresponding to the "Moor" of Shakespeare's Venice, the designation of the Japanese Othello as a "*shin heimin*" produces its own associations and its own logic. Lieutenant General Muro Washirō's success as a military man is the precondition for his being considered Japanese, and this logic is confirmed by the repeated discussion of how one should or should not behave "as a military person." . . . Othello is undone by his passion for a woman, and this is most unmilitary and unmasculine behavior.[17]

The metamorphosis of Othello into Muro Washirō is but one instance of the adaptational mode that characterized much of Meiji theater before the advent of the Free Theater and the Literary Arts Society. Kabuki and New School players also presented adaptations of Samuel Smiles's *Self-Help*, Bulwer-Lytton's *Money*, numerous works of Shakespeare, Schiller's *Wilhelm Tell,* and Sardou's *Tosca,* just to name a few prominent Western examples.[18] As in the case of fiction, an interest in new stories told in familiar yet novel ways took to the stage long before players and audiences developed a taste for the truly radical departure of translated drama. And, again, we find an integral connection between adaptation and a kind of parody that many members of the literati found disturbing and distasteful. From their perspective Kawakami's "Shakespeare" must have looked like a travesty of the worst kind. Its execution on stage was even more "loose" than Suiin's adaptation. Kawakami decided to have the Iago character shot to death at the end of the play, but the people he hired to play the soldiers had nothing to do with the theater, and on opening day they mistakenly shot Othello instead.[19] In his critical meditations on comedy six years earlier, Shōyō had already pointed out that a few slight changes to the text of *Othello* could transform the tragedy into a comedy. In his review of Kawakami's production, which he attended upon opening day, Shōyō remarked that it was on the verge of doing just that.[20]

Subject to Translation: The Theatrical Body Vernacularized

What reform-minded intellectuals shared in common was a desire to make the Japanese stage more literary, to elevate it to the hallowed status of (Western) text. Following a logic that had already been well established in the case of the modern vernacular novel, they also agreed that this could only be achieved by beginning with translation, as opposed to adaptation or even composition. Shōyō's involvement with the translation of Western drama traces back to a time when Osanai and Hōgetsu were still too young to read English literature: in 1884, he published a translation of Shakespeare's *Julius Caesar* titled *Jiyū no tachi nagori no kireaji* (A parting blow from freedom's sword). His response to Kawakami's adaptations of Shakespeare was to translate and produce the same plays himself—specifically, the court scene from *The Merchant of Venice* in 1906 (Kabuki-za) and *Hamlet* in 1907 (Hongō-za). When Osanai wrote that none of the Western plays produced by Kawakami "deserve to be called translation,"[21] he invested the term with the aura reserved for the highest echelons of cultural production. In an open letter to actor Ichikawa Danko, he announced his intention to focus the Free Theater's efforts on the production of translated plays.[22] One year after the production of *A Doll's House*, Hōgetsu concluded that only the translation of Western plays could provide the necessary foundation from which Japanese actors could learn the new genres of modern drama. In his view a Japanese actor would find it nearly unbearable to perform in a Japanese mood play without having first worked with the genre by way of Maeterlinck; the proper order of things was to begin with the translation of an already well-known and critically acclaimed Western work in a particular genre, such as the social problem play, then proceed to an equivalent Japanese composition if a suitable one was available.[23]

From early on, Shōyō had considered Shakespearean drama as the best vehicle for reform, and the complete translation of Shakespeare plays became his lifework. By contrast, the next generation of theater reformers looked to the father of Naturalist drama for their inspiration. In 1907, at the suggestion of Osanai Kaoru and Yanagita Kunio, the Ibsen Society was formed. Its membership included Tayama Katai, Shimazaki Tōson, Hasegawa Tenkei, Kanbara Ariake, Tokuda Shūsei, Masamune Hakuchō, and Akita Ujaku, and their monthly discussions of Ibsen's work were published in the journal *Shinshichō*.[24] If Shōyō's response to Kawakami's Shakespeare could be summed up as an insistence upon translation over adaptation, the next generation's response to both Kawakami and Shōyō could be summed up as an insistence upon the translation of Ibsen over Shakespeare. Looking back on the days of the Ibsen Society, Masamune Hakuchō recalled that "for love of Ibsen even Shakespeare was dismissed as a blockhead" and "for producing Shakespeare Tsubouchi Shōyō's Literary Arts Society was a constant target of their sneers."[25] On November 27, 1909, at the Yūraku-za, Osanai Kaoru's Free Theater presented its first performance, Ibsen's *John Gabriel Borkman*, translated by Mori Ōgai. Almost exactly two years later, Hōgetsu led the Literary Arts Society's production of *A Doll's House (Ningyō no ie)*. At the heart of this divergence over theatrical models was a fundamental disagreement over the proper relationship between the exotic Western text, the Japanese reader-writer, and the Japanese body itself. Briefly stated, Shōyō sought to fuse Western and Japanese conventions in a way that would simply refine the content of the Japanese theater, rather than marking a radical departure from it. By sharp contrast, in choosing to produce Naturalist Western plays translated into the modern Japanese vernacular, both Osanai and Hōgetsu sought to overturn a centuries-old tradition of stage performance and all the painstaking physical training upon which it was built.

Shōyō's second production of *Hamlet* for the Literary Arts Society in May 1911 offers a useful illustration of the differences between himself, Hōgetsu, and Osanai. Having deep personal ties to Edo literature and performing arts, Shōyō was always reluctant to abandon native forms and conventions in his quest to elevate the status of the literary arts to meet the Western standard. Typically he sought more limited changes in content, such as an emphasis on character development or a repudiation of the vulgar themes of the Edo period, while leaving intact basic forms like gabuntai for fiction (as in *Shunpū jōwa* or *Tōsei shosei katagi*) or *jōruri* for the play script (as in *Jiyū no tachi nagori no kireaji*). In short, he was not a great champion of radically exotic forms. To the contrary, his attachment to Shakespeare was fostered in large part by the numerous similarities he found with the popular Japanese theater that had enthralled him as a boy and the many parallels he saw between Meiji Japan and Elizabethan England.[26] Shōyō's *Hamlet* thus became an exercise for the Japanese body to remember and refine native forms of both verbal and bodily stage language, rather than to learn new ones. First, he translated the script into the medieval language of kyōgen plays, on the premise that the language of an Elizabethan playwright should be rendered into a historically equivalent form. Second, he forced the lead actor, Doi Shunshō, to forget everything he had learned from his English acting teacher in favor of the Kabuki-based performance style Shōyō had envisioned for the play.[27] (Incidentally, it was also in this production of *Hamlet* that Matsui Sumako made her stage debut as Ophelia, though it is certainly not the role for which she is most remembered. It was Shunshō's performance of Hamlet, not Sumako's Ophelia, that attracted the most attention at the time. Shōyō's approach to reforming the stage was apparently not conducive to creating a vehicle for the modern actress, an issue to which we shall return later.) In focusing on Shakespeare, Shōyō had set his sights on a "national theater" that would combine the strengths of native conventions with Western realism in a way that he believed would appeal to a broad public. A characteristically outspoken Osanai responded by dismissing Shakespeare as outdated and irrelevant.

Looking at the plays that Kawakami has produced—*Othello, Hamlet, Monna Vanna*, etc.—none of them deserve to be called translations. *The Merchant of Venice* and *Hamlet* put on by the Literary Arts Society, along with Sadanji's *Merchant of Venice* and *L'amour médicin* by Moliére at least had critical value as translations, but they were only fragments of the entire work. And the original works are also old, so their translations did not answer to the needs of the new era.[28]

Even Hōgetsu, Shōyō's prize disciple, remarked that the Literary Arts Society production of *Hamlet* would best be viewed as a classic, since its style of presentation did not speak directly to the contemporary sensibility. Hōgetsu's relationship to Japanese theater was much closer to Osanai's proudly stated position: "We are human beings who have nothing whatsoever to do with today's theater circles. We are simply trying to create our own little world apart, wherein we shall live and offer shelter to our like-minded fellows."[29]

By the tail end of the Meiji era, there were enough like-minded literati to support the "world apart" that New Theater created on the stage, including the strange language of vernacular translation and the exotic body language that necessarily accompanied it. What they looked for in New Theater was not something stylistically familiar that would combine the strengths of two distinct traditions, but rather something radically new and distinctly anticonventional. Young members of the literati especially shared Osanai's passion for the new, as exemplified by Watsuji Tetsurō's almost intoxicated prose.

It is a fact that contemporary Japanese civilization is chaotic and lacking unity. I feel extremely interested by the fact that it is possible to appreciate new Western plays along with those youth who possess a passionate love of the arts of the Edo period. While such youth are earnestly singing the praises of Edo civilization, a person like myself who has abandoned the old traditions without leaving so much as a trace can embrace, from the bottom of his heart, the shabby, half-baked, exotic, and new civilization of recent times. To me, anything that is new looks beautiful. Just like people who love the olden days will unstintingly praise anything that is old.

In terms of seeing plays as well, the experimental productions of the Free Theater bring to me a strong, strong satisfaction. There are people who say that it is strange for Japanese people to put on plays in which they act as Westerners, but what we demand is not the perfect imitation of Westerners' behavior and mannerisms. In acting as Westerners, it is only necessary to give off an exotic air. Even in putting on a Wedekind play, all that has to be done is to pour into the bottom of our consciousness, without our realizing it, the fact that this kind of *life* never existed in the Japan that had Danjūrō and Kikugorō.[30]

In spite of Shōyō's leadership role, the same premium on the new and different ultimately held sway at the Literary Arts Society Theater Institute as well. As a former student of the institute recalled, "In those days we were being tyrannised by the dogma that novelty was nobility, and the old-fashioned was ill-fashioned. . . . In producing plays, everything was geared towards a single principle—Naturalism—indeed so much so that we all felt that we would even die for this cause."[31] If, in the case of the novel, the exoticist impulse was often obscured by the Naturalist rhetoric of truth, the embodiment of translated texts in Japanese New Theater brought it center stage.

Speaking in Texts: The Exotic Language of Translated Drama

Watsuji's account of the Free Theater's 1910 production of Gorky's *The Lower Depths* (1902, English translation 1912) illustrates just how willing the audience was to suspend all manner of disbelief in order to commune with the exotic script.

First the curtain opens. A filthy basement room unfurls before one's eyes. Is the audience constantly aware that this basement room is just a small room on the other side of the footlights of Yūraku-za? No, they surely try immediately to see a corner of life before their eyes. This is the first sign (of translated drama). Next, the audience becomes aware that this basement room is a cheap lodging in Russia. And then their auditory senses are attacked by the familiar voices of Kōjirō (Ichikawa, II) and Sakinosuke (Ichikawa). The audience is aware that the words being manifested by those voices are Japanese. But this awareness momentarily sinks below consciousness, and what enters the mind of the audience are the "human beings" in this dilapidated lodging house; the thoughts and emotions possessed by these "human beings." The costumes and gestures of these human beings constantly furnish a prodding to the depths of audience consciousness that this is not Japan but Russia, while on the surface they attack the minds of the audience with nothing but their expressions as human beings. This is the sign of translated theater. In order to savor this play it is not necessary for the audience to constantly consider the fact that the people in it are Russians. Yet that fact is always lurking at the bottom of their minds, and, when necessary, it rises to consciousness.

For players of translated drama the key to performance is, first of all, how to slip these things smoothly below consciousness and how to hint at them quietly, persistently, and yet without providing undue stimulation.[32]

This kind of double vision—the simultaneous recognition of conspicuous difference and universality in the category of the human being—reflects much more than a willingness to suspend disbelief. The demand for translation in the production of modern drama marks a desire that propelled much of Japanese Naturalist theory and practice: not only to discover felicitous parities between self and other (which, in the case of drama, might be achieved through skillful adaptations), but to forge a conspicuous identification with the foreign, one that would affirm the possibility of a profound identification with the other *in the face of obvious differences*. In other words, the privileging of translation above adaptation and even composition on the modern Japanese stage marks a distinctly exoticist desire to identify with but not assimilate the foreign.

In fact, it might even be said that, for some New Theater proponents, the conspicuous identification with the foreign had already become a kind of second nature, so to speak. As a case in point, Watsuji attacked the adapted play not only for domesticating the foreign text but also for requiring an impossible reconciliation of its exotic and domestic elements in the process. In his view the greatest sin of adapted drama is its demand that the audience *suppress* their knowledge of and associations with the original text and its author.

Whenever I see a Western play that has been rewritten to fit Japanese society, I am horribly repelled. I would have respect for something called an adaptation if it were the case of a Japanese poet who had simply borrowed raw materials and composed something out of Japanese sentiments, but something that has virtually taken the lines and the plot wholesale and simply *edited* them to match Japanese customs is like a woman's face painted with spots of white powder. If the *exotic* quality of the thoughts and emotions is plainly apparent to the eye, then to force the beholder to see this as Japanese custom is a truly unsettling way to manage sentiment.

From my way of thinking, the appearance of Kaburagi Hideko feels laughable. *When put on the stage, Ibsen's artistry will surely become duly manifest*, but how torturous it is for us to have to keep in mind the fact that Hedda's name has been changed to Hideko, and to watch the play while to some degree rolling back our feelings of the exotic. Recently, women like Hedda and Nora have also begun to sprout up in Japan. But whenever I see such new women in Japan, I can't help but think of Ibsen. If we were to depict such a woman, we would surely bring the name of Ibsen into the conversation and create something that would enable people to see the play while thinking of the phantom called Ibsen. And yet when one sees the Hideko play one must forget the name of Ibsen as much as possible.[33] (emphasis in original)

Paradoxically, according to Watsuji's logic, it is a Japanese adaptation's superficial claim to *Japaneseness*—not its superficial relationship to a Western text—that strains the credulity of the well-read audience member, who knows that what really lies beneath the "spots of white powder" is not a Japanese woman's face but an exotic text by a foreign author. We should note that the implied equation here between the naked or "natural" face and the exotic Western text takes the rhetoric of Katai's "Raw Description" and *Futon* to its logical extreme. To the Japanese reader of Western texts who fully expects an experience of the exotic from a trip to the theater, it is the effort to make a Western play appear more Japanese that calls undue attention to itself in the most unnatural way of all.

Although Futabatei's translations certainly laid the groundwork for it, the kind of double vision documented by Watsuji and implied in the practices of Osanai and Hōgetsu was probably inconceivable to the first generation of Meiji literati. In fact, Futabatei explicitly dismissed the notion of a universal "human being" as a basis for literary practice:

Novelists over there [in Russia] often say that, in novels, they manifest the spirit of the age through individual characters. In response, some will surely argue that the thinking of Russian novelists is narrow, that they should rather depict all of life and the human being, but I don't think it is necessarily narrow after all. We may talk about life and the human being, but when it comes to thinking about them and actually writing about them, it turns out that we cannot get beyond life and the human being in the present moment in Japan. Broadly speaking, the human being must include everything from past and present to East and West, but that is ultimately impossible to achieve.[34]

From this perspective the very notion of identifying with the embodiment of a foreign text on the Japanese stage as a representation of the universal human being could only seem absurd. As we have already seen, the exoticist or Futabateian approach to literary translation seeks to preserve linguistic difference even in the attempt to bridge the gap between two languages. The result is a radical transformation of the target language, the creation of a vernacular style that hangs suspended in the phantasmatic space between languages. The attempt to then physically reenact this kind of translation on the stage required not only a grand conceptual leap but also a radical transformation of the body itself.

Genbun-itchi developed as a form of translation, as a foreign use of colloquial diction that elevated spoken diction to the status of writing. We can also see the same process at work in the creation of a body vernacular for the stage. Subjecting the body to translation is the means by which the New Theater achieved this radical transformation: first, it insisted that the actor could only achieve subjecthood as an actor by complete subjugation to the script, an idea that is couched in the rhetoric of faithful translation; second, it offered mainly translated scripts for that process, requiring the complete memorization and verbatim enunciation of the translated text; third, it developed a new type of body language that referred both to the familiar body vernacular of Japanese daily life and to the exotic body vernacular contained in the Western script. While Osanai wrote more prolifically on the theoretical underpinnings for this program of change, it was Hōgetsu who would ultimately succeed in its practical execution.

First, let us look at how the cultural premium on translation informed the New Theater conception of the actor. In language that closely resembles Futabatei's ethic of faithful translation,* Osanai deplored the mode of acting that simply attempts to convey the general meaning of the script.

Of course, just being faithful to the lines of the original work does not add up to faithfulness to the script. In certain cases vocalization demands that one change the position of grammatical particles, skip them, or swallow them. However, the life of the playwright consists in the dialogue between characters. When a playwright writes lines, [he] obviously does not neglect a single word or phrase. Of course, we must assume that the sound and tone of each utterance have been fully considered in the writing process. To casually perform the play with the attitude that all is fine as long as the meaning gets through would be intolerable. Needless to say, the same can be said for the casual insertion of interjections like *that, in other words, it's nothing,* or *wouldn't you say?* here and there in the lines of the original work.[35]

In transposing Futabatei's ethic to the relationship between script and actor, Osanai demanded that actors become transparent windows onto the written text itself. If the best translator refused to neglect even a single comma or period, much less a word or phrase, the true actor would allow himself "to be manipulated by the strings of the script heart in even the movement of a single finger or a single hair." Osanai's language, though directly inspired by Gordon Craig's "Über-Marionette," also echoes the Naturalist call for transparent language in fiction.

The script is a puppet master. The actor is the puppet. The vocation of the actor is to be *the puppet of the script*. But the actor is a living puppet, not an idol made of clay or wood. The value of the actor lies in the fact of being a *puppet possessed of flesh and blood*.

The actor is already a puppet. A puppet has no "ego." The puppet moves in accordance with the will of the puppet master. It is only by becoming *the puppet of the script* that the actor is able to purely become a character in the play.[36]

Here the distinction between puppets "made of clay or wood" and those "possessed of flesh and blood" parallels Katai's opposition of "gold-plated literature" to that which is made from the "blood and sweat" of the writer. The former allude to the puppets of Bunraku and the actors of Kabuki who mimicked them, the latter refer of course to those new actors who will presumably exploit their "nature" as "human beings."

Both Hōgetsu and Osanai demanded the actor's complete subjugation to the (translated) script, an approach to theater that departed quite completely from the performance-centered stages of Kabuki and the New School. At the heart of this demand is a belief in the supremacy of the (Western) text and its potential to not only transcend but even to transform contingencies of performance, language, and cultural context. Osanai even believed that a good script could transform the very being of the Japanese actor, commanding his allegiance by the sheer power of its words:

In any case, as is apparent, the lines [of *John Gabriel Borkman*] are long, so it is a tremendous job just to memorize them. And, unlike Japanese plays, there is little of the extraneous in them. If it were the kind of play that we are accustomed to, one could fumble through by making something up to replace a forgotten line, but this time the only thing that could be done was to skip it entirely. Just knowing that they must not forget their lines forced people to work hard. At first, it seemed the players were studying out of this kind of external impetus, but the power of the script is truly frightening, and as they gradually came to understand the spirit of their roles they were naturally compelled to become truly serious from within.[37]

As mentioned earlier, Hōgetsu considered the translated script the best possible platform for training Japan's new actors and actresses. A similar conviction guided the curriculum of the Theater Institute, where all students spent a full year reading Ibsen's *A Doll's House*, first in English, then in Hōgetsu's translation.

While Osanai and Hōgetsu agreed on many points in their independent attempts to Westernize Japanese theater, their approaches to the Japanese body upon which that theater would be built differed in critical ways. As Osanai famously put it, he was working on "turning players into amateurs," while the Literary Arts Society sought to "turn amateurs into players." In other words, the Free Theater took Kabuki-trained players like Ichikawa Sadanji and Enjaku and tried to make them forget all they had ever learned about the art of acting, while the Literary Arts Society opened up a school to train men and women with no prior theater experience to perform on the New Theater stage. If Osanai's task could be likened to sanding down a finely carved bas-relief to make a flat surface for painting, then the Literary Arts Society began with a blank slate, an advantage that would become all the more obvious with time. Osanai's almost quixotic attempt to transform already developed professional actors speaks to a more fundamental difference between himself and Hōgetsu: Osanai was the vocal ideologue of New Theater, while Hōgetsu was its quiet aesthetician. In his ideological fervor Osanai placed blind faith in the powers of the text, ignoring the body's critical role in theater. It is as if he truly believed the script could simply render the actor immaterial. Hōgetsu, on the other hand, had his faith in the text immediately put to the test when he translated *A Doll's House* for performance. (Although Osanai also had prior experience in translating for the stage, we should note that this experience tested his faith in the theatrical establishment, rather than the text itself, and thus formed the impetus for his Free Theater movement. We might also speculate that his work on *Romeo and Juliet* had exposed the limits of his own abilities as a translator, since he chose to commission Mori Ōgai for the translation of Free Theater scripts.) A great deal more sensitive to the manifold semantic, cultural, and aesthetic difficulties inherent in the New Theater project of translated drama, Hōgetsu took on the nitty-gritty problems of both verbal and bodily translation from the very beginning. As a result he was able, along with Matsui Sumako, to develop a new type of body language that ultimately had a much more decisive impact on the Japanese stage.

As long as we keep the focus on translation, it is quite clear that the primary purpose of Japanese Naturalist theater was to establish an ideologically correct (i.e., properly textual) relationship between the exotic script and the Japanese reader, writer, and actor, *not* to represent some objective reality in a more natural way. This was a matter to which Osanai had given a great deal of thought, and it stood him in good stead during the initial stages of his Free Theater movement. When he presented the first Japanese performance of *John Gabriel Borkman*, its critical success was guaranteed by the emergence of a like-minded audience, one that was more interested in theater as a live representation of literature than as a display of dramatic artistry.

The end of the final act of *Borkman* gave rise to intense, emotional applause. At that moment the minute details of the performance were not a matter of concern. The epoch-making fact that, for the first time, the twenty-nine-year-old Osanai Kaoru and the thirty-year-old Ichikawa Sadanji had transplanted the tree called Ibsen to Japan had inebriated people.[38]

Interestingly, the fact that the actors were *speaking in translated text* especially captivated the literarily inclined members of the audience— so much so that the actors' bodies not only became "transparent," but virtually invisible. In his impressions of *Borkman* Yosano Hiroshi (Tekkan) wrote:

I am not capable of speaking critically about how Sadanji was or how Enjaku did. From the start, that was not my interest in going to see the play, and on the night of the play I was mainly involved in listening with my ears, just as Osanai had requested in his opening greetings, and since I was completely occupied trying to savor the script and listen to Ibsen, the figures of the players hardly even made an impression on my eyes. Until now the main thing in a play has been to see the artistry of the players—or if it wasn't the main thing, the players were at least half the interest—but with this performance of *Borkman* the absolutely main thing was to listen to the script with one's ears. To me that was a new and vivid source of interest. If it hadn't been just a single night's performance, but had gone on for ten days and I had been able to see it three or four times, I am sure that the stimulation of the ears would have dulled and the eyes would have started working, becoming able to see the quality of the players' artistry. I felt happy that, thanks to the Free Theater, I was able to listen to the script without looking at the players for the first time in my life.[39]

If Naturalists were entranced by the strange sounds and rhythms of Futabatei's *Aibiki*, the staging of Mori Ōgai's *Jon Gaburieru Boruku-man* seems to have increased the power of the translated word many times over, temporarily rendering it capable of blinding the audience. This critical event immediately engendered a new discourse on the role of the actor that, in its disdain for conventional concepts of skill and technique, clearly mirrors Katai's embrace of raw description for the novel.

I heard that among those outside actors who came to see this trial production, some said, "All the actors who perform on the stage of the Free Theater are bad. If it were us, we could do it a little better." I have not heard directly from these actors what they meant by "bad," so I am not sure, but I believe that what has hitherto been called skillful on the stage would be, in the case of writing, what is called good in the sense of pretty writing. Just as those who tried to write well ended up running toward the final end of craftsmanship, those actors who pursue skill on the stage lose sight of things like really making their characters come alive and manifesting the overall meaning of the script, so I believe that they have come to focus only on crafting minor details. If this is what is meant by good, then I do not hope for something good in the performers of the Free Theater. It doesn't matter if it is bad or if there is something lacking in the overall finish—what I hope is that they will generally try to very faithfully manifest the character, to leave behind their own personal ideas and forget about the audience, and perform in such a way as to truly translate the work on the stage and convey it to the audience's mind.[40]

Morita Sōhei even went so far as to declare the actor unnecessary in "Haiyū muyō ron," claiming that drama was all in the script, not in the performance.[41] But audiences did not remain blind for long; when the first class of the Theater Institute completed their two-year course of studies and took to the public stage in 1911, they raised the bar for New Theater acting in ways that the all-male, all-Kabuki core membership of the Free Theater simply could not match. The most obvious and important of these, of course, was the revelation of the modern Japanese actress in Sumako's Nora. In essence, what Hōgetsu and Sumako brought to the New Theater stage was the aesthetic, rather than the purely ideological, appeal of translation.

Indeed, I would contend that Hōgetsu's singular contribution to the development of New Theater was the *aestheticization* of New Theater ideology. While Osanai was able to provide enough theoretical and ideological passion to excite his first audiences, that alone was not enough to sustain them for the long term. It was Hōgetsu's attention to the intangible aesthetic questions, the stylistics of speech and body language, that ultimately gained a lasting foothold for the New Theater in Taishō Japan. In his work as both translator and director he was highly sensitive to the desire, exemplified by Watsuji, to forge a conspicuous identification with the foreign without assimilating its most exotic qualities to the banal realm of the domestic. To achieve this precarious balance on the stage would, as a matter of course, prove to be a much greater challenge than that faced by the radical vernacularist novelists we examined in previous chapters. In the shift of venue from the study to the stage, Hōgetsu was made acutely aware of just how much more difficult the translator's task had become. His reflections on the translation of A Doll's House, like Watsuji's accounts of translated drama, reveal a heightened consciousness of language and linguistic difference that certainly does not jibe with the facile ideology of transparent expression as we have so often seen it described.[42]

In putting on A Doll's House, the first thing I felt was the problem of translation. In particular, I became painfully aware of the difference in rigor between a translation to be performed on stage and a translation simply to be read at one's desk. When we translate things from abroad, the characters' gestures, the things around them, and such are completely different from those of Japan. That is what brings about the sense of the "exotic" flavor, as we say in the literary circles—i.e., the general feeling that something comes from a foreign country. There's nothing strange about this, but, at the same time, in the use and order of words themselves, the self-same Japanese can take on the sense of foreignness somewhere, the so-called scent of translation. And this is also the strength that preserves, in no small part, the foreign rhythms in a work of translation. And the foreign atmosphere that is generated when these things come together naturally sparks attention in the eyes of the Japanese, in both good and bad senses. In other words, it stirs enough attention to make a person stop and look, it commands a great deal of interest. As a result, we are able to grasp a work's power, flavor, and the like by entering into details that would elude our attention had we simply glided over the words. In this sense we actually feel more power from foreign works than from Japanese. In other words, it is possible to make a work stronger by borrowing the help of the foreign scent, namely, exoticism. In the case of translation as reading material, it is possible to do this fairly freely. Because of this, at times a work may even generate more power than it originally possessed. A Japanese person may experience as something extremely powerful that which did not particularly impress the Westerner with its strength. Put in positive terms, this is a more profound way of savoring the work; in negative terms, it is an overestimation of the work's value. This is not necessarily limited to Japanese translations; the same phenomenon occurs when Westerners translate works from Japan. . . .

The above is a phenomenon that easily occurs in the case of translations to be read, but when it comes to a play to be put on stage, a slightly different circumstance arises. . . . The true difficulty lies in the nature of theater. It is something that appears on the spot; in other words, with a book it's possible to sit at a desk and read and reread at one's leisure, to put the book down and savor it at one's own pace, quietly ruminating and meditating upon it; this can't be done with drama. The lines are spoken aloud. The gestures are performed on the stage. And, in the meantime, the audience must, willy-nilly, keep pace with the progress of the play. If something is not understood, it simply passes them by. This is the primary difference between art to be read and that to be put on the stage. If it is not done after a great deal of practice, even the smartest person will often find it difficult to understand the (exotic) new words and gestures contained within it upon first viewing. And even if it were possible to understand, it would be difficult to break it down to fully savor it in the mind.[43]

As we can see here and in Watsuji's language, by the end of the Meiji period the term *exotic* was an accepted part of the rhetoric of translation, making explicit what had been an implicit value for Japanese Naturalism. The exoticist approach to translation that gave birth to Japan's modern vernacular had become an attractive model for many readers and writers, and Hōgetsu laments that it is not possible to fully sustain this model in the case of theater. The problem, as he formulates it, is not simply a matter of comprehensibility, but also one of aesthetics. The exotic opacities of style and meaning that had come to lend the translated text its signature appeal could easily become a serious liability for a live performing art: "That which, in the case of reading material, gave a feeling of strength because of the foreign smell interspersed here and there becomes a source of discord when seen on stage, resulting in the evocation of a sense of the comic or the ugly. From this standpoint as well, translation for the stage has less freedom in borrowing the help of the foreign scent."[44] Thus, in spite of his desire to privilege the "exotic flavor" of the Western text,

Hōgetsu was compelled to acknowledge a greater need for compromise in translating for performance.

He presents two specific examples of the kinds of choices he made in translating *A Doll's House* specifically for performance. First, he refers to the use of the word *miracle* at the end of act 3, when Nora tells Helmer that "it would take the greatest miracle of all" for the two of them to become more than strangers again.[45] The Japanese translation of this word, *kiseki,* was not yet familiar enough for most people to understand its connotations upon hearing it spoken aloud. Hōgetsu considered an alternative in the more familiar word *fushigi.* There is no one-word equivalent in English, but we might translate its meaning as both "strange" and "wonderful." While he thought this word would better suit the sensibilities of many in the audience, Hōgetsu nonetheless decided to stick with *kiseki,* with the aim of "better conveying the foreign sense and feeling" of the original term.[46] As an example of a choice he made in the opposite direction, he mentions the word *empty* in Helmer's last line: "Empty. She's gone."[47] While fully aware of the metaphorical valences in the use of the word in this particular context, he weighs the possible Japanese translations and finally decides against attempting to preserve the full depth of meaning in this case.

Even in a case when to yell the English word *empty* on stage would be capable of causing an extremely powerful feeling, in Japanese one simply does not want to say *kūkyo* on the stage. That might be sufficient if one were reading the word, but for a dramatic line one would simply have to translate this as *dare mo inai* [no one is here]. There are many similar cases. The point is that the word *kūkyo* is, in most cases, suitable to be read but not yelled out. The difficulty lies in the fact that to nonetheless make a character yell out the word *kūkyo* would instantly result either in his appearing to be horribly pretentious and insincere or in his seeming like one of those young, hotheaded student types or some such.[48]

In the climactic final scene Nora spouts the Westernesque word *kiseki* while Helmer is limited to the flat, colloquial *dare mo inai.* We cannot help but notice the gender divide here—is it a mere accident that the heroine is permitted to voice the exotic word, while the man is forbidden to shout *kūkyo* for fear that it will make him seem ridiculous? Or is it possible that, coming from a Japanese Nora, even the word *kūkyo* might have become more palatably exotic rather than obnoxiously opaque? It appears that Hōgetsu's acute aesthetic sense included a visceral awareness of that gender divide in modern Japanese literature by which the Westernesque in women could emanate a positively seductive aura, but the Westernesque in men tended to characterize silver-tongued fops in the manner of Seki Kin'ya.

For the purpose of presenting Western drama on the Japanese stage, Hōgetsu considered the medium of the human body to be even less pliant than the spoken text. Unlike Osanai, he fully acknowledged the role of the body in conjuring up the mannerisms, facial expressions, and gestures of the foreign characters of translated drama. For him this body was not the "flesh and blood" of the universal human being, but rather the site of cultural and physiological differences that presented significant obstacles to the transparent expression of the translated script. Enumerating differences in body language (gesture and facial expression), body structure, and the use of voice, Hōgetsu thus concluded that "no matter how hard one might try, a Japanese person's imitation of the gestures of a pure Westerner can never go beyond the point of an imitation that is similar, yet different."[49] Dismissing the use of purely Japanese gestures in translated drama as "discordant," on the one hand, and the complete imitation of the Westerner "every move and gesture" as "intolerably ugly to see,"[50] on the other, Hōgetsu instead sought a felicitous fusion of native and exotic body languages.

At stake in Hōgetsu's pursuit of aesthetic harmony was the critical question of audience identification with the performance, something that he did not assume could be forged by the sheer power of the text alone. "The fact is that, in an art form that is shown to us graphically on the stage, there is a certain ineffable, subtle linkage between word and gesture, and that linkage can mean the difference between something that comes very close to one's heart and something that makes one feel as if one is being shown the problems of other people to whom one bears no relation whatsoever."[51] Contrary to the image of Hōgetsu as a completely passive director who simply watched rehearsals in silence, it is evident that he put a great deal of thought into the finer points of body language, with the stated aim of producing a performance of *A Doll's House* "that does not dispose of the foreign atmosphere and yet bears intimate ties to the spiritual life of the Japanese people."[52] Although this is precisely the aspect of the epoch-making performance that remains the least susceptible to historical documentation and analysis, Hōgetsu did provide us with one concrete example of how the gap between body languages was spanned.

With external matters like how to wear a hat or how to sit in a chair it is easy to do things in a foreign style, but when it comes to a rather strong physical expression, if one wrings one hands while moving one chest in a foreign manner, then a Japanese person's emotional sensibility gets mixed in somewhere. While I can't clearly pinpoint it, there is a certain moment when foreign-style gestures and Japanese-style gestures meet up and harmonize. When that moment is achieved, we settle into a feeling of satisfaction.[53]

If genbun-itchi began as an uneasy coalescence of the native body of speech with the exotic textuality of foreign letters, then embodying the values of that project on the stage also necessitated an attempt to harmonize the Japanese body with the written language of translation and the Western body vernacular it represented. As the above example of one particular fusion of Western and Japanese body languages suggests, Hōgetsu sought to achieve this harmony by means of subtle aesthetic choices that could neither be deduced from nor reduced to the ostensible ideology of Naturalism as transparent expression. The "feeling of satisfaction" that resulted from this process must certainly have derived from the fact that quotidian Japanese gestures thereby assumed the appearance of being immanent, rather than antithetical, to the expression of the Western text.

The notion that truly colloquial Japanese body language was particularly ill-suited to the kind of domestic drama that dominated Western naturalist theater is clearly articulated in Iwaya Sazanami's reflections on having seen *A Doll's House* performed in Berlin.

As I always tell people, on the whole, the stances taken up by Japanese and Westerners in their casual conversation is already quite different. Of course, the construction of homes is different, so isn't it only natural that gestures should differ too?

In comparison to Japanese, Westerners employ far more gestures even in their casual conversation, and, because they sit in chairs, it is very easy for them to stand up or stay still, and in a big house they think nothing of exchanging words as they walk or stand.

By comparison, in Japan, the more serious the conversation, the more one makes an effort to sit properly, without moving one's body. Just try talking and walking or standing indoors. It is so dizzying that one cannot stand to see it.

So in Western plays, even with a monologue, one person can splendidly create the entire stage, but in Japan, even with a dialogue, if the scene gets a bit long it quickly becomes dull.[54]

At first glance Sazanami's account of embodied cultural differences seems a perfectly rational explanation for the modern Japanese theater's reliance upon translated Western drama. Even the most quotidian elements of Western body language have, in his view, an inherent visual, and therefore theatrical, interest that its Japanese counterpart inherently lacked. But there is nothing objective in the aesthetic value he attaches to the simple acts of walking and talking, or standing and talking; rather, it should be said that his demand for pure visual interest in the theater was satisfied by the exotic spectacle of the foreign body vernacular in a way that managed to convert the monotonous verisimilitude of everyday gestures, intended by Naturalist dramatists as a staunch rejection of classical Western notions of theatricality, into a felicitous fusion of realism and visual ornamentation.

One need only look to the postwar films of Ozu Yasujirō for positive proof that the relative stillness of Japanese domestic dialogue can be realistically rendered in a visually compelling way; at the same time, it must be said that the process of discovering in Japanese body language an equivalent to the Western dramatic representation of nature proved a great deal more difficult than it had been for Futabatei to translate Turgenev's descriptions of nature into a new form of Japanese writing or for writers like Doppo and Katai to then project the language of *Aibiki* onto the domestic landscape. As Hōgetsu observed, as a medium of translation, the body is much less malleable than written language. On the one hand, for an actor trained in the physical forms of Kabuki, retraining the body to represent even the most basic aspects of Western body language was excruciating. Indeed, when Ichikawa Sadanji first took on the role of John Gabriel Borkman, he had difficulty with the deceptively simple act of walking and talking at the same time. How much of his lines needed to be spoken in how many steps? The difficulty of coordinating the timing for Borkman actually led Sadanji to fumble some of his lines during the performance.[55] The text-heavy modern Western drama thus rendered obsolete all the painstaking physical training that prepared a Kabuki player to captivate audiences with the intricate coordination of dance, gesture, and the mellifluous recitation of dramatic lines. On the other hand, while the practice of *shasei*—sketching or imitating gestures from daily life—was an important part of the Theater Institute curriculum, its students took to the stage in the roles of European men and women whose daily lives and gestures they knew very little about. The New Theater insistence upon beginning with translation was thus driven by an implicit assumption that no form of Japanese body language—whether tied to theatrical convention or not—was yet capable of revealing the kind of "nature" that its proponents championed.

Like its counterpart in fiction, Naturalist drama sought to strip the stage of all "extraneous" stylistic adornments. Yet the apparent simplicity of purely spoken drama was arguably even more difficult to master than the vernacular style had been for the Meiji novelist. Osanai's attempt to make the body of the Kabuki player conform to a completely different set of theatrical demands was not only painful, but inherently ill-conceived. As Karatani points out with respect to the face, the Kabuki player is in himself "a figure, like kanji" or what Leonard C. Pronko has called "the hieroglyphic actor."[56] By contrast, as we have already seen in *Futon*, the Naturalist concept of the body was that of a transparent window onto the complex interiority of the modern individual. While that was the theoretical ideal, New Theater further added the demand that the body serve as a site for the felicitous fusion of Western and Japanese languages, a task for which there was no possible guide aside from a short history of literary precedent and gut aesthetic instinct. That the body as a set of highly conventional signifiers was antithetical to both these demands would become most clear in the performance of New Woman roles on the New Theater stage.

Gender Drag, Culture Drag, and Female Interiority

Nakamura Kichizō, codirector for the Literary Arts Society's production of *A Doll's House,* expounded a theory of the proper place of the actress on the Japanese stage that helps to explain the particular meaning invested in Sumako's performance of Nora, and the reasons for its immediate acclaim. He wrote that it was only in the modern social drama, with its "highly advanced realistic tendencies and descriptions of individuals," that the actress could find firm ground to exhibit her special strengths.[1] According to him, most Japanese theater pundits were in agreement that Kabuki, which relied on stereotypical characters and emotions, did not require the special qualities of the actress. To the category of theater that does not need actresses, he also added the New School and even Western classics such as Shakespeare. As we recall, Sumako's performance in *Hamlet* was lacking in some critical element that would earn her the crown of the first modern actress in Japan. In confirmation of Nakamura's theory, it seems that the only way to become a modern actress in Japan was to play the part of a modern woman. As his process of elimination—not Kabuki, not New School, not even Western "classics"—shows, the identity of the modern actress was defined by contrast to a host of other types of performers and performance precedents: the male *onnagata* (female role specialist) and his performances in Kabuki, New School, and New Theater productions, the Western actress, the *onna yakusha* (woman player) who appeared in Kabuki and New School, and, finally, the New School actress. In order to better understand what becoming the first modern Japanese actress required, let us examine how she emerges in relation to her fellow thespians.

The male actors who specialized in female roles (*onnagata*) in Kabuki represented the most complete contrast to the modern actress: their performances were appreciated precisely because of their artificiality, not in spite of it. As the onnagata had been the mainstay of popular Japanese theater for roughly three centuries, it is no surprise that contemporary debates over the pros and cons of the actress typically compared her to him. Kano's summation of these debates sees a binary distinction between actresses and onnagata that aligns "women with what they are 'essentially,' 'physically,' and 'naturally,' as opposed to 'the male onnagata's 'patterns,' his 'art,' or 'artifice.'"[2] In her view the only difference between the factions is that "the pro-actress faction values woman's natural expression, rooted in her body, over the onnagata's artificial one, while the anti-actress faction values the onnagata's superior art over woman's inferior nature, also rooted in her body."[3] While this schematization of the terms of the debate does not fully address the complexities of the actress question as it was perceived and described at the time—for instance, most theater pundits assumed a critical distinction between Japanese and Western women that would effectively nullify the notion of a universal female "essence"; some also characterized the modern (Western) woman as a more *masculine* type, a fact that would necessarily complicate any overarching binary view of the gender issues at hand; and *all* were aware of the presence of *female onnagata*, women who by definition straddled the ostensible divide between "nature" and "artifice"—the sharp contrast between nature and artifice does hit upon a critical point in the emergence of the modern actress: namely, that she would have to make her name in a theatrical form that laid claim to the virtues of naturalness rather than artifice.

The direct contrast between Osanai's use of onnagata in the Free Theater's productions of modern European drama and the Literary

Arts Society's deployment of the modern actress brought concrete differences to bear on what had otherwise been a mostly hypothetical debate. At the level of theory Osanai not only acknowledged the actress as an integral part of modern drama, he also translated interviews with Western actresses for the edification of Japanese theatergoers. But, in practice, he persisted in producing modern translated drama with virtually all-male casts at a time when the Literary Arts Society was actually training actresses. Thanks to his production of Hauptmann's *Lonely Lives* in October 1911, we can say that the first actual Japanese embodiment of Anna Mahr was a man—namely, the Kabuki onnagata Ichikawa Enjaku. A month earlier, Sumako had played the role of Nora for a private performance of *A Doll's House*; a month later, she would take to the public stage in the same pathbreaking role. Now young critics were less willing to overlook the shortcomings of Osanai's use of Kabuki actors. In a highly critical review, Komiya Toyotaka wrote:

Even with Sumizō's wife Käthe, the external appearance of innocence and helplessness was well done, but one wanted to see more of the spiritual aspect of her helplessness and her clinging dependence upon her husband. With his performance, it is just enough to elicit sympathy for a woman whose own lack of positive action led her husband's feelings to stray to another woman, but one cannot see a woman who is at a loss because of an awareness of her own spiritual inferiority, as a result of which there is the weak nervous condition of a woman suffering from hysteria, but not the feeling of helplessness of a weak woman based on her own self-awareness. . . .

Within this script, the schoolgirl Anna is the poorest in execution, and at the same time, if one were so inclined, one could easily question the reasons for her coming and staying. Even so, Enjaku's performance was full of sweetness only, and did not have enough of a bitter flavor. [He] looked very pretty, but was lacking in a more decadent aspect, the aspect that would show some disdain for Braun and condescend to and care for Johannes as a younger brother. Without displaying the sparkle of the kind of genius that can enthrall a person with a manner of conversation, and not just with a face, it seems like Johannes was simply infatuated with Anna because of her pretty face, and not anything else. Thus it ends up that, aside from a pretty face, the qualifications Anna has for attracting a man are no different from the qualifications possessed by the wife Käthe.[4]

Komiya's complaint about both Sumizō and Enjaku is that they were only able to approximate the external trappings of these female characters instead of manifesting the subtle signs of their interiority— Käthe's self-conscious sense of inferiority and Anna's intangible yet irresistible brilliance. He was even more critical of Sadanji's Johannes: "To a certain extent Johannes's external form had been imitated, but there was no apparent sign that he had tried to enter deeply into Johannes's psyche; he didn't try at all to evoke the core lyricism of Johannes, he just screwed up his face, sharpened his voice, and made a great show of being *upset*."[5] Komiya's main point was not that men did not have the "essence" needed to portray women on the stage, but rather that Kabuki actors lacked the intellectual wherewithal to fully understand and portray the psychologically developed characters of modern drama. Put in another way, what they were lacking was neither nature nor artifice, but brains—an idea that Osanai and other New Theater advocates had expressed repeatedly in their critiques of Kabuki and New School.

Nagata Hideo had also doubted that Kabuki-trained onnagata could really perform the roles of Käthe and Anna in *Lonely Lives*. As for their actual performances,

I thought Enjaku would have done better in the role of Vockerat's wife Käthe. Anna Mahr is a new woman of Russia. And she is a woman whose nerves and emotions have extremely sharp movements. In the end, Enjaku's Anna was distasteful, being strangely sentimental. The character of Käthe was a very ordinary type that could be easily seen in Japan as well, but Sumizō's performance was terribly awkward.[6]

Here Nagata implies that there is a particular difficulty in portraying the "new woman of Russia," while "a very ordinary type [of woman] that could easily be seen in Japan" should have been easy even for an onnagata to play. Thus, in addition to the notion that Kabuki actors are poorly suited to representing the complex interiority of a woman

FIGURE 2A Onoe Kikugorō VI as Yaegaki-hime (*left*) in *Honchō nijūshikō* (Twenty-four Japanese paragons of filial piety, Ichimura-za). *Engei gahō*, December 1909.

FIGURE 2B Kawai Takeo as Tsubaki-hime (*right;* literally, "Princess Camellia," based on Dumas's *La Dame aux Camèlias*), *Engei gahō*, May 1911.

Both of these male onnagata are able to achieve stunningly feminine appearances. Onoe Kikugorō worked the Kabuki stage while Kawai Takeo worked exclusively with the New School. Notice the striking similarity in makeup and the delicate hand gestures.

FIGURE 3 The Free Theater's production of *Lonely Lives*, October 1911 (Teikoku gekijō). All major roles were played by actors. (*Clockwise from top center*) Ichikawa Sadanji as Johannes, Ichikawa Ennosuke as Braun, Ichikawa Enjaku as Anna Mahr, Ichikawa Sumizō as Käthe, and Enjaku as Anna Mahr again. In the center are Ichikawa Sahachi as Johannes's mother (*right*) and Genjūrō as the nurse (*left*). Note the difference in Enjaku's poses. At the top, with glasses, he stands defiantly upright, almost glaring. At bottom, without glasses, he shows the delicate hand gestures and demure look that were much more familiar to onnagata. *Courtesy of the Waseda University Theatre Museum, Tokyo (F54-05483)*

on the stage, we find that there is also something about a particularly Western—i.e., distinctly non-Japanese—type of woman that will
elude their art as well. This is an important point with respect to the
emergence of the modern Japanese actress, for the binary opposition of Japanese versus Western formed the very basis for the debates
on the actress versus the onnagata. In the debates over the so-called
actress question that began in 1912, we find that there is an almost
unanimous recognition of the place of the actress on the *Western*
stage.[7] Most defenses of the actress are based upon this model, and
most objections to the actress on the Japanese stage are articulated
in terms of the perceived shortcomings of *contemporary Japanese
women*. As Kano writes,

Those who argued that actresses are unnecessary usually based their judgment on physical criteria, especially the observation that women, specifically Japanese women, lacked the physiological and congenital qualities
necessary to perform on stage. Japanese women were said to be too short,
their voices too soft, their hips too large and unshapely. Others added that
Japanese women's noses are too flat, their faces not striking enough, and
their gestures not forceful enough.[8]

Thus the modern Japanese actress was not only compared with the
Japanese onnagata but implicitly with Western actresses as well.
Indeed, Kawakami Sadayakko's resounding success on the Western
stage—i.e., her proven ability to compare favorably to the Western
actress—was a primary factor in establishing her name as an *actress* in
Japan.[9] It was the fine comparison she made with Western actresses,
rather than any comparison she might have made with the Kabuki
onnagata or even the onna yakusha, that ultimately counted the most
for her stage career in Japan. In terms of the hierarchy of cultural
legitimacy that emerges from the discourse on the actress in Japan,
it is the Western actress who stands unchallenged at the top of the
totem pole, with the onnagata and the Japanese actress battling it out
for second place.

While Komiya and Nagata were both skeptical about the onnagata's ability to successfully portray the women of modern Western

drama, Osanai asserted that, at least in the short term, the onnagata was better suited to this task than was the Japanese actress. His reasoning is quite intriguing. In a dialogue on the pros and cons of the actress, Osanai wrote:

"Well then, what about translated drama?"
"Of course, it must be performed by the actress."
"In that case, it must be rather comical to use the traditional onnagata for modern drama in translation, right?"
"In the future, that is sure to be the case. Or rather, it must *become* the case. But with things as they are now, it is terribly discouraging to think about when this will be felt as 'comical.' From my perspective, in the case of the here and now, the strain of a Japanese onnagata playing a woman is a much lighter crime than a Japanese actress playing a woman in a Kabuki play. In fact, I believe that the onnagata, a man by birth, is much more suited to the modern woman than today's Japanese actresses, who have terribly little of the manly element in them."[10]

Here, we find Kano's theory about essence turned upside down and stood on its head: it is the onnagata's *masculine nature*—the fact that he is "a man by birth"—that makes him better suited than the Japanese actress to play a modern woman. It is tempting to dismiss Osanai's comment as nothing more than the twisted logic of misogyny, yet another way to rob (Japanese) woman of "agency" by implying that "masculine nature" is the wellspring of all "art." But there is more to it than that. In her encyclopedic study of Meiji New Theater, Matsumoto Shinko records the change in Osanai's attitude toward the Japanese actress from hope to disdain. Specifically, she cites Osanai's response to a 1907 production of *Merchant of Venice* by Ichikawa Sadanji that debuted, among others, two daughters of the late Danjurō IX. Here too, while he strikes a more hopeful note on the potential of Japanese women on the stage, praising these actresses for a "splendid first performance," he also laments their overly feminine—or rather, *Japanese feminine*—attributes:

One thing that was disappointing is that all of them are still lacking in facial expression. This is a general misfortune for all Japanese women, who are taught from their ancestors that "facial expression" is a kind of "evil." The woman who wants to become a new actress of Japan must first break through this old morality and experiment prolifically with facial expressions everyday, even while sitting or standing. And another thing was that the cloying sweetness at the ends of lines in all cases followed the "Noshio" style. I believe this could be quickly resolved by practicing cutting off the voice in a masculine manner.[11]

Echoing the Naturalist rhetoric we encountered in Katai, the desire to see more variety in "facial expression" is informed by an assumption that the typical Japanese woman is nothing but a set of conventions, so strictly bound to their forms that she either possesses no interiority to speak of or that that interiority is so deeply submerged beneath the thick layers of socially encoded femininity as to be irretrievable for the purposes of Naturalist art. What we cannot but notice here is the critical ways in which the terms *feminine* and *masculine, female* and *male, actress* and *onnagata* are all informed by an overarching distinction between Japanese and Western, feudal and modern, convention bound and liberated, particularly as deployed in Naturalist discourse. While none of these terms are stable, even within the relatively restricted context of late Meiji theater discourse, it is nonetheless clear that the latter half of the second set of binaries—Western, modern, and liberated—consistently bears the greatest weight of all. Osanai's disappointment in the Japanese actress, who was in large part equated with the Japanese woman, was first expressed as a disappointment in her Japaneseness, and then, in the later dialogue on the actress, as a disappointment in her femininity. In both cases the *modern Western actress* remains in the background as the ultimate ideal.

The perception of the modern woman as more "manly" was not limited to Osanai, nor was it particularly endemic to a misogynistic or anti-actress agenda. In fact, we find a similar assumption at work for an opposing end in Tamura Toshiko's defense of the Japanese actress. Before becoming a novelist Tamura had herself flirted with a career on the stage, studying with Ichikawa Kumehachi and briefly considering entering the Theater Institute, so she had a particularly strong interest in the actress question.

Seeing recently that the part of Nora played by a woman for the Literary Arts Society enjoyed much greater acclaim than that of [Anna] Mahr played by a man for the Free Theater, I got the sense that the path to future success for the actress in contemporary drama had already been opened up. Though it is of course impossible to expect a male actor trained in Japanese Kabuki theater to understand the role of an awakened woman, or a woman with a well-developed, scientific mind who has received a modern education, the man who played the woman's role of Mahr tried to portray a complex, educated woman by making his voice ridiculously thick, so he ended up sticking to the unnaturalness of a man's natural voice. In the case of Nora, a graceful actor like Kawai [Takeo] would probably be able to do the parts where she butters up her husband or frolics innocently about, but, from the point of her awakening, a man simply wouldn't work, you know. It is because a woman strains her naturally fine voice to strike the bold tones of anger that the word "self-awareness" resonates so strongly in the minds of the viewers. This cannot be achieved by a man spouting emotions in an artificial woman's voice. And if he tries to make his voice thick because the character has become self-aware, then the man's natural voice will emerge. If this is done with artistry, the flavor will be lost. I am sure that the favorable reception of Nora was because the effect was particularly conspicuous in this area.[12]

According to Tamura, the aspect of the modern woman that most completely eludes the external art of the onnagata is precisely her *masculinity*: the bold expression of anger by which she "strains her naturally fine voice." At first glance she seems to be making a universal claim for the "natural" superiority of women over men in the performance of female roles. In particular, as Kano points out, her comparison of the natural voice and the falsetto posits a biological difference that cannot and should not be overcome through artistry. Given such a position, the final lines of her opinion piece come as a surprise: "When it comes to actresses and onnagata in New School theater, it seems that the onnagata are better. And if a newly emerging actress should try to follow this path, such a person wouldn't even be worth talking about."[13] It turns out that Tamura's interest in what is or is not natural applies only to the representation of the intellectually advanced or awakened women of modern drama. To her, representations of women in the mongrel theater of the New School were so far beneath contempt that she not only conceded to, but even encouraged, the dominance of onnagata on that particular stage. What Tamura's argument does is to shift the relative weight between the linked terms *modern, Western* and *actress* in such a way that the male Kabuki actor is made to represent the negative side of all three binary sets: he is backward or feudal, and therefore incapable of understanding the "modern woman," and this is quite typical of the *Japanese man*. As we can see so far, the modern Japanese actress, who must land on the positive side of all three binary sets, already has her work cut out for her.

Shimamura Hōgetsu himself also participated in this gender-blending discourse. In his preface to *Botan bake* (Peony brush, 1914), a collection of Matsui Sumako's essays and short pieces that was often attributed to Hōgetsu himself, he wrote of his lover as an artist who combined a masculine spirit with the feminine habits of mind and body typical of a Japanese woman:

The art created by Miss Sumako's body is the reflection of the strength of conviction and forcefulness of her spirit. As strength of conviction and forcefulness are symbols of man, her art naturally comes to assume a masculine hue. On the other hand, the hue that Miss Sumako creates through painstaking inscription is that of feminine indirection. Thus nature always stands on top of artifice.

By masculine I of course mean nothing more than that masculine hue that appears in a woman. The hue of a Japanese woman with which you were naturally endowed is not something that will vanish on account of that. When you first rehearsed the part of Nora in *A Doll's House,* your outstretched arm could not stand to hold a straight line for long, and it seems that it took quite a lot of practicing before you could make a splendidly straight line. And again, it must have taken quite some time for your stage voice to stop sounding like the chirping of birds, as they say, or for your laugh to stop pursing up like the mouth of a jar. In the end, the gentle softness of the Japanese woman still remains and is being stretched taut by your fervid love for your art.

Shades of feminine pliancy added to a rough sketch of masculine force-fulness—this is Miss Sumako's art, and this is where both her strengths and weaknesses come from.[14]

Kano cites the above passage as evidence of Hōgetsu's need to defend Sumako's *feminine* and *Japanese nature* against the Westernized and masculinized image created by her training and success as an actress.[15] But if we read the passages that precede and follow it, we find that, for Hōgetsu, Japanese femininity was not a virtue worthy of preserving but rather a limitation to be overcome. After praising the "heroic" strength by which she perseveres as an artist in the face of harsh public attacks, he says that she is also a "weak woman standing at a crossroad fretting over whether to choose art over the world at large or to choose the world over art."[16] Acutely aware of the tremendous pressure that constantly bore down upon Japan's first modern actress, Hōgetsu exhorted her to be "a strong person," to rely upon the strength of her art. Finally, he praises her for having gone beyond the limits of the Japanese woman on the stage and pushes her to do the same in her daily life as well:

The feverish force and the vivid and intense facial expressions you release in a torrent onto the stage transcend the limits that today's Japanese woman is capable of reaching.

But daily life, which moves slowly and changes quietly, still only appears within the bounds of the clever Japanese woman. I believe that the future of your self-cultivation lies in this direction.[17]

Whereas the Naturalist rhetoric of transparent language sought a seamless union between art and life, Hōgetsu points to the actual gap between Matsui Sumako's "art" and her "daily life" in a way that neatly encapsulates the double bind that textual exoticism helped to create for the modern Japanese woman. If the Japanese woman was seen as finally capable of manifesting expressions no less vivid and intense than her Western counterpart, the characterization of her daily life as deeply mired in conventional gender behaviors left these expressions strangely untethered to a stable source of subjectivity.

FIGURE 4 (*left*) A photograph commemorating Kobayashi Masako's graduation from the Toita Women's School of Sewing, July 1903.

FIGURE 5 Matsui Sumako as Nora in *A Doll's House* (Teikoku gekijō, November 1911). *Courtesy of the Waseda University Theatre Museum, Tokyo (F30-08447)*

FIGURE 6 Matsui Sumako as the eponymous heroine in *Magda* (Yūraku-za, May 1912). By the time of her second starring role as a professional actress, Sumako had already begun to exude a kind of self-assurance that cannot be found in the earlier photograph of Nora. Her makeup is much less conspicuous, and she even seems to wear her costume with more ease. *Courtesy of the Waseda University Theatre Museum, Tokyo (F54-03765)*

Aside from the onnagata and the Western actress, there is one more significant other for the modern Japanese actress to whom I would like to draw attention: that of the onna yakusha (woman player) as opposed to the *joyū* (actress). As mentioned above, this figure fundamentally problematizes any simple binary between actress and onnagata as nature and artifice. Of particular interest is the career of Meiji Kabuki's foremost woman player, Ichikawa Kumehachi. While it is a well-known fact that women were banned from the Kabuki stage in 1629, it is generally less known that professionally trained female entertainers known as *okyōgenshi* continued to perform for women of the *daimyō* class whose high social status precluded them from seeking amusement outside the home. When the daimyō class was dismantled by the Meiji restoration in 1868, all of these women entertainers lost their jobs, but one of them would go on to become a significant presence on the Meiji stage. Impressed by her performances, Danjūrō IX himself accepted Kumehachi as a disciple, and she came to be known as the "woman Danshū" ("Danshū" was a popular nickname for Danjūrō). As noted above, Kumehachi was most commonly identified as a woman player, an onna yakusha, rather than as an actress. Theater pundits of the early twentieth century had many strategies for distinguishing between the two, including personal and sexual mores (woman players being associated with the lax sexual mores of the Tokugawa era, actresses with the strict sexual propriety of an "enlightened" society), but since Kumehachi was known for the impeccability of her personal life, the only distinction setting her apart from the actress was her professional training in the forms of the old theater that she had mastered all too well.[18]

In an interview on the subject of how to become an onnagata, Kumehachi recalled that her own training included techniques for imitating the movement of puppets and the subtle distinction between a puppet trying to look like a living person and a real person trying to look like a puppet trying to look like a living person.[19] Despite the fact of her biological womanhood, she undertook the same training as any male onnagata. Even as a new concept of theatrical realism was taking hold of certain Kabuki players and politically motivated theater reformers, Kumehachi's sex was not an asset that she could actively exploit on the stage. In fact, she remarked that for a woman to successfully play a woman's role on a stage dominated by men, she had to approach the performance with the same mental preparations required by the male roles.[20] Kumehachi considered the gender performances of other Kabuki players before the gender of the roles she played, which included both male and female characters throughout her career. Indeed, as her nickname reminds us, she learned much of her art by imitating a man, Danjūro IX himself. Recalling the first time he saw Kumehachi perform, Okamoto Kidō wrote that in her female roles Kumehachi's voice had become thick and gruff from playing so many male roles, on top of which she strove to employ a feminine falsetto in the style of Danjūro. At the same time, he felt that her depiction of Yaegaki-hime had a beauty and elegance that more than made up for the flaws in her voice.[21]

As her training and career illustrate, on the Kabuki stage form took precedence over the sex of the players. There was no great demand on the part of the audience, nor any significant desire on the part of the Kabuki establishment, for women to play women's roles. At the same time, there was enough public interest in female players in Meiji Tokyo to support the Misaki-za, a theater led by Kumehachi with an all-female cast, in which women regularly portrayed both men and women. As Kano points out, the fact that such women preceded the emergence of the *actress* can only mean that "the definition of actress involves more than a woman performing."[22] Although these women players never enjoyed the public prominence of Kawakami Sadayakko, their careers nevertheless coincided peacefully with hers—indeed, Kumehachi shared the stage with her more than once. But, with the emergence of a new generation of "actresses" in 1911, the very term *woman player* was summarily abjected and virtually erased from cultural memory not long after.[23] This virtually forgotten history of women on the Meiji stage illuminates a key point in the public reception of the actress: her identity was defined not only in opposition to the onnagata and the Western actress but also to the woman player of Meiji theater. Nakamura Kichizō wrote that "just as the literary circles have shifted from the so-called age of the *gesaku-sha* to today's age of the *bungaku-sha* (man of letters), I fervently hope for the prompt arrival of a day when the theater circles will be marked by the transition from the age of the *woman player* to the new age of the *actress*."[24]

FIGURE 7 (*top, left page*) Ichikawa Kumehachi in the female role of Hanako in *Kyōganoko Musume Dōjōji* (Miyako-za, April 1909). *Courtesy of the Waseda University Theatre Museum, Tokyo (FA1-05574)*

FIGURE 8 (*bottom, left page*) Danjūrō IX in the role of Hanako (Kabuki-za, March 1890). *Courtesy of the Waseda University Theatre Museum, Tokyo (FA1-05572)*

FIGURE 9 (*above*) *Ataka kanjinchō* (The subscription list) performed by the all-female troupe of the Misaki-za. *Engei gahō*, November 1909. The starring role of Benkei (*second from the left*) is played by Fujimura Tsurue, now a forgotten name. Based on the photograph alone it would not be possible to identify the gender of the players.

As we have seen, the ideal of the modern Japanese actress developed by theater critics was a tall bill to fill. First, by implication the modern Japanese actress would have to compare favorably to the eminent Western actress, a hurdle that Kawakami Sadayakko had already crossed without actually "settling" the actress question. In addition to what Sadayakko had already achieved, the truly epoch-making Japanese actress would also have to project a more natural image of woman than the onnagata, she would have to be more "modern" and more Westernesque than both the onnagata and the onna yakusha, and she would have to distinguish herself from virtually all other Japanese players by exhibiting a special talent for manifesting the subtleties of "female psychology."[25] This latter requirement necessarily narrowed the actress's ken to modern (i.e., Naturalist and post-Naturalist) European plays, which often centered around New Women. In order to understand and represent such women, the actress would also have to be a New Woman herself. And perhaps the most difficult of all, she would have to achieve all this by speaking convincingly in the exotic language of translation. Critics like Osanai Kaoru and Morita Sōhei claimed that Japanese women were still too simple-minded and intellectually underdeveloped to portray the complex women of modern Western drama, much less to assume the social and artistic status enjoyed by the great actresses of the West.[26] To the majority of her audience, however, Sumako spectacularly overturned these prejudices.

By the accounts of those who knew her before she became Matsui Sumako, Kobayashi Masako seemed a most unlikely candidate for the modern actress. Indeed, we can find no telltale signs in Masako's personal history that would foreshadow Sumako's brilliant career on the stage. Born in 1886 as the ninth and last child of a once prominent samurai family of Matsushiro (Nagano Prefecture) whose fortunes had rapidly declined after the Meiji Restoration, she completed the compulsory eight years of elementary education while living as the adopted daughter to a related family. Her adopted father died when Masako was around fifteen years old,[27] whereupon she was returned to her birth family, only to lose her biological father in the same year. Soon after, she moved to Tokyo to live with her older sister's family, helping out at their confectioner in Azabu. In an apparent effort to prepare her for the typical life course of a woman of her time and place, Masako was then sent to study at the Toita Women's School of Sewing. One woman who knew her when she was working in her sister's confectioner described Masako as a "quiet person . . . who could have married into a good family" if only she had not become an actress.[28] After four or five years in Tokyo, she did initially marry into a "good family" in Chiba. But, after a year, she was mysteriously ejected from what, according to her own accounts, was a state of much-longed-for domestic tranquillity,[29] when the Torigai family sent her back to Tokyo with an apparently misdiagnosed illness and a divorce.[30] While this traumatic event does establish the ground for Masako's subsequent transformation into a self-proclaimed New Woman, it does not shed light upon her decision to pursue a career on the stage.

Masako's second marriage did prove fateful, however. Arranged by the same family that had served as go-between for her first marriage (and divorce), Masako's marriage to Maezawa Seisuke, a high school teacher with an amateur interest in theater, in fact provided the direct impetus for her career in acting. Not long after their marriage, Maezawa began teaching at the Actors' Training Institute, and their home was frequented by his friends and associates from the theater world. According to those who knew her at the time, before her entrance into the Theater Institute Masako's knowledge of theater was all secondhand, based on what she had heard from Maezawa and his friends. According to Sumako herself, she came to the Theater Institute with no formal training in any of the performance arts.[31] It was originally Maezawa who encouraged his wife to consider becoming an actress. When he heard about the opening of the Theater Institute, he encouraged her to apply and secured a letter of introduction from a theater friend, Masumoto Kiyoshi, on her behalf.

If it had not been for Masumoto's introduction, Masako's educational background and ignorance of the theater would surely have disqualified her as an applicant—she failed the entrance examination, but Shōyō decided to give her a chance based on her physical potential alone. In terms of cultural expectations, Masako's classmates Kamiyama Uraji and Hayashi Chitose—both highly educated young women who were already accomplished readers of literature and English—would have seemed obviously more promising as candidates for the new and Westernesque career of the modern actress.

Masako was clearly the odd one out in a cast of characters who had sought entrance into the Theater Institute based on a longstanding personal interest in the cultural vanguard, a group of students who already shared the same language(s). As Masumoto put it, somewhat harshly, "The students of the Theater Institute had each been motivated by their own ambitions, so they had some knowledge of the theater, but Sumako alone was a woman who had obviously come straight down from the mountains, and since she couldn't even tell the difference between the top and bottom of the stage, it is a fact that she was kept at a distance by the other students."[32]

We have already seen Hōgetsu's account of Sumako's transformation from a shy woman with typical Japanese mannerisms into a physically impressive and powerful vehicle of modern Western drama. One of the most vivid descriptions of Kobayashi Masako's apparent lack of potential as an actress comes from Tanaka Eizō, a friend of Maezawa's who tutored her in English after she entered the Theater Institute. Maezawa had asked for Tanaka's help in finding a way for his wife to fulfill her (his) ambition of becoming an actress.

Maezawa introduced the woman with the words, "This is Maa-chan." I thought his words of introduction were too lax, but what surprised me even more was the woman who said she wanted to become an actress. She could not give the greeting for a first meeting, nor even really say anything at all. She simply made a half-seated bow. . . . Her looks were well below average. Her face and body were large, but her movements were rough, lacking in composure. And her flat nose was an eyesore.[33]

The first step in Kobayashi Masako's transformation into the modern actress was plastic surgery: before her interview for the Theater Institute, she had a paraffin injection to raise the profile of her "flat nose." Although this procedure was apparently a common enough practice among the actors of her day—Masumoto had taken Masako to see the nose of one such actor as proof that a "flat nose" would not automatically disqualify her for a career onstage[34]—one is also led to suspect that the male desire for a more Western type of Japanese woman was not simply a matter of interiority.

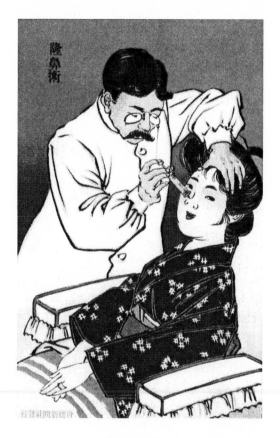

FIGURE 10 Picture postcard of a woman receiving a paraffin injection to raise the profile of her nose. *Ehagaki sekai*, September 1908; reprinted by Chikuma Shobō under the title *Miyatake Gaikotsu Kokkei shinbun bessatsu Ehagaki sekai*, 1985.

Kobayashi Masako was utterly bereft of the kind of cultural capital that would have seemed necessary to successfully pursue the new cultural identity that would become synonymous with Matsui Sumako. The transformation from Masako to Sumako was not a matter of personal destiny, but rather an achievement that was enabled by the felicitous meeting of happenstance and an inexplicable degree of personal determination. Tanaka remarked that Matsui Sumako must have been the only person to have headed straight from the ABC's of English to the reading of Shakespeare. Masako's total devotion to her studies cost her the marriage with Maezawa, who was unable, in spite of his role as initiator, to tolerate playing second fiddle to his wife's suddenly paramount career goals. The couple divorced in 1911, before Sumako took to the stage. Before she assumed the name of Matsui Sumako, Masako herself had thus already chosen between pursuing a personal ambition—even if it had not initially been "her own"—and fulfilling a woman's domestic duties. Given her prior experience with the institution of marriage, it is not unreasonable to surmise that Masako's choice had been informed by a healthy skepticism with regard to the promise of stability it offered to the economically dependent sex. This was the critical turning point in her life, the point at which Masako finally opted out of a mode of existence that was directed by husband and family. The alternative she chose was not entirely of her own making, nor was it the kind of career that easily lent itself to fulfilling the aims, requirements, and illusions of autonomous selfhood, a notion she herself may have only begun to entertain. The critical difference was that Masako chose to entrust herself to an institution much larger than the family—one that, though still dominated by men, nevertheless offered her a previously unimagined possibility of being recognized by a large, live, and, for the most part, anonymous, audience. Given Masako's background, making this choice required a leap of the imagination that cannot easily be accounted for in the conventional terms of cultural history or literary biography.

Gradually, hard work earned Masako two starring roles under a new stage name. Hōgetsu had already begun to notice Sumako's potential in the performance of Ophelia; a fateful attraction was sparked as he watched her grow into the role of Nora and deliver the lines of his own carefully crafted translation. The Literary Arts Society's production of *A Doll's House* at the Imperial Theater headed a longer program that included three original dance plays by Tsubouchi Shōyō and a scene from *Merchant of Venice* performed by Tōgi Tetteki. Yet Sumako's Nora proved so compelling that both contemporary audiences and theater history easily forgot about the rest of the program as well as the other actors and actresses.

The three dance plays that came second were beautiful in execution, but to people like us, who were then completely rapted by modern drama, they were irrelevant. Next the curtain opened on that famous scene from *Merchant of Venice*. There could be nothing bad about it, since the Literary Arts Society had so often worked on it, but throughout that night's performance the only thing that moved before my eyes was Matsui Sumako. There was nothing else—not the Imperial Theater, which was the most beautiful stage in Japan, nor the dance plays, nor Tōgi's Shylock with his bulging eyes. There was only Nora. Above all, when she awakened and answered Helmer with a strong voice, "I am taking off the clothes of a doll," the scene of her concealing herself in the next room left a very powerful impression on me.[35]

Sumako's performance answered the growing demand for something new in the representation of nature, women, and Western plays on the stage. What made her performance of Nora a watershed event was the fact that she convinced so many of the critics in her audience that it was not only theoretically desirable for women to play women in modern drama, but that it was practically possible for a *Japanese woman* to compellingly portray a woman from modern Western literature on the stage. In a review of the private performance of *A Doll's House*, Kawamura Karyō wrote,

I am deeply, deeply happy that, for the first time, I was able to hear natural lines spoken from the lips of an actress born in Japan and, at the same time, though it is surely the result of Matsui Sumako's great effort, I also thought that the power of the directors, Shimamura-sensei and Nakamura-sensei, must surely have had an immeasurable impact.[36]

As specific examples of "natural lines," he cited the following, seemingly insignificant moments:

When [Nora] is explaining to Helmer the toys she bought for the children, I was extremely surprised when I heard the lines "a rocking cradle and doll," followed by the lines "they're a bit too ordinary, but [she will] end up breaking them soon anyway." I just thought this was amazing! In that it manifests the intricate change in mood that occurs before and after, this kind of line represents the highest level of difficulty even just in terms of elocution, and when we also look at the gestures that go with it, it is not at all the facile kind of thing that can be done by just any woman. This type of line can also be seen where Nora puts the sweets in the mouths of Rank and Mrs. Linde and says, "one, at the most two."[37]

What Kawamura seems to be describing is the first successful representation of the quotidian on the Japanese stage. We can well imagine what an absurdity it would be for an actress to recite these humble lines in a Kabukiesque declamatory style—the results would be much like the Shakespearean recitation of a soup label. Kawamura sums up by praising Sumako's style of delivery, which broke away from Japanese theatrical precedent:

First, the lines are natural, and the way of saying them made perfect sense, on top of which there was nothing of that awful dramatic accent that follows actresses around; on these points, Sumako was head and shoulders above all the other actors and actresses on the stage, and that made up for the weakness of relatively poor facial expression and depth of gesture.[38]

In his words, Sumako's Nora offered her audience the thrill of seeing a Western ideal literally embodied by a woman "born in Japan." Part and parcel of this experience, particularly for the generation of theatergoers who supported New Theater, was the actress' representation of the Western text. This is an area where Sumako simply outstripped all competition. The women who preceded her on the Japanese stage had no relationship whatsoever to the text-centered paradigm of modern Western drama; the Kabuki actors who preceded her in the Free Theater's performances of modern Western drama had barely been able to memorize their lines. By contrast, Sumako would become famous for her rapid and perfect memorization of lines and for her assiduous rehearsing.[39] As Hōgetsu's earlier observation on the difficulties of translated drama suggest, Sumako's perfect memorization and thorough rehearsing of the strange language of the translated script must surely have contributed a great

deal to an apparently *natural* delivery, particularly when we understand this term in relation to other types of performers and performances in her day.

The quality of the lines themselves was also a critical element
of Sumako's meteoric rise. As we have already seen, in translating *A Doll's House* Shimamura Hōgetsu set his sights on preserving as much exotic flavor as possible without crossing the line
into incomprehensibility or inadvertent parody. In this respect
his script departed quite radically from the inherited language of
Kabuki, which continued to dominate the stage. As Ishizawa Shūji
observes, even the opening lines of Mori Ōgai's translation of *John
Gabriel Borkman* combine the contemporary spoken style with
the 7–5 syllabic pattern of Kabuki, a style that was also commonly
used for New School adaptations. In his estimation it would have
been impossible for a radically new type of theater to emerge from
Kabuki players performing a script written in this style.[40] On the
other hand, once Ōgai's script departs from the 7–5 model it loses
rhythm altogether, falling into a stiff, written type of colloquial dec-
lamation. By contrast, Hōgetsu's *Ningyō no ie* reads much more like
the dialogue of a vernacular novel. Moreover, it has a rhythmic flow
that breaks from the traditional 7–5 pattern while still maintaining
mellifluous enunciability.

Finally, another important area in which Sumako must have surpassed her competition was in the physical translation of the Western
body vernacular, the particular kind of body language embedded in
Naturalist drama. Although this is the one sign system that proves
the least susceptible to historical analysis, since there are virtually no
texts from which to form a judgement, it is a critical element in the
emergence of a Naturalist style of Japanese acting, and hence worth
an extra effort to extrapolate from what we do know. As we have
already observed, both Kabuki and New School theaters were driven
by the performance rather than the text. Accordingly, the acting
styles for both theaters relied more heavily on the bold expressions
of physical gesture than on the subtleties of verbal expression. In the
case of Kabuki these gestures were based upon a set of physical signs
known as *kata* or "patterns" that had been developed and handed

down through many generations of Kabuki actors, constituting a kind of body writing. In what might be described in terms of a shift from heavily patterned movement (dance, stylized gesture, emphatic pose) to "live action" (especially in the depiction of fight scenes), the New School imitated the bold outlines of the Kabuki style without really learning or adhering to its language, enabling its actors and actresses greater freedom in the development of new body signs. The primacy of gestural language for both Kabuki and New School can be gleaned from many of the promotional stage photographs that were published in the theater journals of the day. Compared to the body language demanded by New Theater, both these theatrical styles appear to be "exaggerated" and "grotesque." (The same could be said of Western theater prior to Naturalism, as Zola's diatribes against theatrical convention attest.) As we have already seen, the sheer volume of spoken lines in modern Western drama presented quite an ordeal for the Kabuki actor and certainly necessitated a completely different kind of body language. By comparison to the thespians of Kabuki, New School, and of course the Free Theater, Matsui Sumako had the advantage of being a complete amateur (*shirōto* in Japanese, a term that approximates the sense of tabula rasa) when she embarked upon a stage career. Before her training at the Theater Institute, she had no knowledge of any kind of kata she might be tempted to imitate. During her two years at the institute, she simultaneously studied Japanese dance, the English language, classic and modern Western play scripts in English and Japanese translation, Tsubouchi Shōyō's art of elocution, and the practice of "life studies" (gestural sketching). All these languages were equally new to Masako, and some of them were still in the process of being formed. As a true newcomer to the stage, she was thus particularly well situated to make a vernacular translation, rather than a conventional adaptation, of Western body language: having no old forms into which she might pour the contents of a given role, she in fact had no choice but to create something new.

In terms of the logic of modern Japanese literature, to translate was to bring something new into existence in Japanese by faithfully adhering to the form and substance of a Western text; to adapt was to transfer something Western into preexisting Japanese forms. If others before her had only adapted, putting Western women characters into forms that had been developed by the onnagata, Matsui Sumako's Nora was a translation. This translation was a much more complex process than that undertaken in the novel. Based upon the work of both the actress and the translator/director, it began with Hōgetsu's translation of Ibsen's script into Japanese, then Sumako's complete memorization and felicitous recitation of the lines, and ended with her physical transformation into the character of Nora—makeup, costume, facial expression, gesture. At every level a careful blending of Japanese colloquial languages and sign systems with Western text and images was required to create a sense of the natural.

While contemporary reviews suggest that Sumako's Nora was far from perfect in its attempt at "naturalness," her May 1912 performance as Magda in the Literary Arts Society's followup production of Hermann Sudermann's *Heimat* cemented her reputation as the shining star of the New Theater movement. The alchemy of Sumako's art of theatrical translation can be measured by its effect on Hōgetsu himself: with the production of *Maguda* not only did Hōgetsu fall in love with the woman who was so good at rendering his carefully crafted translations onstage, he also gained a new confidence in the accessibility of translated drama. Half a year after *Maguda*'s run in Tokyo, Hōgetsu wrote:

People often say that with Western plays the flavor doesn't fully come through, so they want Japanese plays, but I have my doubts about this notion. Do we really sense a big difference in flavor between a well-performed Western play and a well-performed Japanese play? So long as the work and the production method are good, then it makes almost no difference whether the costumes, gestures, and proper nouns are Western or Japanese—isn't this degree of cosmopolitanism the state of our tastes today?[41]

It is at this point that the relationship between Japanese signifier and Western signified (Japanese language, Western text; Japanese actress, Western woman) becomes "transparent." The Hōgetsu who

明治座三月狂言當二番目（鈴）「材長怨案の場」

明治座三月狂言當二番目（鈴）「材長怨案の場」

遠方アイテント　隣眠郎の龍　左曜方のマシアス　荒郎の振例長　市川寺リタスチシ

市川市十郎のマリシ　中村又五源郎のハプンス　市左左源方のマシアス　市川左并テアラテの齢

FIGURE 11 (*top, left page*) Kawakami Otojirō and Sadayakko in *Momijigari* (Hunting autumn leaves), 1901. This photograph offers one of the most extreme examples of the primacy of gesture on the New School stage. *Courtesy of Kawakami Hatsu*

FIGURE 12 (*bottom, left page*) Ichikawa Sadanji makes a dramatic entrance on the New School stage, suggesting the continuing primacy of gestural language. *Suzu* (The bell), Meiji-za. *Engei gahō*, April 1911.

FIGURE 13 (*above*) Ichikawa Danjūrō strikes a famous pose as the eponymous hero of *Sukeroku* (Kabuki-za, 1896). *Engei gahō*, July 1909.

had talked about the manifold differences between Japanese signifier and Western signified that hindered the faithful translation of
a script for performance has been replaced by a cosmopolite who
firmly believes in a transcendental aesthetic. Surely it was Matsui
Sumako who established the standard for the kind of "well-performed Western play" that could make the audience see nature in
the opacities of style and meaning inherent to translated drama.
Indeed, so effective was her art that audiences began to read her performances of Western plays in the self-referential mode of Kataian
Naturalist fiction.

If Sumako's Nora established an association between the modern
actress and the persona of the awakening New Woman, her performance of Magda established the persona of the modern actress herself as a paragon of the New Woman. Taking up where Nora left off,
Sudermann's heroine has already defied her father's orders to marry,
left her parents' home, and established a career for herself as a singer.
The play opens with her return home eight years later, and the ensuing family conflict provides its central drama. During the production
of this play in Osaka in 1912, the professional relationship between
Hōgetsu and Sumako gave way to romantic involvement, an increasingly public scandal that ultimately led Tsubouchi Shōyō to dissolve
the Literary Arts Society in the following year. As Kano deftly points
out, "by translating the word 'Sängerin' (singer) of the original as *opera
joyū* (literally 'opera actress'), Hōgetsu's translation strengthened the
association between the character Magda and the actress performing
it."[42] When Hōgetsu and Sumako's affair developed into a full-fledged
domestic and professional partnership—Sumako was dismissed from
the Literary Arts Society by Tsubouchi Shōyō, Hōgetsu left his wife
and job, and together they founded the Literary Arts Theater (Bungei-
za) in July 1913—the self-referential mode of producing and reading
the plays would expand to include the director himself, and of course
the relationship between director and actress. Akita Ujaku notes that
during the period he calls "the victory of love," when Hōgetsu and
Sumako had first taken up residence together and were struggling to
establish a solid foundation for their Literary Arts Theater, "the works
they handled were mostly triangle relationship stories that spoke

of their own position, and Matsui Sumako would play the heroine and attract the attention of the public. The major plays were *Monna Vanna, The Lady from the Sea, Magda, Anna Karenina, The Power of Darkness, and The Living Corpse.*[43] Finally, in a strange twist of fate that once again identified the actress with her role, Matsui Sumako took to the stage as Isabella in D'Annunzio's *Dream of a Spring Morning* (*Sogno d'un Mattino di Primavera,* Japanese *Midori no asa*) on November 6, 1919, the day after Shimamura Hōgetsu's unexpected death from the Spanish flu. Sumako had been rehearsing this part when Hōgetsu died. In the play the character of Isabella loses her sanity after discovering her lover Giuliano murdered as he lay asleep next to her. When Sumako first appeared on stage on opening night, the audience fell silent for a moment, then broke out into spontaneous applause.[44]

The public nature of Hōgetsu and Sumako's affair had both immediate and long-term consequences. Having lost the financial backing of the Literary Arts Society, they were now forced to contend with public tastes and opinion in order to guarantee the survival of their troupe. This certainly became an important factor in their choice of plays and perhaps even the reason why they abandoned New Woman plays altogether. Hōgetsu had already been forced by police censorship to change the ending to *Maguda*, which they claimed to pose a grave threat to public morals. Instead of Magda's steadfast refusal to compromise with her father, the Osaka version of the play ended with Magda begging forgiveness for her sins.[45] We can easily imagine that once Hōgetsu and Sumako had themselves violated the code of public morals, they would have to tread lightly on such potentially explosive ground. By the end of her career in 1919, Sumako had become most powerfully associated with three distinct types of roles: the New Women of her first years, the fallen woman of Tolstoy's *Resurrection,* and the voluptuous femmes fatales of *Salomé* and *Carmen.*

In the long term, harshly critical views of Sumako—particularly among the actors and young male intellectuals who admired Hōgetsu and initially sympathized with him—would combine to create a composite portrait that connects Sumako with the femme fatale persona she played so well on the stage rather than the New Woman personae that originally cemented her reputation as Japan's first modern actress. As Phyllis Birnbaum vividly puts it,

On the list of women who have singlehandedly wrecked the lives of Japanese literati, Matsui Sumako has been given a prominent place. Now dead and unable to speak a word in protest, Matsui has long been at the mercy of her lover's writer friends, who have written denunciations of her in numerous biographies and reminiscences. Over the years, Matsui has been held responsible for the bouts of fever her beloved suffered, his financial dilemmas, the lonely look in his eye. It is said that she put impure ideas into the mind of her unfortunate partner, Shimamura Hōgetsu , whose only indulgence had been drinks at a second-floor noodle shop.[46]

Upon quitting the troupe in 1914 one disgruntled actor of the Bungei-za, Sasamoto Kōgo, had particularly acerbic things to say about Sumako.

The life of this new theater simply cannot be reconciled to a system that gives priority to the troupe leader. In the case of theater some compromise may be reached if the troupe leader is a humble artist with true understanding, but in a troupe sullied by the star status of an actress as self-centered and lacking in understanding as Sumako, one would do better trying to write on flowing water than to entertain high expectations. . . . In other words, to leave Sumako as she is now would neither benefit her nor [Shimamura] Sensei. It is also extremely disadvantageous for art itself. . . . These days I have the feeling that a certain death deity is shadowing Sensei. If it were an Otowaya-style death deity [i.e., a Kabuki player of the Onoe Kikugorō house], there might be some redeeming sense of black humor . . . but the death deity shadowing Sensei is dangerous. . . . Sensei surely cannot see it, but we can vaguely make out its figure and we are terribly frightened. Please be careful!![47]

In its comparison of Matsui Sumako to a dangerous "death deity," this diatribe may seem an extremely prescient foretelling of Hōgetsu's death five years later. But it would be more accurate to say that the bitter resentment against Sumako, shared by many of Sasamoto's peers, provided the ground upon which they later interpreted Hōgetsu's death and Sumako's career. Indeed, we could even go a step further to propose that pervasive hostility toward Sumako by Hōgetsu's many male admirers was the real death deity that drove Sumako, not Hōgetsu, to an early grave.

When Kawamura Karyō looked back on his initial reaction to *A Doll's House* eight years later (just after Sumako's death), he recalled being particularly interested in the resemblance of Sumako's enunciation of her lines and her accent to the mannerisms of Shimamura Hōgetsu himself, which led him to believe that Hōgetsu must have taught her how to say virtually every line. Because of his own ambition of becoming a director, he had seen this performance as a "beautiful and most precious instance of the director's passion, and Sumako's ability to become a doll for Shimamura-sensei."[48] Matsui Sumako thus appeared to fulfill the expectations laid out by Osanai, with the minor but significant difference that here the actress is a puppet for the director himself rather than the script. This fantasy of the perfectly understanding female disciple whose language reflects the heart and soul of her mentor is by now a familiar theme in the narrative of the Westernesque femme fatale, as is the betrayal necessarily built into it. In the love story of Hōgetsu and Sumako—retold so often (mostly by Sumako's male detractors) as to eclipse both their careers—we observe the ease with which a common fiction of the Westernesque woman could be transferred to the biography of the first Japanese woman to embody the images of modern Western women on the stage. As with Osei and Yoshiko, Sumako's sirenlike allure derived from her apparent fluency in an idealized, exotic language of the self, but her self-conscious manipulation of that language ultimately laid the foundation for her bitter betrayal of (and *by*) the entranced male subject. Sumako paid a high price for her position as Japan's first modern actress: she committed suicide on January 5, 1919, exactly two months after Hōgetsu's death. In the process of her physical and theatrical transformation, from a typical country woman to the New Woman and the tragic Westernesque femme fatale, we see the literary fascination with the Westernesque extended beyond the realm of media and gender image to leave an indelible impression upon the female body itself. The same exoticist sensibility that gave Naturalist drama the face of a new type of woman would also present a conundrum for Japanese women, both inspiring them to awaken to their identities as individuals and creating a powerful theatrical association between modern female self-consciousness and the treacherously calculated performance of the femme fatale.

Final Reflections
Gender, Cultural Hierarchy, and Literary Style

The biography of Japan's first modern actress—here defined as the first Japanese woman to successfully perform the modern Western woman's awakening to selfhood on the stage—presents a conundrum for literary history. Writers' lives are typically narrated in terms that lead more or less directly to their eventual careers in letters—the educational and reading résumés that illuminate their literary baselines and influences, the personal encounters that bring them to a career in writing, and the life experiences that shape the thematic terrain their brushes and pens will plow. But there is nothing in the early life of Kobayashi Masako that would suggest an inevitable desire to take to the stage, much less express herself in an art that had yet to be realized. Some of the short personal essays in *Botan bake* do attempt to bridge the gap between Sumako and Masako, pointing to a young woman's process of mastering the performative interaction between seller and buyer in the family confectioner where she works, or a girl's awakening to the opposite sex in the process of playing a part in a wedding ceremony, as instances of a budding actress's interest in everyday performance.[1] But these retrospective connections are so meager and tenuous as to suggest that even Sumako herself was hard-pressed to account for her own transformation in the conventionally prescribed manner. Indeed, it would be most accurate to say that Matsui Sumako was not the sum product of the life of Kobayashi Masako, but rather a radical break from that life catalyzed by the twenty-three-year-old Masako's sudden and intense engagement with modern European drama in translation. There was little or nothing in Masako's life that could have prepared her for the experience of going straight from the "ABC's of English" to Shakespeare, much less Ibsen. Moreover, as the depictions of a physically robust and hardworking but culturally challenged country bumpkin attest, the way in which that experience affected and transformed Kobayashi Masako clearly confounded all expectations.

The sharp discontinuity between the lives of Masako and Sumako has made the actress even more susceptible to the historical tendency to ascribe a woman's achievements to the men around her—in this case producing the frequent contentions that all that was right in her performances belonged to Hōgetsu, while all that was wrong with them belonged to Sumako alone. What is missing from the historical portrait of Matsui Sumako is her identity as a *reader* and any serious consideration of how her acts of reading enabled her stunning transformation from an unsophisticated woman of the backwaters of Matsushiro to the triumphant Japanese female embodiment of theatrical modernity. It would be no exaggeration to say that Matsui Sumako's acts of reading have been summarily dismissed in the rhetoric of memorization, which leaves ample room for the idea that the successful actress need not read her lines, but only render a perfect imitation of them. In this sense she is another example of the facility with which the cultural productivity of imitation, of submitting oneself to the seduction of a text written by another, can be retrospectively erased by the politics of the moment. One need only reinscribe the text with ultimate authority (originality) to cast its smitten reader as a hollow mimic, a person without a proper "self" of his or her own. But, as I have demonstrated, the sheer difficulty of satisfying the contemporary audience's desire for a performance of the modern woman that would deploy both the exotic and the quotidian in the creation of a new vernacular for the stage could not have been surmounted through "mere imitation."

The stigma of hollow imitation that haunts the East-West divide was displaced onto the figure of the Westernesque femme fatale, whose linguistic acts all turn out to be performative rather than referential—treacherous rather than truthful. This is how the history of vernacular textual exoticism created a double bind for the modern Japanese woman: by insisting that she both represent the purported freedom of spoken language *and* possess the kind of subjectivity that can only be formed by submission to the authority of the hallowed (and, in this case, Western) text. If the performative aspect of language was thus denigrated by male vernacularist authors, it would be well worth the effort to investigate how female writers working in the vernacular negotiated the apparent contradiction between the performative aspects of language and gender and the pursuit of modern selfhood. Although it is beyond the scope of the present study, the work of Tamura Toshiko, a woman whose career not only straddled both the classical and vernacular styles but also included a brief stint as an actress on the pre-Naturalist stage, offers fertile ground for such an inquiry.[2]

The initial inspiration for this study came many years ago from a graduate seminar in modern Japanese literature offered by Paul Anderer, which first introduced me to the phenomenon of the culturally hybrid femme fatale in the Modern Girl heroines of 1920s Japanese fiction. At the time I was mainly interested in what these popular media figures, whose depictions by Tanizaki and Kawabata seemed to resonate so clearly with the familiar eroticism of Euro-American images of the exotic other, could tell us about the particularities of Japanese modernity. What could be extrapolated from the fact that the hybrid figures of Westernesque Japanese women became the privileged objects of an eroticizing-exoticizing gaze unleashed by Japanese male writers? Put in another way, if the Western exoticist gaze directed itself at objects that were imagined to represent an undiluted otherness, how might an exoticism that stays at home and directs its gaze at a culturally hybrid female icon revise our understanding of the way in which self and other are constituted beyond the familiar bounds of the East-West divide?

These were the simple questions with which I set out to investigate the phenomena of the Westernesque woman in modern Japanese literature. In a manner somewhat vaguely inspired by the work of Northrop Frye, I began with the ambition of making meaning from a literary archetype and identifying a modern Japanese variety of exoticism that could, at the very least, relativize the implicit claims of the Euro-American exoticist project. However, I quickly realized that the greatest obstacle to this goal was posed by the multiple ways in which the figure of the Westernesque woman could be seamlessly recuperated to commonly held images of both Japan and the West. It is all too easy to read her as a mere by-product of global political, economic, and cultural hierarchies, to surmise that these were what made her a privileged object of Japanese male desire, one that was always circumscribed by the *real* exotic other of the West—a notion of otherness produced by Western exoticism itself. Such a reading would not only reconfirm the status of the Western exoticist gaze as a privileged form of modern subjectivity but would also implicitly reduce the writing of desire by modern Japanese authors (and actresses) to the status of semiconscious imitation that merely reflects a global reality without seriously reflecting *upon* it, thus failing to create anything new.

It was not until I moved out of the 1920s, the era of Japanese modernism, to trace the genealogy of the Westernesque woman back to the Meiji period that I began to see the problem from a different perspective: the relationship between modern literary style and translation. Although questions of literary form have always been a particular interest of mine, the question of literary style itself was not originally a central part of my inquiry. It was the work of Futabatei Shimei, both in its original conception and its later reception, that opened up this third path for me.

Analyses of literary texts that merely "discover" in literature something that could easily be deduced from the historical and theoretical narratives that already guide our understanding of literary context deserve to be regarded with suspicion. This kind of analysis can be done without actually reading works of literature. By its very nature, however, the study of Japanese literature within the American academy makes it difficult to avoid the mode of reading literature *only insofar as* it represents something else. We continually confront the problem of representativeness, which forces us to ask ourselves to what extent we study "Japan" and to what extent we study "literature." The deceptively simple answer is that we do both. But it is not an easy matter to balance the two. The problematic question of "Japan" or "literature" applies with even greater force to the study of *modern* Japanese literature. With its prominent literary and cultural differences, the study of premodern Japanese literature comes with a built-in raison d'être for the American scholar: between the two simple facts of the ubiquity of poetry and the unparalleled importance of female writers of the Heian court, she already has all she needs to justify her contribution to the study of world literature, both to her students and to that imagined field of interested American scholars whose baselines are defined by (often modern) Western traditions. By contrast, the inherently diluted and convoluted differences in Japan's modern literature constantly force the American scholar to question the broader relevance of what she has—out of some ineffable and perhaps truly inexplicable sense of personal affinity—chosen as her primary field of inquiry. The modernity of Japan does not afford the special appeal of postcolonial studies, which directly rewrites the history of English literary culture and identity formation from the perspective of its most significant others, its very own colonial subjects. If anything, the case of modern Japan deserves comparison to that of modern Russia, the original example of an empire that inhabits the liminal space between the West and the rest, being fated to switch sides according to the dictates of the political moment. When modern Japan has spoken directly to the West—here understood to mean Western Europe and the United States—it has been by means of either military or economic force or by an aesthetic seduction that is all the more suggestive for its political prostration. These are the basic facts with which any American scholar of modern Japanese literature is forced to contend, especially if she wants to address issues that do not apparently speak to the academy at large in an easily consumable form.

The approach that first brought modern Japanese literature to the attention of the American public in the postwar era was to show how very "Japanese" this literature was, in spite of Western influences, and to show how "literary" Japan has always been. In this scenario it is because Japan has always been so "literary" (i.e., aesthetically oriented) that *she* was able to withstand the potentially flattening forces of modernization = Westernization and retain a culturally distinct identity. Put in terms that are commonly accepted today, the original image of modern Japanese literature was constituted as part of the Orientalist production of knowledge and the fetishistic embrace of the aesthetic other that forms its counterpart. This is the disciplinary precedent against which all contemporary American scholars of Japanese literature must work. The project of revising that original image has included critical attention to writers who did not easily accommodate the Orientalist vision of modern Japan, literary histories that undermined such essentialist myths as "Japanese sincerity," and ideological issues that brought academic discussions of modern Japan out of the area studies ghetto and into the sights of contemporary Western theory. Among these critical approaches, I would submit that very little *concrete* attention has been paid to the issue of literary style, whether in translation or in expository discourse.

The reasons for this oversight should be obvious by now—to fully attend to the question of modern Japanese literary style in a way that goes beyond the mere categorization of types and vague suggestions of an individual author's "originality" requires a dizzying process of shuttling back and forth between English and Japanese in an attempt not to account for the "uniqueness" of the Japanese language but rather to evoke the interstitial quality of a language engendered by the encounter with modern Western literary languages.[3] If the work itself is arduous, the result is not necessarily reader-friendly, particularly if one hopes to reach an audience that does not already possess specialized knowledge of the field.

Nevertheless, I would propose that close attention to matters of literary style in fact constitutes one of the few compelling justifications for the work that we do as American scholars of modern Japanese literature. Indeed, it may very well be the only area of inquiry that enables us to discuss the modern Japanese writer *as writer*. This mission would seem to be built into our job descriptions, but the conditions in which we work continue to frustrate its actual execution. To focus on content alone requires the reader-scholar-critic of non-Western texts to identify a narratological or topological difference from the established image of modern Western writing in order to make her work worthy of perusal by the Western specialist. This suspicion was painfully confirmed for me when a highly sophisticated reader of my dissertation informed me that the Japanese authors I discussed had contributed nothing "new" to what had already been said in Western languages. My point then, and my point now, is that "newness" is not simply a matter of *content* (i.e., what was said). The sad fact is that what Japanese writers *write* is still seen by the non-specialist (and, even more sadly, often by the specialist herself) solely in terms of what they *said* and not what they *wrote*. In other words, despite the apparent superiority of Western literary and critical theory, the work of the non-Western writer is still reduced, by even the most apparently sophisticated of Western readers, to the status of mere content, more raw material for the production mill.

To avoid any misunderstandings, I should specify that by writer I do not mean to signify some kind of genius, in the romantic tradition, who is possessed of the awe-inspiring power to single-handedly create something new out of nothing. Although my depiction of Futabatei Shimei's stylistic invention does, admittedly, skirt the border of a romantic notion of originality, it is undertaken with the express intent of relativizing the notion of translation as merely derivative. Moreover, proper attention to literary style also demands that we acknowledge the inventiveness of a writer like Katai, who could otherwise be legitimately seen as a pathetic hack. It also requires that we acknowledge the innovations of not only Shimamura Hōgetsu but also Matsui Sumako, whose personal history as an inventor of language remains hazy at best. In the cases of Katai, Hōgetsu, and Sumako, it was their profound impact on both readers and other writers that determines their status as deft manipulators of written language. In this sense to discuss the modern Japanese writer as writer is also to discuss the modern Japanese reader as implicit *critic*. Although we may certainly debate the quality of the criticism, reading itself is never a passive act of reception. Nor is reading entirely constricted by the kind of "culture" that serves as the object of anthropological inquiry. While these facts are most clearly demonstrated by the written texts that acts of translingual reading have produced, the perfect memorization of *Ningyō no ie* by Matsui Sumako should, at the very least, stand shoulder to shoulder with the memorization of *Aibiki* by Naturalist writers like Katai and Doppo.

In its final formulation this study of modern Japanese vernacular literature as a form of exoticism aims to shed light on the linguistically based desire that gave birth to the Westernesque femme fatale. It is my hope that this focus on literary style—as opposed to mere content (including the more obvious questions about gender and culture)—will also open up new possibilities for *reading* modern Japanese literature in *all* its formal complexities, as an alternative to simply comparing its contents and structures against the monolithic, universal, and absolutely authoritative Western text.

Notes

Introduction

Segalen, *Essay on Exoticism*, 46. *Essai sur l'exotisme* is a posthumously published collection of Segalen's notes written from 1904–18.

1. Celéstin, *From Cannibals to Radicals*, 220.

2. Taussig, *Mimesis and Alterity*, xv.

3. Karatani, *Origins of Modern Japanese Literature*.

4. This condition is already suggested in Karatani's analysis of genbun-itchi, particularly in his assertion that Mori Ōgai's *Maihime*, in its relation to Western syntax, actually constituted an advance, rather than a retreat, for the genbun-itchi style. Ibid., 49–50.

5. Yonekawa, "Meiji, Taishō no ryūkōgo."

6. Mizuno, "Jogakusei-bi."

7. Silverberg, "The Modern Girl as Militant."

8. Nakamura, *Fūzoku shōsetsu ron*, 13–18.

9. Pierre Loti, "Les Femmes japonaises" (1890), *L'exilée* (Paris: Calmann Levy, 1896), 236–37.

10. Marjorie Garber, *Vested Interests: Cross-Dressing and Cultural Anxiety* (New York: Routledge, 1992).

11. Barthes, *Empire of Signs*, 6.

12. Berman, *The Experience of the Foreign*, 8.

13. Karatani, "Nationalism and Écriture," 17–18.

14. Friedrich Schleiermacher, "On the Different Methods of Translating" (1813), trans. Susan Bernofsky, in Venuti, *The Translation Studies Reader*, 62. For a thorough introduction to the discourse and practice of literary translation in the formative period of modern German literature see Bernofsky, *Foreign Words*.

15. Goethe, "Translations," 64.

16. Ibid., 64.

17. Ibid., 64–65.

18. Ibid., 65.

19. Geertz, "Thick Description," 9.

20. Appiah has also used this term, though in a much broader sense ("Thick Translation"). I have therefore deemed it more useful to define the term methodologically within the context of this study, rather than introduce Appiah's usage, only to reorient it toward my own.

Part 1. Foreign Letters, the Vernacular, and Meiji Schoolgirls

Futabatei, *Futabatei Shimei shū*, 38. The translation approximates the syllabic structure of the original, which very roughly follows the traditional 7–5 pattern of Japanese verse in accordance with the conventions of the *gabuntai* literary style. In addition, the translated quotes presented here attempt, as far as possible, to preserve the balance between Chinese and Japanese diction through the use of Latinate and native English terms, respectively.

1. Despite its longstanding position at the beginning of the canon of modern Japanese fiction, *Ukigumo* has never enjoyed a broad audience, in part because of Futabatei's hasty abandonment of novel writing and his steadfast refusal to join the literary circles of his day.

1. Translation as Origin and the Originality of Translation

1. See Isoda, "Yakugo 'bungaku' no tanjō," in *Rokumeikan no keifu*, 7–40. Isoda points out that the introduction of this particular concept of literature in Japan took place at a time when the concept of literature in the European context itself was still in a transitional phase from "learning, skill in letters" (Samuel Johnson) to the written arts of poetry, drama, and fiction.

2. Quoted in Itō, *Nihon bundan shi 1: Kaika no hitobito*, 17. I am indebted to Nakajima Fumi for explicating the puns in this passage. We were unable to determine an alternative meaning for *roshia* (Russia) with any certainty.

3. Ibid., 162–63.

4. Tokuda, *Meiji shōsetsu bunshō hensen shi*, 13. According to Tsubouchi Shōyō, this work was actually written by Katō Asatori (*Kaki no heta*, in *Shōyō senshū*, vol. a4, bessatsu 4, 407).

5. Ishii also documents a boom in spoken *kango* in *Meiji jibutsu kigen*, 82.

6. Kimura, *Meiji hon'yaku bungaku shū*, 395–96.

7. Ryan, *Japan's First Modern Novel*, 100.

8. On the importance of the *bōdoku* style of *kanbun* in enabling modern Japanese narratives that were not inscribed with linguistic markers of class hierarchy, see Kamei, *Transformations of Sensibility.*

9. Ryan, *Japan's First Modern Novel*, 43. The passage from Shōyō's *Shumpū jōwa* can be found in *Shōyō senshū*, bessatsu 2, 39. The lines of the original text are not separated as in Ryan's romanized transcription.

10. *Aibiki* was first published in *Kokumin no tomo*, vol. 3, nos. 25 and 27 (July and August 1887).

11. Futabatei, "Yo ga hon'yaku no hyōjun," *Futabatei Shimei zenshū* 4:167; originally published in *Seikō* (January 1906).

12. Futabatei, "Shōsetsu sōron," *Futabatei Shimei zenshū* 4:7–8. Originally published in *Chūō gakujutsu zasshi* (April 1886).

13. Quoted in Ebiike, *Meiji bungaku to eibungaku*, 44. The original passage is from *Chūgaku sekai* (November 1906).

14. Ibid., 44–45.

15. Yamamoto, "Genbun-itchi-tai," 318–19. Specifically, Yamamoto cites Ōtsuki Gentaku's *Kangaku kaitei* (1783) and Ōba Sessai's *Yaku waran bungo* (1855–57). Genbun-itchi advocate Maejima Hisoka was also a Dutch translator for the Edo Bakufu.

16. Although, of course, there are crucial differences between the Japanese and European situations. In the European context the movement toward the vernacular was a form of resistance against the hegemony of Latin, a prestige language. In Japan this kind of vernacularization had already been realized long before the threat of Western hegemony, in response to the hegemony of China and Chinese characters. In this sense the Japanese parallels to the work of Dante, Luther, and Chaucer can already be found in such "ancient" (classical) works of Japanese literature as the *Man'yōshū, Kojiki, Kokinshū,* and *Genji monogatari.* By the time that Japan confronted the threat of Western hegemony, the vernacular as a "native or indigenous" idiom had already been well established as a literary language for certain genres such as Japanese poetry (as opposed to the Chinese poetry with which it coexisted), narrative fiction, and nativist studies. Thus the "native" language of "Japanese" was already a written language, but it was not the common parlance of contemporary Japan, nor could it function as the written language of modern Japan. Whereas the prestige language of Latin served as a model for vernacular writing in the European context, then, it was the vernacular writing of Europe that served as a model for genbun-itchi.

17. It is worth noting that in *Ukigumo* Futabatei often circumvented the final copula altogether, preferring to use the circumlocution of the conjunctive *de* instead.

18. Yamamoto, "Genbun-itchi-tai," 316, 332. It has also been suggested that the use of *desu* was particularly reminiscent of the language of the pleasure quarters. Bimyō himself switched from *da* to *desu,* while writing for the women's education magazine *Iratsume,* in what may have been an attempt to appeal to female readers by using a more polite (and also more feminine) form of the vernacular.

19. Turgenev, *A Sportsman's Notebook,* 266.

20. Futabatei, *Futabatei Shimei zenshū,* vols. 2, 5. All citations are from the first version of *Aibiki,* as published in *Kokumin no tomo.*

21. Ryan, *Japan's First Modern Novel,* 122.

22. Ishibashi, "*Aibiki o yonde*" (1888), in *Futabatei Shimei zenshū,* bessatsu, 345.

23. Turgenev, *A Sportsman's Notebook,* 266.

24. Tsubouchi and Uchida, *Futabatei Shimei,* 79.

25. Unlike modern English, both written and spoken Japanese encompass

a multiplicity of first-person pronouns. According to Daniel Sullivan's count, there are at least twenty-five first-person pronouns from which to choose. Until Futabatei's *Aibiki*, *jibun* had never been an option for the first-person pronoun in writing. First of all, first-person statements in writing, whether in "Japanese" or "Chinese," did not necessarily require the use of a first-person pronoun, since the first-person nature of a statement could be articulated by verb form alone. However, in cases that required the explicit articulation of a first-person pronoun, the options for writing were generally dominated by "Chinese" usages such as *yo* and *wagahai* for men, and *warawa* for women. The former two examples, belonging to the lexicon of the learned lingua franca, fall somewhere between "I" and the royal "we" in English, while the latter example, which marks the female gender of the enunciator, stands somewhere between "I, being a mere woman" and "I, being simply a woman but still an educated woman." The first-person pronoun *jibun* derives from the spoken lexicon. In English the closest approximation for *jibun* is "oneself," in the sense that *jibun* may be used to refer to the "self" of the speaker or the "self" of people in general. As opposed to other options from spoken Japanese such as *watakushi, boku,* or *atashi,* which can only refer to the enunciator, *jibun* has a more neutral resonance, as it does not clearly mark the relationship between speaker and addressee in the social hierarchy.

26. Yamada, "Preface to *Fūkin shirabe no hitofushi*," in *Iratsume*, vol. 1 (July 9, 1888): 14–15.

27. Futabatei, "Yo ga genbun-itchi no yurai" (1906), *Futabatei Shimei zenshū* 4:171–73.

28. Yamada, *Fūkin Shirabe,* 15–16.

29. Yamada, *Natsu kodachi,* 49; originally published in *Garakuta bunko,* vols. 15–16 (December 1887–February 1888).

30. Ishibashi, "*Aibiki* o yonde," 345.

31. Karatani, *The Origins of Modern Japanese Literature,* 49–51.

2. Meiji Schoolgirls in and as Language

1. Tsubouchi, *Shōyō senshū,* vol. a4, bessatsu 4, 418–19. *Omai* and *ore* are casual first- and second-person pronouns of spoken Japanese; *sō kai* is a casual question form, and *sō shina* is a casual imperative form. When Shōyō

offers kanbun-kuzushi as an alternative to such expressions, his reference to the form *kou naninani se yo* should replace *sō shina*, not *sō kai.*

2. Mill, *History of British India*, 383–85. That Mill was simply making an argument for the moral superiority of England over India and other countries, and not for the equality of the sexes, is amply demonstrated by his later arguments against women's suffrage.

3. A list of those works that focus specifically on Western women would include *Saigoku retsujo den* (Biographies of heroic women from Western countries; Tajima Shōji, 1881); *Rokoku kibun Retsujo no gigoku* (Strange tales from Russia: Heroic women in prison; Someda Sakutarō, 1882); *Kakumei yobun Yūfu Tereeze den* (Overheard at the revolution: Biography of Therese, woman of courage; Kawazu Hiroyuki and Komiyama Tenkō, 1882); *Joketsu zenden kadofu* (Woman of courage Joan of Arc; Matsumura Misao, 1884), an adapted biography of Joan of Arc; *Kaiten iseki Futsukoku bitan* (Heroic acts: A French tale of virtue; Kuriya Kan'ichi, 1884), another biography of Joan of Arc; *Naou gaiden Keishū bitan* (Biography of Napoleon's wife: A tale of female virtue; Akiba Kiyotarō, 1885), a translation of a biography of Josephine; *Teisō Eikoku bitan* (Fidelity: An English tale of Virtue; Yarita Shujin, 1886), a translation of John Cooke's *My Lady Pocahantas*; and *Taisei jojōfu Roran fujin den* (A Western woman stalwart: The life of Madame Roland; Tsubouchi Shōyō, 1886), a translation of a biography of Madame Roland.

4. Of course, a discursive connection between the feminine and the native in Japan can already be seen in the work of Motoori Norinaga. Yet this is still a step removed from the explicit connection between historical and legendary female figures and the Japanese nation that emerges in the Meiji period.

5. Yamakawa, *Onna nidai no ki*, 30–31. Nakamura Masanao was a friend of Kikue's grandfather and encouraged him to send his daughter Chise (Kikue's mother) to his school. Her account is based on the recollections of her mother and grandfather.

6. Nakamura, "Zenryō naru haha o tsukuru setsu."

7. *Iratsume*, vol. 1, from the journal's statement of purpose.

8. First initiated by Christian missionaries, the history of Meiji women's education was further propelled by the government's institution of compulsory elementary education for both sexes in 1872, the establishment of the exclusive Takehashi Jogakkō (for the education of high-ranking bureaucrats' daughters) in the same year, the Joshi Shihan Gakkō (Normal School for

Women, forerunner to Ochanomizu Joshi Daigaku) in 1875, and a host of privately managed girls' schools.

9. Masaki and Nakagawa, "How to Unify the Writing of Men and Women," in *Dainippon kyōiku zasshi*, nos. 73 and 74 (March and April 1888). The essay contest was sponsored by Mori Arinori, then education minister.

10. Nakagawa, "*Iratsume* to genbun-itchi"; quoted by Yamada Yūsaku in the "Kaidai" (commentary) to the reprint of *Iratsume* (Fuji shuppan, 1983), 11.

11. *Iratsume* 1:16–18.

12. *Iratsume* 3 (September 10, 1887): 19. The *Tempō era*, from 1830–44, was commonly used as a pejorative epithet meaning "backward" or "behind the times." While a second-person pronoun is not expressly articulated in Bimyō's text, I have used "you" here to capture the attack the narrator implicitly directs at both Okaku and any reader who might identify with her. This implication is particularly clear in the final line, which directly addresses either the reader or Okaku herself or both: "Oi, sore de mo shukujo ka."

13. Ibid., 19–20.

14. Bimyō begins the first chapter of his next *Iratsume* novel, *Fukusa zutsumi*, with an account of a young woman who visits him to lodge the complaint that *Fūkin* is inappropriate material for a women's education magazine. She suggests that he write about more exemplary women, and offers the story of her own life as material. *Iratsume* 4:7–10.

15. At the end of the final installment of *Fūkin*, Bimyō appends several comments by unnamed critics, one of whom states that "in a women's education magazine, even if it's a case of true love, there's no good in imitating the likes of Lytton. Most people will see it in the same way as Tamenaga, you know." *Iratsume* 3:24.

16. *Iratsume*, 2 (August 13, 1887): 22–23.

17. See the June 24, 1889, entry in Futabatei's journal *Ochiba no hakiyose futakagome* in *Futabatei Shimei zenshū* 5:75 and Saganoya, "*Ukigumo* no kushin to shisō."

18. Futabatei, "Sakka kushindan" (1897), in *Futabatei Shimei Zenshū* 4:151. In an interview eleven years later, Futabatei gave a slightly different version of his models for writing, naming Goncharov as the main influence on volume 3 ("Yo ga hansei no zange" [1908]), in *Futabatei Shimei Zenshū* 4:288–97. While the difference between Dostoevsky and Goncharov is far

from insignificant, making this discrepancy a source of consternation for Futabatei scholars, it is not particularly important to the discussion at hand, so I have adhered to Futabatei's original account for the sake of simplicity.

19. Uchida, *Omoidasu hitobito*, 20.

20. Gotō, "Konketsu to bunretsu," 251–52. The phrase "Slavic spirit, Western knowledge" is a play on the Meiji slogan "Japanese spirit, Western knowledge" (*wakon-yōsai*).

21. Gotō makes a persuasive case for Dostoevsky's *The Double* as the essential subtext for *Ukigumo*, upsetting the longstanding emphasis on Goncharov and Turgenev in Futabatei studies.

22. Ibid. Futabatei studied Russian at the Tōkyō Gaigo Gakkō (Tokyo School of Foreign Language). See Ryan, *Japan's First Modern Novel,* for an account of his education and upbringing.

23. Futabatei, "Roshia no fujin-kai," *Futabatei Shimei zenshū* 4:62–70 (1904).

24. For instance, see headnote 6 and supplementary notes 48, 51, and 53 to *Ukigumo* in *Futabatei Shimei shū*, 72, 429, and 430, annotated by Hata and Yasui, with commentary by Tanaka Yasutaka.

25. Futabatei, *Shinpen Ukigumo* 1:30–34. A note on the style: as the above transcription of the original text illustrates, Futabatei used very little punctuation for the first two volumes of *Ukigumo*. There are only a few commas and brackets to set off speech, with no periods at all, and no paragraph breaks except to set off passages of dialogue. Because of the sheer length and quantity of the quotations, I have broken Futabatei's rule of translation and refrained from strictly following the orthography of the original text. For the rest of the quotations from *Ukigumo* I have cited the edited text from *Futabatei Shimei shū*, with page numbers given in parentheses. The above passage can be found on pp. 50–51 in that volume.

26. In this case, *bungaku* refers to learning, rather than *literature* in the modern sense. Sekii Mitsuo pointed out to me that the name Bunzō also derives from the year of the character's birth, Bunkyū 3 (1863).

27. The term probably derived from the German *Wahrheit*.

28. Hata and Yasui cite the following passage as an example: "To start with, a fixed truth is immutable throughout the ages; hence it is said that the world should change course in accordance with the truth, but the truth should never change with the times"; "Shūkyō shinkaron," *Jogaku zasshi*, December 15, 1886, *Futabatei Shimei shū*, supplementary note no. 53, 430.

29. Lippit's analysis of the eruption of foreign words as a symptom of psychological breakdown in the work of Akutagawa Ryūnosuke originally alerted me to a similar trend in *Ukigumo*. See "The Disintegrating Machinery of the Modern."

Part 2. Tayama Katai and the Siren of Vernacular Letters

1. A brief catalogue of relevant examples would include *Makaze koikaze*, *Hototogisu* (Tokutomi Roka, 1898), *Konjiki yasha* (Ozaki Kōyō, 1897–1902), *Onogatsumi* (Kikuchi Yūhō, 1899–1900), *Seishun* (Oguri Fūyō, 1905–6), *Sanshirō* (Natsume Sōseki, 1908), and *Baien* (Morita Sōhei, 1909).

3. Portrait of the Naturalist as a Young Exote

1. Tayama, *Tōkyō no sanjūnen*, 19–21.

2. Katai's hometown of Tatebayashi (currently part of Gunma Prefecture) was on a particularly fast track to the periphery: as the former domain of a house that had served the Tokugawa Shogunate for centuries, its history was not favorable to its prospects under the new regime. For the Tayama family, low-ranking retainers to Tatebayashi's Lord Akimoto, the Meiji restoration theoretically brought the promise of an upward mobility that had been foreclosed to them in the Tokugawa era; in reality, it stripped them of security and the modicum of social standing that had made their already low standard of living tolerable. The search for better prospects would inevitably point in the direction of the new capital. See Yanagida, *Tayama Katai no bungaku 1: Katai bungaku no botai*.

3. See Richter, "Marketing the Word," and Kinmonth, *The Self-Made Man in Meiji Japanese Thought*.

4. Tayama, "Yo no tōshoka jidai," *Bunshō sekai*, vol. 3, no. 13; quoted in Yanagida, *Tayama Katai no bungaku II: shōnen Katai no bungaku*, 86.

5. Tayama, *Tōkyō no sanjūnen*, 24–25.

6. Ibid., 34–35.

7. Ozaki, *Ninin bikuni Iro zange*, in *Ozaki Kōyō shū*, 4.

8. Kitani, *Ozaki Kōyō kenkyū*, 40. When Kōyō later revised this work, he

deleted this sentence. Kitani provides a detailed analysis of the differences between the original version of *Ninin bikuni* and its later revision for the *Kōyō zenshū*.

9. On Saikaku's idiosyncratic style of punctuation, see Ihara, *The Great Mirror of Male Love*, 22–23. For those who are not familiar with classical Japanese and Chinese writing, it is important to note that there were no universally accepted rules for punctuation in these systems; most often, writers used no punctuation at all. Kōyō's punctuation in *Iro zange* was both idiosyncratic and eclectic—his use of white periods derives from the work of Ihara Saikaku, while the dashes and ellipses come from English, yet their usage departs from the English model. By contrast, Yamada Bimyō introduced the rules of English punctuation in his usage of commas and periods; he defined his own use of the white comma as something between a black comma and a period, like the English semicolon.

10. Kitani, *Ozaki Kōyō kenkyū*, 40.

11. Ibid., 43. Kitani argues that Kōyō's attempt to fashion a new style, coupled with his rejection of the genbun-itchi model, led to a reliance on dashes and ellipses as innovative replacements for the copular sentence ending. She also notes that Kōyō jettisoned most of these foreign elements when he rewrote *Ninin bikuni* for publication in the *Kōyō zenshū*.

12. Tayama, "Kōyō Sanjin o tou," *Tōkyō no sanjūnen*, 43–48.

13. Tayama, "Bunshō o tsukutte kita keiken," in *Bunshō sekai*, vol. 7, no. 3 (February 1912).

14. Yanagida, *Tayama Katai no bungaku 2: Shōnen Katai no bungaku*, 203. Furthermore, the magazine's circulation was strictly limited to its paying members. This rather odd stipulation can only lead to one of two possible conclusions: that the magazine was based on the *Eisai shinshi* model, in which the writers were also the readers and consumers, or that the Ken'yūsha members expected the magazine's membership to function as its writers, readers, and noncommissioned distributors. In either case the enterprise could be called exploitative.

15. See Itō, *Nihon bundan shi 3: Nayameru wakōdo no mure* (1995 [1955]), 120–21.

16. Tayama Katai, *Kindai no shōsetsu* (1923), in *Katai zenshū shinshū*, bekkan (Bunsendō shoten, 1974), 256.

17. In passing we should note that, before Futabatei, Mori Ōgai had ful-

filled this function for Katai. In several of his memoirs Katai recalls his youthful admiration for Ōgai's translation style and his erudition in Western letters, stating that Ōgai showed him an important alternative to the literary mainstream dominated by Kōyō. In fact, Katai even published several poems in Ōgai's first journal, *Shigarami sōshi*. Yet later Ōgai would repeatedly critize Katai's fiction in his second critical journal, *Mezamashi gusa*, a slight that may have contributed to Katai's belated conversion to Futabatei.

18. Uchida Roan, "Gendai bungaku" (1891), in *Uchida Roan shū*, 166–72.

19. Tayama, "Bunshō o tsukutte kita keiken."

20. Tayama, "Futabatei Shimei-kun," in Tsubouchi and Uchida, *Futabatei Shimei*, 47.

21. Tayama, *Tōkyō no sanjūnen*, 34.

22. Tayama, *Meiji no shōsetsu*, as quoted in Yamamoto Masahide, *Genbun-itchi no rekishi ronkō: zokuhen*, 563.

23. Tayama, "Rokotsu naru byōsha," 198.

24. Tayama, *Kindai no shōsetsu*, 245–46.

25. *Sekai daihyakka jiten* (Heibonsha, 1955), quoted in Yanabu, *Hon'yaku no shisō*, 40–42.

26. Yanabu, *Hon'yakugo seiritsu jijō*, 133.

27. Yanabu, *Hon'yaku no shisō*, 126.

28. As quoted ibid., 113–14.

29. To illustrate the intellectual impasse created by the coexistence of these two contradictory meanings in *shizen*, Yanabu cites the 1889 "literature and nature" debate between Iwamoto Yoshiharu and Mori Ōgai (a false opposition that he finds repeated in Nakamura Mitsuo's critique of Katai). The debate was sparked by Iwamoto's claim that the greatest literature depicts nature just as it is—"shizen no mama ni shizen o utsusu." Ōgai objected that such was the province of scientific writing, while artistic writing aims to capture the *Geist = seishin* of *Natur = shizen*. Yanabu convincingly argues that because Ōgai used *shizen* as a Japanese synonym for the German *Natur*, he misunderstood Iwamoto's meaning. As their debate unfolded, it became evident that Iwamoto's *shizen* not only included the *Geist* of *Natur* but also served as the all-encompassing source of the writer's ideals and tastes. As such, Iwamoto's *shizen* could not be an object for the writer to observe and purify in writing, as Ōgai insisted it should be, because it was the ultimate source of everything, including subjectivity itself. Yanabu's account of the debate conjures an image

of Ōgai and Iwamoto arguing over what they fail to recognize as false cognates. We should also note, however, that another crucial difference between the debaters was their grounding in so-called Western thought—Ōgai was trained in the medical sciences in Germany, while Iwamoto was educated and converted by American Protestant missionaries. If the two ended up with significantly different versions of Western thought, it seems reasonable to suspect that those differences might have also reflected some of the incongruencies in the various cultures of the West, rather than an essential difference between traditional Japan and the modern Western monolith. If Ōgai was mainly interested in attacking Iwamoto's failure to grasp the difference between natural phenomena and human artifice, science and art, Iwamoto seemed particularly dedicated to demonstrating the superiority of nature—creation in the Christian sense—over human endeavor, chastising the arrogance of man by reference to the omnipotence and omnipresence of God. As usual, the Japan-West binary creates an illusion of native versus Western culture that grossly oversimplifies a much more complicated scenario.

30. Tayama, "Rokotsu naru byōsha," 201.

31. Ibid., 199 and 201, respectively.

32. Tayama, "Ozaki Kōyō to sono sakuhin" (1912), in *Tayama Katai zenshū*, 15:244–47.

33. Kōyō's father, Takeda Sōzō, was well-known not only for his carving skills but also as a *hōkan*, a professional host who tended to guests in the pleasure quarters, at theaters, and at sumo tournaments. Kōyō's mother was the daughter of a Chinese doctor, and he was raised by his maternal grandfather. His patrilineage was apparently a source of great embarrassment to him. See Itō, *Nihon bundan shi*, 3:212–13.

34. Tayama, "Ozaki Kōyō to sono sakuhin," 248.

35. Ozaki, "Dokusha hyōbanki 3—hiiki no kakeai," *Momochidori*, vol. 4 (October 20, 1889). As quoted in Yamamoto Masahide, *Kindai buntai hassei no shiteki kenkyū* (Iwanami shoten, 1965), 735. For some reason, this portion of the text has been omitted from the *Ozaki Kōyō zenshū*.

36. Oka, *Ozaki Kōyō no shōgai to bungaku*, 44–45.

37. Emi, *Ken'yūsha to Kōyō*.

38. Nakamura, *Fūzoku shōsetsu ron*, 18–19.

39. Ibid., 37–38.

4. Literary Desire and the Exotic Language of Love

1. Kamei, *Transformations of Sensibility*, 45.

2. Tokutomi Sohō, "Comments on the Boom in Political Novels" ("Kinrai ryūkō no seiji shōsetsu o hyōsu"), *Kokumin no tomo*, no. 6 (July 1887), 11; quoted and translated ibid., 44.

3. Tayama, "Kisu izen," in *Kataishū*, 287–88.

4. Tayama, *Tōkyō no sanjūnen*, 43. The names, both poetic tropes of autumn, suggest a particularly felicitous match.

5. Kamei, *Transformations of Sensibility*, 34.

6. Bun'en expounded a philosophical and aesthetic ideology that shared much in common with Futabatei Shimei's idealism and Mori Ōgai's romanticism. In "Chōzetsu shizen ron" (*Shinbundan*, no. 1), Bun'en stated that the phenomena of nature were not the proper model for literature, but rather that literature should target the essence of phenomena. Katai recalls that it was Bun'en who first introduced him to the work of Futabatei (*Tōkyō no sanjūnen*, 49–52). Since Bun'en wrote very little and quickly fell into obscurity, it is difficult to trace his intellectual lineage or the precise nature of his influence on Katai, but he was an early bridge between Katai and Futabatei.

7. Takase, "Bungaku iken," in *Yamada Bimyō Ishibashi Ningetsu Takase Bun'en shū*, 358. Originally published as a supplement to *Wakaba* (Shun'yōdō, 1893). Presumably Bun'en's concept of the poet as a transcendental literary artist derived from the introduction of romantic literary ideals in the pages of *Shigarami sōshi*, the magazine of literary criticism launched by Mori Ōgai shortly after his return from Germany. By 1892 this idea was circulating well beyond the pages of Ōgai's magazine.

8. See Tayama Mizuho, "Mukashi no shokan—Takase Bun'en ni tsuite," ibid., 389–98, for a thorough account of Bun'en's response to "Shōshijin," including his letters to Katai and an unpublished review of the novella.

9. Tayama, "Shōshijin," in *Tayama Katai zenshū*, Shinshū bekkan:122. Page numbers for the following quotations are given in parentheses.

10. "At the time, it was after Kunikida had separated from that woman Onobu, and he was living in a house on a hilltop in the Shibuya suburbs. I had not only already heard the story from [Miyazaki] Koshoshi, but was also interested in his love story, as well as being impressed by his fresh, vivid

writing, so after visiting Koshoshi's place in Dōgen-zaka, I suddenly called on him at his house on the hilltop." Katai, *Tōkyō no sanjūnen*, 102.

11. Kobayashi, *Tayama Katai kenkyū*, 2:400–1.

12. Tayama, "Kisu izen," 288.

13. Saeki, *Iro to ai no hikaku bunkashi*, 36–40.

14. Tayama, "K to T," in *Tōkyō no sanjūnen*, 113–16.

15. Ibid., 135.

16. Tayama, *Kindai no shōsetsu* (1923), in *Tayama Katai zenshū*, Shinshū bekkan:241.

17. Tayama, "D no shishū," in *Bunshō sekai*, August 1918, quoted in Kobayashi, *Tayama Katai kenkyū*, 7:442.

18. Tayama, *Jokyōshi*, *Tayama Katai zenshū*, 14:475–76; page numbers for the following quotations are given in parentheses.

19. Tayama, *Teikoku bungaku* (July 1903); quoted in Kobayashi, *Tayama Katai kenkyū*, 3:444.

20. Ibid., 444–45.

21. Tayama, "Shōjo-bi," 8.

22. Tokuda Shūsei: "In general, I like women who are full of expression. No matter how good her face might be, I don't like the kind of regular facial features that fit into a mold. The same can be said about her demeanor; a grace that unwittingly moves men's hearts, in other words, a rich expressiveness, is good. In terms of her comportment as well, she must be spirited and expressive." ("Bijin to wa?" 1–2) Mizuno Yōshū: "For us [the schoolgirl] has a certain demeanor and expression that completely breaks free of the old mold and ventures forth into a new realm of freedom, which brings us into contact with impressions and feelings that we do not find in other types of women. What I meant by 'high-collar' was precisely this free expression and an air of having broken free from the inherited mold" ("Jogakusei-bi," 10).

23. Honda, *Jogakusei no keifu*.

24. Yanabu, *Hon'yakugo seiritsu jijō*, 98–100. The translation of Aizan is from Suzuki, *Narrating the Self*, 75.

5. Haunting the Laboratory of Vernacular Style

1. Kobayashi, *Tayama Katai kenkyū*, 3:444.

2. Tayama, "Shōjobyō," in *Tayama Katai shū*, 70. Page numbers for the following quotations are given in parentheses. A note on the translation: I have supplemented third-person pronouns in brackets where necessary for the sake of clarity.

3. Tayama, *Bibun sahō*, in *Teihon Katai zenshū*, 26:4–8.

4. Tayama, *Shōjo sekai* (May 1906), quoted in Kobayashi, *Tayama Katai kenkyū*, 4:192–94.

5. "*Katai shū* gappyō," *Shumi* 3, no. 5 (May 1908), 66.

6. Sōma, "*Futon* gappyō," 1:53.

7. Mitani, "Kindai shōsetsu no gensetsu." In a similar line of reasoning Noguchi Takehiko also argues that the use of *ta* in modern Japanese fiction is not so much a matter of tense but of person; *Sanninshō no hakken made*.

8. Even a vernacularist like Futabatei, who clearly modeled his style after Western writing, heavily exploited this indigenous rhetorical device in his fiction. The frequent use of the present tense and clipped sentences in early genbun-itchi fiction may also suggest a visceral resistance to some of the Western rhetorical conventions upon which it was initially based. A work by Ozaki Kōyō offers a convenient case study. Written in the vernacular, *Tonari no onna* (The woman next door, 1893) was an adaptation of Zola's *Pour une nuit l'amour*, which Kōyō had read in an English translation lent to him by Matsui Shōyō. A decade later Matsui published a literal translation of the same work in *Bungeikai*. Kitani Kimie's detailed comparison of the two texts illustrates key differences between a Japanese style largely dictated by the rhetorical conventions and grammatical expectations of a Western language and the kind of felicitous Japanese style that Kōyō hoped to develop even in the use of the vernacular. Kōyō uses the present tense in 93 percent of his sentences, whereas Matsui's translation is predominantly past tense (59.5 percent), and while Matsui only employs the nominal sentence ending once, *Tonari no onna* avails itself of this technique in thirty-seven instances. These striking differences mark Matsui's effort at faithful translation, on the one hand, and the keen sensitivity to native linguistic sensibilities and antipathy for the buttery stench of translationese that enabled Kōyō to create a more

easily digestible form of the vernacular style, on the other. Kitani, *Ozaki Kōyō kenkyū*, 89.

9. The name most commonly associated with the *da* sentence ending is Futabatei Shimei, who referred to himself as a proponent of the "*da* style" in the interview "Yo ga genbun-itchi no yūrai" (The origins of my vernacular, 1906, in *Futabatei Shimei zenshū* 4:171–73). But, in actual fact, Futabatei almost never used the final *da* in any of his writing. In early translations like *Aibiki* and *Meguriai* he chose the past-tense expository copula *de atta* (which he later revised to the present-tense *de aru* following Kōyō's example). In *Ukigumo* I have only been able to locate a single instance of the final *da* in any of the narrative passages, and it punctuates a harshly acerbic narratorial comment, "iya ourayamashii koto da" (*Shinpen Ukigumo*, 1:2). The sense of the statement translates as something like "It is oh-so enviable"). Contrary to the common misconception of Futabatei as the progenitor of the *da* style vernacular, in *Ukigumo* he consistently *avoided* the final copula, frequently resorting to the circumlocution of its conjunctive form *de* when other options such as the nominal sentence ending did not avail. What he meant by the "*da* style" was clearly not his use of this particular form of the copula but rather his choice of informal verb endings, as opposed to Bimyō's preference for the more formal *desu/masu* declensions.

10. Ozaki, *Kōyō zenshū*, 5:483.

11. Katai adopted this style for *Nanashigusa* (Nameless grasses), February 1896. See Yamamoto, *Genbun-itchi no rekishi ronkō*, 188. Katai's first use of the *de aru* style was in *Rakka-son*, published in *Kokumin shimbun* from March 27 through June 19, 1892. Katai then abandoned this style in favor of nonvernacular models for several years, finally settling into the vernacular style around 1899 with *Ukiaki*. See Yamamoto, *Genbun-itchi no rekishi ronkō: zokuhen*, 568–609.

12. See Fujii, "Between Style and Language: The Meiji Subject and Natsume Sōseki's *Neko*" for an analysis of the ways in which "*Neko* definitively breaks with Tokugawa literature"; *Complicit Fictions*, 103–25.

13. Tayama, *Bibun sahō*, in *Teihon Katai zenshū*, 26:265.

14. Of the remaining four examples of the *da*-final sentence, two express the narrator's aesthetic appraisal of particular young women whom Sugita encounters, one represents Sugita's internal exclamation directly in the narrative passage, and one describes Sugita's personal knowledge of the com-

muting patterns of young women on his route. Notably, in most of these cases there is a strong potential to blur the boundary between the subject positions of narrator and protagonist. At the same time, however, the use of the spoken *da* precludes the possibility of fusing either subject position with that of a neutral, objective observer.

15. Tayama, *Futon, Tayama Katai shū*, 71–72. Page numbers for the following quotations are given in parentheses.

16. Yanabu, *Hon'yakugo seiritsu jijō*, 197–98.

17. Ibid., 210.

18. Ibid., 199–202.

19. Ibid., 210–11.

20. A note on the translation: in order to give the reader a better sense of the specific role played by "superfluous" personal pronouns in the original text, I have attempted an interlineal translation that ignores English rhetorical norms. In many places the result reads like diary shorthand, which is not an accurate representation of the original text. Rather, what I had hoped to reveal is the fluidity of subject positions made possible in Japanese—which does not require the overt articulation of a grammatical subject—when the narrative adopts the expository, rather than spoken, idiom. In the absence of the occasional "he," we might reasonably read this as a first-person narrative. Instead we find ourselves meandering between first- and third-person perspectives.

21. Amano, "Tayama Katai-shi no *Futon*."

22. Nakamura, *Fūzoku shōsetsu ron*, 38.

23. Yanabu, *Hon'yaku seiritsu jijō*, 212.

24. Sōma, "*Futon* gappyō," 1:50.

25. In October 1906 Katai wrote an essay entitled "Jijitsu no jinsei," or "Factual Life." Numerous critics have seen this work as evidence of Katai's increasing estimation of the literary value of actual facts and a major impetus for the particular form of Naturalism he practiced.

26. Sōma, "*Futon* gappyō," 1:51.

27. For a thorough examination of the relationship between truth and sexuality in Japanese Naturalism, see Suzuki, *Narrating the Self*, 79–88.

28. Futabatei, *Ukigumo*, 109.

29. On this point I am indebted to Iida Yūko's work on Natsume Sōseki's *Sanshirō* for illuminating the significance of the emphasis on female facial

expression in the fiction of the Meiji forties. See "Onna no kao, Mineko no fuku."

30. *Makaze koikaze* (Winds of demons, winds of love, 1903) by Kosugi Tengai was a very popular novel about the tragic love affair of a poor, orphaned schoolgirl. *Konjiki yasha* (The gold demon, 1905) by Ozaki Kōyō was an even more popular novel about a schoolgirl's betrayal of her beloved in favor of a rich suitor.

31. See Watanabe, "Tayama Katai *Futon*." The *Mainichi* series was published from September 20 to November 17, 1905.

32. Fujimori, "*Futon* ni okeru futatsu no kokuhaku."

33. See Saeki, *Iro to ai.*

34. Suzuki, *Narrating the Self*, 79–88.

35. Futon *o meguru shokan shū*, 298. Letter dated July 6, 1903.

36. Ibid., 329. Letter dated August 20, assumed to have been written in 1903.

37. Ibid., 329–30.

38. Fujimori, "*Futon* ni okeru futatsu no kokuhaku," 406.

39. Shimamura Hōgetsu, "*Seishun* o hyōsu," *Waseda bungaku* (April 1905), in *Hōgetsu zenshū*, 2:26–7.

40. Oka, "Shigeru, Sayoko, soshite Mineko-ra."

Part 3. Staging the New Woman

1. Rolf Fjelde points out that "Ibsen titled his play *Et dukkehjem*—A Doll *House*, without the possessive 's" in order to indicate the "universality of reference" by which Torvald was as much of a "doll" as Nora (*Ibsen: The Complete Major Prose Plays*, 121). Nevertheless, I have chosen to follow the earlier English translation convention, complete with a possessive and an emphasis on Nora, as it more aptly reflects the interpretation of the text in late Meiji Japan. Although there is certainly no absolute grammatical basis for reading the "no" of the Japanese translation *Ningyō no ie* as a possessive, I believe that such a reading duly reflects both the process by which the play was translated (from the English, not Norwegian) and the manner in which it was received.

2. Shimamura, "Shinkyū engeki no zento."

3. Ōzasa, *Nihon gendai engeki shi*, 86.

4. Kano, *Acting Like a Woman in Modern Japan*, p. 204. Kano's work also provides one of the few thorough examinations in English of the life and career of Kawakami Sadayakko, the most famous actress of the New School.

5. Ibid., 8.

6. Sasaki, *"Atarashii onna" no tōrai*, 240–46.

6. Setting the Stage for Translation

1. Osanai, with Ichikawa, *Jiyū gekijō*, 92.

2. Kawatake, *Sakigakeru monotachi no keifu*, 14–48. For a detailed account of the "modern formation of theater" in Japan, see Kano, *Acting Like a Woman in Modern Japan*, 33–35 and 57–84. For a detailed account of Morita Kan'ya XII's Westernized theater, see Brandon and Leiter, *Kabuki Plays on Stage*, 7–9.

3. See Itō, *Nihon bundan shi*, 1:131–32, quoted in English in Karatani, *The Origins of Modern Japanese Literature*, 55, and Kobitsu, *Nihon shingeki rinen shi Meiji zenki hen*, 172–73.

4. Itō, ibid., 132. The translation, slightly modified, is from Karatani, ibid., 55.

5. Karatani, *The Origins of Modern Japanese Literature*, 55–56. I have made minor modifications to the translation.

6. Kobitsu Matsuo provides a detailed account of the public reception of Danjūrō's early *katsureki*. Danjūrō's habit of prefacing his longer monologues is recounted by a contemporary eyewitness in *Meiji bungaku zenshū geppō*, no. 22, 1.

7. Matsumoto, "Osanai Kaoru's version of *Romeo and Juliet*, 1904," 62.

8. For those who are not familiar with Meiji history, it is important to note that the boom in political novels and political plays was part and parcel of the people's rights movement of the 1880s. People like Sudō and Kawakami were not actually employed politicians, but rather political advocates during a time when political parties in themselves had no officially recognized function (the Diet was not opened until 1890).

9. *Kawakami Otojirō senchi kenbun ki* (Kawakami Otojirō's account of things heard and seen on the battlefield), performed in December 1894 at Ichimura-za.

10. Matsumoto, "Osanai Kaoru's version of *Romeo and Juliet*, 1904," 54–66.

11. Kano, *Acting Like a Woman in Modern Japan*, 66.

12. While it is often said that Sadayakko's stage debut was in the United States, the historical record shows that she in fact took to the stage with the Kawakami troupe just before she and Otojirō departed for the United States. See Inoue, *Kawakami Otojirō no shōgai*, 62.

13. Kano cites the following plot summary from a March 2, 1900 review of the New York performance: "A beautiful geisha falls in love with a knight who is challenged by a jealous rival. They fight, but are separated by the geisha. Thereupon the lucky knight is claimed by his bride, whom he has neglected for the sake of the geisha, and is carried off. They flee into a sacred temple. The geisha tries to follow them, but is prevented by the monks. She dances to please them, and then slips into the temple. She soon returns with the unfortunate bride, and in a rage of jealousy tries to kill her, but is prevented by the knight, in whose arms she dies of a broken heart"; *Acting Like a Woman in Modern Japan*, 88.

14. Kawatake, *Sakigakeru monotachi no keifu*, 84–85. English title as translated by Brandon and Leiter, *Kabuki Plays on Stage*, 11. For a detailed account of the play, see Yoshihara, "Japan as 'Half-Civilized.'" According to Brandon and Leiter, this play "was set in Tokugawa-period Japan, populated by standard Kabuki merchants and officials, and featured the theme of Buddha's mercy. While spectators were aware that the story was foreign, their experience was of a typical domestic drama (*sewamono*)."

15. Ishizawa, *Shingeki no tanjō*, 29–30, 130–31; Kano, *Acting Like a Woman in Modern Japan*, 59. Kano plays on the meaning of *straight* to construct an interesting argument on the new normative ideologies of gender and performance that emerged from Kawakami's theater, by which "many aspects of *Kabuki* became coded as 'queer' and abjected."

16. The troupe "did not have the time to translate, or even understand the words of the original; they simply imitated the gestures of Irving and Terry and mouthed gibberish to suit the action." Kano, *Acting Like a Woman in Modern Japan*, 106.

17. Ibid., 107.

18. As the status of Meiji fiction rose, popular works like Ozaki Kōyō's *Konjiki yasha* (The gold demon), Kikuchi Yūhō's *Ono ga tsumi* (My sin), and even Natsume Sōseki's *Wagahai wa neko de aru* (I am a cat) were also adapted

to the stage. Initially these dramatizations were undertaken by professionally trained Kabuki playwrights such as Kawatake Mokuami and work-hungry *gesaku-sha* like Kanagaki Robun, who relied upon oral retellings of the original plot lines by informed literary associates. Gradually the roster of dramatizers also came to include prominent members of the Ken'yūsha and other outside writers.

19. Ishizawa, *Shingeki no tanjō*, 132, citing Emi Suiin, "Hon'an geki *Osero no hanashi*," *Waseda bungaku*, no. 257.

20. Kawatake, *Sakigakeru monotachi no keifu*, 70.

21. Osanai, "Kyakuhon no hon'yaku ni tsuite," 92.

22. Osanai, "Haiyū D-kun e" (1909), in Osanai, with Ichikawa, *Jiyū gekijō*, 79.

23. Shimamura, "Hon'yaku geki no koto" (1912), in *Hōgetsu zenshū*, 2:438–40.

24. The formation of the Ibsen Society strongly suggests that Zola was not necessarily the most important frame of reference for Japanese Naturalism. Although it is beyond the scope of the present study, greater attention to the cross-fertilization of Japanese Naturalism with European naturalist drama, rather than only fiction, might significantly illuminate many of the purported idiosyncrasies of Japanese Naturalist literary theory and practice.

25. Masamune Hakuchō, "Hōmei o tsuioku suru," *Masamune Hakuchō zenshū*, 13 vols. (Shinchōsha, 1965–69), 12:252; quoted in Horie-Webber, "Modernization of the Japanese Theatre, 161.

26. See especially Tsubouchi, "Hamuretto ni tsuite," *Kabuki*, no. 131 (May 1911): 26–29.

27. Kawatake, *Kindai engeki no tenkai*, 173.

28. Osanai, "Kyakuhon no hon'yaku ni tsuite," 92–93.

29. Osanai, "Atarashiki tochi o eyo," 91.

30. Watsuji, "Hon'an geki no kachi," 103.

31. Takeda Shōken, "Shokoku onna banashi," in Matsumoto, *Nihon shingeki shi* (Tsukuma shobō, 1966), 48; quoted in English in Horie-Webber, "Modernization of the Japanese Theatre," 161.

32. Watsuji, "Jiyū gekijō shokan"; quoted in Ōzasa, *Nihon gendai engekishi*, 108.

33. Watsuji, "Hon'an geki no kachi," 104–5. *Kaburagi Hideko* is the title of Doi Shunshō's adaptation of *Hedda Gabler*.

34. Futabatei, "Sakka kushin dan" (1897), *Futabatei Shimei zenshū*, 4:156.

35. Osanai, *Engeki shinsei*, 218–19.

36. Ibid., 209–10.

37. Osanai, "Jiyū gekijō no shien o oete," 119.

38. Toita, *Engeki gojūnen*, 60.

39. "*Borukuman* geki ni taisuru shoka no iken," *Kabuki*, no. 114 (January 1911): 49–50.

40. Yosano Tekkan, "Jiyū gekijō kansō roku," *Kabuki*, no. 121 (July 1910), 96.

41. Morita Sōhei, "Haiyū muyō ron," *Tōkyō Asahi shinbun*, December 1, 1910; quoted in Matsumoto, *Meiji engeki ron shi*, 998.

42. For instance, Kano writes: "Moreover, New Theater demands two kinds of allegiances from the translation: allegiance to the original text, and allegiance to the naturalness of the text as spoken on stage. Not surprisingly, the two allegiances are often at odds with each other. Yet the ideology of New Theater does not recognize there to be a contradiction since it believes that it should be possible to translate European texts faithfully into Japanese and to transcribe the resulting text faithfully onto the stage. If European texts embody universal ideas of culture, and if Japan is becoming a cultured nation, why should Japanese theater not be able to represent universality on stage? The only hindrance to such a staging would be conceived as Japanese particularity, and this in turn is understood to be Japanese backwardness: peculiarities of Japanese language and physique, timeworn habits of the mind and the body. But according to New Theater, these are vestiges of the old Japan, which are to be overcome through education, training, and technique. New forms of discipline will scrub away old habits until we end up with a Japan that is like the universal West in every respect"; *Acting Like a Woman in Modern Japan*, 171. Here, we find a curiously disembodied ideology, one with beliefs of its own that exist in apparent autonomy from the actual practitioners of New Theater. The evidence clearly shows that key figures like Osanai and Hōgetsu had a much more sophisticated appreciation of the numerous contradictions involved in their undertaking. From their perspective it was not Japan's "becoming a cultured nation" that would make it possible to translate and represent universality on stage, but rather the other way around: it was the process of translation that might enable Japan to become cultured, and the success or failure of this process was very

much in their hands. It is worth differentiating between the desire to establish *parity* between Japan and the West and the purported desire to create "a Japan that is like the universal West in every respect." Aside from some of the well-known excesses of the Rokumeikan period, during which some Westernists even called for the adoption of English as the national language, or for all Japanese to marry and produce children with Westerners, Japanese intellectuals were well aware that the only way to achieve true subjecthood as a modern nation-state would be to produce a society and culture that was commensurate with the universal Western model, while at the same time manifesting Japanese *particularity*. Translation was often seen as an important first step toward that goal.

43. Shimamura, "*Ningyō no ie* to hon'yakugeki (*Ningyō no ie* no butai kantoku ni tsuite no kansō)" (1912), *Hōgetsu zenshū*, 2:380–82.

44. Ibid., 383.

45. English translation from Rolf Fjelde, *Ibsen: The Complete Major Prose Plays*, 196.

46. Shimamura, "*Ningyō no ie* to hon'yakugeki," 385.

47. Fjelde, *Ibsen*, 196.

48. Shimamura, "*Ningyō no ie* to hon'yakugeki," 385.

49. Ibid., 383.

50. Ibid.

51. Ibid., 384.

52. Ibid.

53. Ibid., 385.

54. Iwaya, "Nora no geki o miru," 66–67.

55. Osanai, "Jiyū gekijō no shien o oete," 126.

56. Pronko, "*Kabuki:* Signs, Symbols, and the Hieroglyphic Actor," 239.

7. Gender Drag, Culture Drag, and Female Interiority

1. Nakamura, "Nihon no joyū ni tsuite," 212–15.

2. Kano, *Acting Like a Woman in Modern Japan*, 22.

3. Ibid., 23.

4. Komiya, "Jiyū gekijō no *Sabishiki hitobito*," 100–1.

5. Ibid., 98–99.

6. Nagata, *Shingeki no reimei*, 98.

7. See especially Kuwano, *Joyūron*, and *Engei gahō*, January 1912.

8. Kano, *Acting Like a Woman in Modern Japan*, 21.

9. For an account of Sadayakko's critical reception in the West, see ibid., 89–95.

10. Osanai, "Onnagata ni tsuite," in *Osanai Kaoru engekiron zenshū*, 1:20; originally published in *Engei gahō* (October 1914).

11. Matsumoto, *Meiji engekironshi*, 935. The "Noshio" style refers to Bandō Noshio, daughter of Kabuki actor Bandō Shūchō II and wife of Shūchō III.

12. Tamura, "'Ne' hanashi," *Engei gahō* (January 1912), 146.

13. Ibid., 146.

14. Shimamura, "Jo ni kaete," in Matsui, *Botan bake*, 5–6.

15. Kano, *Acting Like a Woman in Modern Japan*, 138–40.

16. Shimamura, "Jo ni kaete," 4.

17. Ibid., 6–7.

18. Matsumoto Shinko points out that, strictly speaking, the terms *joyū* and *onna yakusha* were not applied in a way that would consistently maintain a distinction between professional players (including geisha cum players) and amateurs (i.e., those who, like Matsui Sumako and other women of her generation, had never been initiated into the older arts of Kabuki and geisha performance before embarking upon a stage career); however, she also acknowledges that while women like Kumehachi and her underlings at the Misaki-za were being called *joyū* in the newspapers by the 1900s, at the same time the constant call for the need to raise actresses in Japan suggested that these women did not quite fill the bill; *Meiji engekironshi*, 927.

19. Ichikawa, "Onnagata no kokoroe," 110–15.

20. Ibid., 113. See also "Geidan hyakuwa," *Engei gahō* (April 1907): 85.

21. Okamoto, *Ranpu no shita nite*, 159–60.

22. Kano, *Acting Like a Woman in Modern Japan*, 32.

23. This is especially clear in Kuwano Tōka's *Joyūron*, in which he accuses the new "actresses" of the Teikoku gekijō and other commercial theaters of being nothing more than "woman players" borrowing the name *actress*. Notably, he treats the actresses of the Literary Arts Society as a separate category altogether and holds them up as an ideal to be followed.

24. Nakamura, "Nihon no joyū ni tsuite," in *Saikin gekiron to gekihyō*, 218.

25. Nakamura, "Yo no mitaru gaikoku no joyū to Nihon no joyū," in *Saikin no gekiron to gekihyō*, 231.

26. Osanai, "Onnagata ni tsuite," and Morita Sōhei, "Joshi wa oshiyubek-arazu," *Engei gahō* (January 1912).

27. Biographical accounts of Masako, as well as Sumako's own autobiographical fictions, presumably employed the Japanese count for years. They all concur that these personal losses happened when Masako was "sixteen," which would translate to either fourteen or fifteen by the Western count.

28. Tanaka, "Matsui Sumako," 72.

29. Matsui Sumako, "Osanai namida" and "Horo," in *Botan bake*, 48–49 and 54–63.

30. Although various rumors have circulated about the real reasons for Masako's dismissal from the Torigai family, I have followed the account by Machida Hisen, whose family was related to Masako by marriage, served as go-between for her marriage to Torigai Keizō, and also ran a clinic of their own. According to Machida, Masako was sent back with an illness that the Torigai family had mistaken for tuberculosis. It turned out to be a "female illness" contracted from Keizō, by which Machida obviously means a sexually transmitted disease. Masako underwent treatment at a clinic that specialized in such illnesses, after which she returned to the Machida home and helped out at the clinic while her next move was being pondered. Her second marriage to Maezawa Seisuke was then arranged by the Machidas, and Hisen served as go-between. In his words, this was not a marriage based on "love," but rather on necessity and mutual agreement; "Masako no toki kara Sumako ni naru made," in Akita Ujaku and Nakagi Teiichi, eds., *Koi no aishi Sumako no isshō* (Nihon hyōron sha shuppan-bu, 1919; rpt., Ōzora-sha, 1999), 259–67. In passing, I would mention that the longer biography of Masako/Sumako that constitutes the bulk of *Koi no aishi* is quite obviously bent on narrating Masako's life as though it somehow led inevitably to the birth of the first modern Japanese actress; having been filtered through this lens, the biographical information that it reports as "facts" frequently contradicts firsthand accounts by Sumako and others.

31. Matsui, "Matsui Sumako to kataru," 97.

32. Masumoto, "Maezawa fujin jidai no Sumako," in Akita and Nakagi, *Koi no aishi*, 274–75.

33. Tanaka, *Shingeki sono mukashi*, quoted in Toita, "Matsui Sumako," 318.

34. Masumoto, "Maezawa fujin jidai," 270–71.

35. Ibid., 135–36.

35. Kawamura, "Shienjō to *Ningyō no ie*," *Kabuki*, no. 137 (November 1911); quoted in Matsumoto, *Meiji engeki ron shi*, 952.

36. Ibid., 952. The Japanese lines are "Yurikago ni ningyō . . . koryaa, chitto heibon sugimasu kedo, jiki kowashichimaun desu kara ne" and "hitotsu, seizei futatsu."

37. Ibid.

38. Ibid.

39. See Akita Ujaku, "Hito oyobi haiyū to shite no Matsui Sumako" and Kamiyama Uraji, "Shugyō jidai no kotodomo," in Akita and Nakagi, *Koi no aishi*, 192 and 285–86.

40. Ishizawa, *Shingeki no tanjō*, 135–36.

41. Shimamura, "Hon'yaku geki no koto," 439–40.

42. Kano, *Acting Like a Woman in Modern Japan*, 203.

43. Akita, "Hito oyobi haiyū to shite no Matsui Sumako," 195.

44. Toita, *Monogatari kindai Nihon no joyū shi*, 72.

45. Iwasa, "'Kokyō' jōen o megutte."

46. Birnbaum, *Modern Girls, Shining Stars, and the Skies of Tokyo*, 2.

47. *Engei kurabu* (April 1914), quoted in Matsumoto, *Shingeki no yamanashi*, 37. "Otowaya" is the house name for Onoe Kikugorō and his disciples.

48. Kawamura Karyō, "Joyū to shite no Sumako," in Akita and Naka, *Koi no aishi*, 302–3. It is impossible to determine the degrees of fantasy and reality that may have contributed to Kawamura's impression of a resemblance between Sumako's elocution and Hōgetsu's habits of speech. Sumako was, by all accounts, the most conscientious student in Hōgetsu's class on Ibsen. It was also said that Tsubouchi Shōyō's style of elocution exerted such a powerful influence over his students that they could not help imitating him on the stage.

Final Reflections

1. Matsui, "Mise no hito" and "Mechô," in *Botan bake*, 1–36.

2. Although neither address the question of performative language per se, both Seki Reiko's *Ichiyô ikô no josei hyôgen: Sutairu, media, jendaa* (Kanrin

shobô, 2003) and Yamasaki Makiko's *Tamura Toshiko no sekai: Sakuhin to gensetsu kūkan no hen'yô* (Sairyūsha, 2005) offer compelling analyses of the relationships between style and gender in Tamura Toshiko's work.

3. The same should clearly be said for the study of classical Japanese literary styles, which cannot be fully comprehended in isolation from classical Chinese literature. In this sense the study of classical Japanese literary styles in English presents an even more daunting task.

Bibliography

Unless otherwise noted, all Japanese language books were published in Tokyo.

Akiyama Yūzō. *Hon'yaku no chihei: hon'yakusha to shite no Meiji no sakka.* Kanrin shobō, 1995.

Amano Itsujin. "Tayama Katai-shi no *Futon.*" *Myōjō,* October 1907; rpt. *Futon sakuhinron shūsei* 1:57. Ōzorasha, 1998.

Appiah, Kwame Anthony. "Thick Translation." In Lawrence Venuti, ed., *The Translation Studies Reader,* 389–401. 2d ed. New York: Routledge, 2004.

Arishima Takeo. *Aru onna.* 2 vols. Sōbunkaku, 1920; rpt., Kindai bungaku kan, 1974.

Ashiya Nobukazu. *Kunikida Doppo: Hikaku bungakuteki kenkyū.* Izumi shoten, 1982.

Barber, Charles. *The English Language: A Historical Introduction.* Cambridge: Cambridge University Press, 1993.

Barthes, Roland. *Empire of Signs.* Trans. Richard Howard. New York: Hill and Wang, 1982.

Bassnett, Susan, and André Lefevere, eds. *Translation, History, and Culture.* London: Pinter, 1990.

Berman, Antoine. *The Experience of the Foreign: Culture and Translation in Romantic Germany.* Trans. S. Heyvaert. Albany: State University of New York Press, 1992.

Bernofsky, Susan. *Foreign Words: Author-Translators in the Age of Goethe.* Detroit: Wayne State University Press, 2005.

Birnbaum, Phyllis. *Modern Girls, Shining Stars, and the Skies of Tokyo.* New York: Columbia University Press, 1999.

Bongie, Chris. *Exotic Memories—Literature, Colonialism, and the Fin de Siècle.* Stanford: Stanford University Press, 1991.

Brandon, James R., and Samuel L. Leiter, eds. *Kabuki Plays on Stage,* vol. 4: *Restoration and Reform, 1872–1905.* Honolulu: University of Hawaii Press, 2003.

Céléstin, Roger. *From Cannibals to Radicals: Figures and Limits of Exoticism.* Minneapolis: University of Minnesota Press, 1996.

Chow, Rey. *Primitive Passions: Visuality, Sexuality, Ethnography, and Contemporary Chinese Cinema.* New York: Columbia University Press, 1995.

—— *Woman and Chinese Modernity: The Politics of Reading Between East and West.* Minneapolis: University of Minnesota Press, 1991.

Clifford, James, and George E. Marcus, eds. *Writing Culture: The Poetics and Politics of Ethnography.* Berkeley: University of California Press, 1986.

Ebiike Toshiharu. *Meiji bungaku to eibungaku.* Meiji shoin, 1968.

Emi Suiin. "Ken'yūsha sokumen shi matomaranu kioku". In Togawa Shinsuke, ed., *Meiji bungaku kaisō shū.* Vol. 2. Iwanami bunko, 1999 [1926].

—— *Ken'yūsha to Kōyō.* Kaizōsha, 1927; rpt. Nihon tosho sentaa, 1983.

Fujii, James. *Complicit Fictions: the Subject in the Modern Japanese Prose Narrative.* Berkeley: University of California Press, 1993.

Fujimori Kiyoshi. "*Futon* ni okeru futatsu no kokuhaku: yūwaku to shite no kokuhaku kōi." *Nihon kindai bungaku*, May 1994; rpt. "*Futon*" *sakuhinron shūsei* 3:401–13. Ōzorasha, 1998.

Fukuda Kiyoto. *Ken'yūsha no bungaku undō.* Sankai-dō shuppan-bu, 1933; rpt. Nihon tosho sentaa, 1992.

—— *Ozaki Kōyō.* Kōbundō, 1941; rpt. Nihon tosho sentaa, 1987.

Futabatei Shimei. *Futabatei Shimei shū.* Ed. Hata Yūzō and Yasui Ryōhei. Nihon kindai bungaku taikei 4. Kadokawa shoten, 1971.

—— *Futabatei Shimei zenshū.* 8 vols. Chikuma shobō, 1984–93.

—— *Shinpen Ukigumo.* 2 vols. Kinkōdō, 1887; rpt. Kindai Nihon bungakukan, 1973.

—— *Ukigumo.* Part 3. *Miyako no hana,* nos. 18–21 (July 7–August 18, 1889).

Futon o meguru shokan shū. Tatebayashi: Tatebayashi-shi kyōiku iinkai bunka shinkō ka, 1994.

Geertz, Clifford. "Thick Description: Toward an Interpretive Theory of Culture." In *The Interpretation of Cultures: Selected Essays,* 4–30. New York: Basic, 1973.

Goethe, Johann Wolfgang von. "Translations." Trans. Sharon Sloan. In Lawrence Venuti, ed., *The Translation Studies Reader,* 64–66. 2d ed. New York: Routledge, 2004 [1819].

Gotō Chūgai. *Meiji bundan kaikō roku.* Okakura shobō, 1936; rpt. Nihon tosho sentaa, 1983.

Gotō Meisei. "Konketsu to bunretsu: Nihon kindai bungaku ni okeru 'watakushi.'" In *Shōsetsu no kairaku,* 239–60. Kōdansha, 1998.

—— "Shōsetsu wa doko kara kita ka." *Gunzō* (January 1993): 322–27.

Hirano Ken. *Geijutsu to jitsu seikatsu.* Kōdansha, 1958.

Hirota Eitarō. *Kindai yakugo kō.* Tōkyōdō shuppan, 1969.

Honda Masuko. *Jogakusei no keifu.* Seidosha, 1990.

Horie-Webber, A. "Modernization of the Japanese Theatre: The Shingeki Movement." In W. G. Beasley, ed., *Modern Japan: Aspects of History, Literature and Society,* 147–65. Berkeley: University of California Press, 1975.

Howland, Douglas R. *Translating the West: Language and Political Reason in Nineteenth-Century Japan.* Honolulu: University of Hawaii Press, 2001.

Hsieh, Yvonne Y. *Victor Segalen's Literary Encounter with China: Chinese Moulds, Western Thoughts.* Toronto: University of Toronto Press, 1988.

Ibsen, Henrik. *Ibsen: The Complete Major Prose Plays.* Trans. Rolf Fjelde. New York: New American Library, 1978.

Ichikawa Kumehachi. "Geidan hyakuwa." *Engei gahō* 1, no. 4 (April 1907).

—— "Onnagata no kokoroe." *Kabuki,* no. 84 (July 1907).

Ihara Saikaku. *The Great Mirror of Male Love.* Trans. Paul Schalow. Stanford: Stanford University Press, 1990.

Iida Yūko. "Onna no kao to Mineko no fuku." *Sōseki kenkyū,* no. 2 (1994): 130–41.

Inagaki Tatsurō and Oka Yasuo, eds. *Zadankai Shimamura Hōgetsu kenkyū*. Kindai bungaku kenkyūjo, 1980.

Inoue Seizō. *Kawakami Otojirō no shōgai*. Ashi shobō, 1985.

Ishibashi Shian. "*Aibiki* o yonde." In *Futabatei Shimei zenshū* bessatsu, 345. Chikuma shobō, 1993 [1888].

Ishii Kendō. *Meiji jibutsu kigen*. Vol. 1: *Daiichihen Jinjibu*. Chikuma gakugei bunko, 1997 [1944].

Ishizawa Shūji. *Shingeki no tanjō*. Kinokuniya shoten, 1964.

Isoda, Kōichi. *Rokumeikan no keifu*. Kōdansha bungei bunko, 1991.

Itō Sei. *Nihon bundan shi*. 18 vols. Iwanami bunko, 1994–97 [1952–73].

Iwasa Sōshirō. *Hōgetsu no beru epokku*. Taishūkan shuppan, 1998.

—— "Kokyō' jōen o megutte." *Nihon kindai bungaku*, no. 53 (October 1995).

Iwaya Sazanami. "Nora no geki o miru." *Waseda bungaku*, July 1906.

Jakobson, Roman. "On Linguistic Aspects of Translation." In Rainer Schulte and John Biguenet, eds., *Theories of Translation: An Anthology of Essays from Dryden to Derrida*, 144–51. Chicago: University of Chicago Press, 1992.

Kamei Hideo. *Transformations of Sensibility*. Ed. and trans. Michael Bourdaghs. Ann Arbor: Center for Japanese Studies, University of Michigan, 2002.

Kano, Ayako. *Acting Like a Woman in Modern Japan: Gender, Theater, and Nationalism*. New York: Palgrave, 1995.

Karatani Kojin. "Nationalism and Écriture." *Surfaces* 5, no. 201.1 (January 11, 1995): 5–25.

—— *The Origins of Modern Japanese Literature*. Ed. and trans. Brett de Bary. Durham: Duke University Press, 1993.

Katō Shūji, ed. Futon *sakuhinron shūsei*. 3 vols. Ōzorasha, 1998.

Kawabata Yasunari. *Asakusa kurenaidan*. Senshinsha, 1930; rpt., Kindai bungakukan, 1982.

Kawatake Shigetoshi. *Shingeki undō no reimeiki*. Yūzankaku, 1947.

Kawatake Toshio. *Kindai engeki no tenkai*. Shin NHK shimin daigaku sosho 11. Nihon hōsō shuppan kyōkai, 1982.

—— *Sakigakeru monotachi no keifu*. Tōseisha, 1985.

Kimura Ki. "Kaidai." *Meiji hon'yaku bungaku shū*, 395–410. Meiji bungaku zenshū 7. Chikuma shobō, 1972.

—— "Nihon hon'yaku shi gaikan." In *Meiji hon'yaku bungaku shū*, 375–94. Meiji bungaku zenshū 7. Chikuma shobō, 1972.

Kindai bungaku hyōron taikei. Vol. 3. Ed. Yoshida Seiichi and Wada Kingo. Kadokawa shoten, 1972.

Kinmonth, Earl. *The Self-Made Man in Meiji Japanese Thought: From Samurai to Salaryman.* Berkeley: University of California Press, 1981.

Kitani Kimie. *Ozaki Kōyō no kenkyū.* Sōbunsha shuppan, 1995.

Kobayashi Ichirō. *Tayama Katai kenkyū.* 10 vols. Ōfūsha, 1976.

Kobitsu Matsuo. *Nihon shingeki rinen shi Meiji chūki hen.* Miraisha, 1998.

—— *Nihon shingeki rinen shi Meiji zenki hen.* Hakusuisha, 1988.

Komiya Toyotaka. "Jiyū gekijō no Sabishiki hitobito." *Engei gahō,* December 1911.

Kosugi Tengai. *Makaze koikaze.* 2 vols. Iwanami bunko, 1999 [1903].

Kunikida Doppo. *Kunikida Doppo shū.* Gendai Nihon bungaku zenshū 57. Chikuma shobō, 1956.

Kuwano Tōka. *Joyūron.* Sanbōya shoten, 1913.

Leiter, Samuel L., ed. *A Kabuki Reader: History and Performance.* Armonk, NY: Sharpe, 2002.

Lippit, Seiji. "The Disintegrating Machinery of the Modern: Akutagawa Ryūnosuke's Late Writings." *Journal of Asian Studies* 58, no. 1 (February 1999): 27–50.

Loti, Pierre. *Aki no Nihon fūbutsushi.* Trans. Shimoda Yukio. Keisō shobō, 1953.

—— "Les Femmes japonaises," in *L'exilée.* Paris: Calmann Lévy, 1896 [1890].

—— *Rochi no Nippon nikki: Okikusan to no kimyō na seikatsu.* Trans. Funaoka Suetoshi. Yokohama: Yūrindō, 1979.

Liu, Lydia H. *Translingual Practice: Literature, National Culture, and Translated Modernity—China, 1900–1937.* Stanford: Stanford University Press, 1995.

Maeda Akira. *Meiji Taishō no bungakujin.* Sagoya shobō, 1942; rpt. Nihon tosho sentaa, 1983.

Matsui Sumako. *Botan bake.* Shinchōsha, 1919; rpt. Fuji shuppan, 1986.

—— "Matsui Sumako to kataru" [Interview]. *Engei gahō* (March 1912): 97.

Matsumoto Kappei. *Nihon shingekishi: shingeki binbō monogatari.* Chikuma shobō, 1967.

—— *Shingeki no yamanami*. Asahi shorin, 1991.

Matsumoto Shinko. *Meiji engekironshi*. Engeki shuppansha, 1980.

—— "Osanai Kaoru's version of *Romeo and Juliet*, 1904." In Minami Ryūta, Ian Carruthers, and John Gillies, eds., *Performing Shakespeare in Japan*, 54–66. Cambridge: Cambridge University Press, 2001.

Mayama Seika. "Oguri Fūyō ron." *Shinchō*, September 1907.

Meiji hon'yaku bungaku shū. Meiji bungaku zenshū 7. Chikuma shobō, 1972.

Meiji no joyū ten. Nagoya: Nagoya tetsudō kabushikigaisha, 1986.

Mertz, John Pierre. *Novel Japan: Spaces of Nationhood in Early Meiji Narrative, 1870–88*. Ann Arbor: Center for Japanese Studies, University of Michigan, 2003.

Mill, James. *A History of British India*. New York: Chelsea House, 1968. [1817]

Mitani Kuniaki. "Kindai shōsetsu no gensetsu—joshō." In Komori Yōichi, ed., *Kindai bungaku no seiritsu*, 118–28. Yūseidō, 1986.

Mizuno Yōshū. "Jogakusei-bi." *Shumi* 3, no. 7 (July 1907): 9–10.

Mori Ōgai. *Maihime*. In Miyoshi Yukio, ed., *Mori Ōgai shū*. Nihon kindai bungaku taikei 11. Kadokawa shoten, 1974.

Morita Sōhei. *Baien*. Uetake shoin, 1914; rpt. Kyoto: Kokusai Nihon bunka kenkyū sentaa Nichibunken sōsho, 1999 [1909].

—— "Joshi wa oshiyubekarazu." *Engei gahō* 5, no. 1 (January 1912).

Nagata Hideo. *Shingeki no reimeiki*. Guroria sosaete, 1931.

Nakagawa Kojūrō. "*Iratsume* to genbun-itchi." In *Bimyō senshū* 1. Ritsumeikan shuppan-bu, 1935.

Nakamura Kichizō. *Saikin gekiron to gekihyō*. Okamura shoten, 1913.

Nakamura Masanao. "Zenryō naru haha o tsukuru setsu." *Meiroku zasshi* no. 33 (March 1875).

Nakamura Mitsuo. *Fūzoku shōsetsu ron*. Shinchō bunko, 1994 [1950].

Nakane Komajūrō, ed. *Kunikida Doppo*. Shinchōsha, 1908; rpt. Nihon tosho sentaa, 1990.

Natsume Sōseki. *Sanshirō*. In *Sōseki zenshū*, vol. 7. Iwanami shoten, 1956 [1908].

Niranjana, Tejaswini. *Siting Translation: History, Post-Structuralism, and the Colonial Context*. Berkeley: University of California Press, 1992.

Niwa Jun'ichirō. *Karyū shunwa*. In *Meiji hon'yaku bungaku shū*, 3–109. Meiji bungaku zenshū 7. Chikuma shobō, 1972.

Noguchi Takehiko. *Sanninshō no hakken made*. Chikuma shobō, 1994.

—— *Shōsetsu no nihongo*. Nihongo no sekai 13. Chūōkōronsha, 1980.

Oguri Fūyō. *Seishun*. 3 vols. Iwanami bunko, 1994 [1906].

Oka Yasuo. *Hyōden Oguri Fūyō*. Ōfūsha, 1971.

—— *Ozaki Kōyō no shōgai to bungaku*. Meiji shoin, 1968.

—— "Shigeru, Sayoko, soshite Mineko-ra." In *Meiji bungaku ronshū 2— suimyaku no uchisoto*, 182–91. Shintensha, 1989.

Okamoto Kidō. *Ranpu no shita nite*. Iwanami bunko, 1993 [1935].

Osanai Kaoru. "Atarashiki tochi o eyo." *Engei gahō* 3, no. 4 (April 1909).

—— "Borukuman no shien ni tsuite." *Kabuki*, no. 113 (December 1909).

—— *Engeki shinsei*. Tōundō shoten, 1911.

—— "Jiyū gekijō no shien o oete." *Engei gahō* 4, no. 1 (January 1910).

—— *Osanai Kaoru engekiron zenshū*. Vol. 1. 5 vols. Miraisha, 1964–68.

Osanai Kaoru, ed., with Ichikawa Sadanji. *Jiyū gekijō*. Jiyū gekijō jimusho, 1912.

Ozaki Kōyō. "Dokusha hyōbanki," *Momochidori* 4 (October 20, 1889).

—— *Kōyō zenshū*. 6 vols. Hakubunkan, 1904.

—— *Ozaki Kōyō shū*. Meiji bungaku zenshū 18. Chikuma shobō, 1965.

Ōzasa Yoshio. *Nihon gendai engeki shi*. Meiji Taishō hen. Hakusuisha, 1985.

Pálsson, Gisli, ed. *Beyond Boundaries*. Oxford: Berg, 1993.

Pronko, Leonard C. "*Kabuki*: Signs, Symbols, and the Hieroglyphic Actor." In Samuel L. Leiter, ed., *A Kabuki Reader: History and Performance*, 238–52. Armonk, NY: Sharpe, 2002.

Richter, Giles. "Marketing the Word: Publishing Entrepreneurs in Meiji Japan." Ph.D. diss., Columbia University, May 1999.

Rodd, Laurel Rasplica. "Yosano Akiko and the Taisho Debate on the 'New Woman.'" In Gail Lee Bernstein, ed., *Recreating Japanese Women, 1600– 1945*, 175–98. Berkeley: University of California Press, 1991.

Ryan, Marleigh Grayer. *Japan's First Modern Novel: UKIGUMO*. New York: Columbia University Press, 1965.

Saeki Junko. *Iro to ai no hikaku bunkashi*. Iwanami shoten, 1998.

Said, Edward W. *Culture and Imperialism*. London: Chatto and Windus, 1993.

—— *Orientalism*. New York: Vintage, 1979.

Saitō Tsuyoshi. *Meiji no kotoba: Higashi kara nishi e no kakehashi*. Kōdansha, 1977.

Saganoya Omuro. "*Ukigumo* no kushin to shisō." *Shinshōsetsu*, June 1909.

Sasaki Hideaki. "*Atarashii onna*" *no tōrai: Hiratsuka Raichō to Sōseki*. Nagoya: Nagoya daigaku shuppan kai, 1994.

Sawa Toyohiko. *Tayama Katai no shi to hyōron*. Chūsekisha, 1992.

Segalen, Victor. *Eguzotisumu ni kansuru shiron/Kiryo* [Essai sur l'exotisme]. Trans. Kinoshita Makoto. Gendai kikaku-shitsu, 1995.

—— *Essay on Exoticism: An Aesthetics of Diversity*. Ed. and trans. Yaël Rachel Schlick. Durham: Duke University Press, 2002.

Shimamura Hōgetsu. *Hōgetsu zenshū*. 8 vols. Ten'yūsha, 1919–20.

—— "Shinkyū engeki no zento." *Shumi* 1, no. 6 (November 1906): 46–54.

Shimazaki Tōson. "Jiyū gekijō kansō roku." *Kabuki*, no. 121 (July 1910).

Silverberg, Miriam. "The Modern Girl as Militant." In Gail Lee Bernstein, ed., *Recreating Japanese Women, 1600–1945*, 239–66. Berkeley: University of California Press, 1991.

Sōma Gyofū. "*Futon* gappyō." In *Waseda bungaku* (October 1907), 38–54; rpt. Katō Shūji, ed., *Tayama Katai Futon sakuhinron shūsei* 1:37–53. 3 vols. Ōzorasha, 1998.

Sōma Kokkō. *Mokui*. Josei jidaisha, 1939; rpt. Nihon tosho sentaa, 1983.

Suga Hidemi. "Reishō suru orientarizumu." *Hihyō kūkan* 2, no. 16 (January 1998).

Suzuki, Tomi. *Narrating the Self: Fictions of Japanese Modernity*. Stanford: Stanford University Press, 1996.

Takase Bun'en. *Yamada Bimyō Ishibashi Ningetsu Takase Bun'en shū*. Meiji bungaku zenshū 23. Chikuma shobō, 1971.

Takitō Mitsuyoshi. *Kunikida Doppo ron*. Hanawa shobō, 1986.

Tanaka Sumie. "Matsui Sumako." In Enchi Fumiko, ed., *Gei no michi hitosuji ni*, 67–104. Jinbutsu Nihon no josei shi 9. Shūeisha, 1977.

Tanizaki Jun'ichirō. *Chijin no ai*. Chūōkōronsha, 1985 [1925].

Taussig, Michael. *Mimesis and Alterity: A Particular History of the Senses*. New York: Routledge, 1993.

Tayama Katai. *Futon, Jūemon no saigo*. Shinchō bunko, 1996 [1907, 1902].

—— *Katai shū*. Ekifūsha, 1907.

—— *Meiji no shōsetsu*. Shinchōsha, 1926.

—— *Meiji shōsetsu naiyō hattatsu shi*. Bungaku fukyū-kai, 1914.

—— "Rokotsu naru byōsha." In *Kindai hyōron shū* I. Nihon kindai bungaku taikei 57. Kadokawa shoten, 1972, pp. 198–200. [1904]

—— "Shōjo-bi." *Shumi* 3, no. 7 (July 1908).

—— *Tayama Katai shū.* Meiji bungaku zenshū 67. Chikuma shobō, 1968.

—— *Tayama Katai zenshū.* 16 vols. plus 1 Shinshū bekkan. Bunsendō shoten, 1973–74.

—— *Teihon Katai zenshū.* 12 vols (numbered 17–28 as a continuation of *Tayama Katai zenshū*) plus 1 bekkan. Rinsen shoten, 1994–95.

—— *Tōkyō no sanjūnen.* Iwanami bunko, 1981 [1917].

Todorov, Tzvetan. *On Human Diversity.* Trans. Catherine Porter. Cambridge: Harvard University Press, 1993.

Toita Yasuji. *Engeki gojūnen.* Jiji tsūshinsha, 1956.

—— *Monogatari kindai Nihon no joyū shi.* Chūōkōronsha, 1980.

Toki Michiko. "Joyū no keifu." In Enchi Fumiko, ed., *Gei no michi hitosuji ni,* 220–48. Jinbutsu Nihon no josei shi 9. Shūeisha, 1977.

Tokuda Shūsei. "Bijin to wa?" *Shumi* 3, no. 7 (July 1908).

—— *Meiji shōsetsu no bunshō hensen shi.* Bungaku fukyū kai, 1914; rpt. Nihon tosho sentaa, 1982.

Tsubouchi, Shōyō. "Hamuretto ni tsuite." *Kabuki,* no. 103 (February 1909).

—— *Shōyō senshū.* Shun'yōdō, 1926–27.

—— *Tsubouchi Shōyō shū.* Nihon kindai bungaku taikei 3. Kadokawa shoten, 1974.

Tsubouchi, Shōyō, and Uchida Roan, eds. *Futabatei Shimei.* Ekifūsha, 1909; rpt. Kindai bungakukan, 1975.

Turgenev, Ivan. *A Sportsman's Notebook.* Trans. Charles and Natasha Hepburn. London: Everyman's Library, 1992.

Uchida Roan. *Omoidasu hitobito.* Iwanami bunko, 1994 [1925].

—— *Uchida Roan shū.* Meiji bungaku zenshū 24. Chikuma shobō, 1978.

Unno Hiroshi. *Modan gaaru no yūwaku.* Heibonsha, 1989.

Venuti, Lawrence. *The Scandals of Translation: Towards an Ethics of Difference.* London: Routledge, 1998.

—— *The Translation Studies Reader.* 2d ed. New York: Routledge, 2004.

—— *The Translator's Invisibility: A History of Translation.* London: Routledge, 1995.

Wada Kingo. *Byōsha no jidai.* Sapporo: Hokkaidō daigaku tosho kankō kai, 1975.

Watanabe Masahiko. "Tayama Katai *Futon,*" In *Gunma kenritsu joshi daigaku kokubungaku kenkyū* (March 1992), 13–26; rpt. *Futon sakuhinron shūsei* 3:247–60. Ōzorasha, 1998.

Watsuji Tetsurō. "Hon'an geki no kachi." In *Shinshichō* 2, no. 3 (November 1911): 103–7.

—— "Jiyū gekijō shokan." In Osanai Kaoru and Ichikawa Sadanji, eds., *Jiyū gekijō*, 9–16. Jiyū gekijō jimusho, 1912.

Yamada Bimyō. *Fūkin shirabe no hitofushi*. In *Iratsume* 1–3 (July 9–September 10, 1888).

—— *Fukusa zutsumi*. In *Iratsume* 4 (October 10, 1888).

—— *Natsu kodachi*. Kinkōdō, 1888; rpt. Kindai bungakukan, 1981.

Yamada Hiromitsu. *Kitamura Tōkoku to Kunikida Doppo: Hikaku bungakuteki kenkyū*. Kindai bungeisha, 1990.

Yamada Yūsaku. "Kaidai." Reprint of *Iratsume*. Fuji shuppan, 1983.

Yamakawa Kikue. *Onna nidai no ki*. Tōyō bunko, 1975.

Yamamoto Masahide. *Genbun-itchi no rekishi ronkō*. Ōfūsha, 1971.

—— *Genbun-itchi no rekishi ronkō: zokuhen*. Ōfūsha, 1981.

—— "Genbun-itchi-tai." In *Buntai*, 311–48. Iwanami kōza Nihongo 10. Iwanami shoten, 1977.

Yanabu Akira. *Hon'yakugo seiritsu jijō*. Iwanami shinsho, 1982.

—— *Hon'yakugo no ronri*. Hōsei daigaku shuppan kyoku, 1972.

—— *Hon'yaku no shisō: "shizen" to NATURE*. Heibonsha, 1977.

Yanagawa Shun'yō. "Katai shū gappyō." *Shumi* 3, no. 5 (May 1908).

Yanagida Izumi. *Tayama Katai no bungaku*. 2 vols. Shunjūsha, 1957–58.

Yokota Murakami Takayuki. *Sei no purotokoru*. Shin'yōsha, 1997.

Yonekawa Akihiko. "Meiji, Taishō no ryūkōgo." *Kokubungaku kaishaku to kyōzai no kenkyū* 42, no. 14 (December 1997): 21–31.

Yoshida Seiichi. *Shizenshugi no kenkyū*. 2 vols. Tōkyōdō, 1955–58.

Yoshihara Yukari. "Japan as 'Half-Civilized': An Early Japanese Adaptation of Shakespeare's *Merchant of Venice* and Japan's Construction of Its National Image in the Late Nineteenth Century." In Minami Ryūta, Ian Carruthers, and John Gillies, eds., *Performing Shakespeare in Japan*, 21–32. Cambridge: Cambridge University Press, 2001.

Index